The Trumpet of Prophecy

James A. Beckford

The Trumpet of Prophecy

A SOCIOLOGICAL STUDY OF JEHOVAH'S WITNESSES

A Halsted Press Book
JOHN WILEY & SONS
NEW YORK

Library of Congress Cataloging in Publication Data

Beckford, James A

    The trumpet of prophecy.

    "A Halsted Press book."
    Bibliography: p.
    Includes indexes.
      1. Jehovah's Witnesses.   2. Religion and sociology.
I. Title.
BX8526.B4   289.9   75–14432
ISBN 0–470–06138–3

Printed in Great Britain

CONTENTS

TABLES AND FIGURES

To Julie for
Louisa and Charlotte

INTRODUCTION

It is a curious fact about the historical development of sociological studies of religion in Britain that greater aggregate effort has been expended on the study of small, so-called sectarian movements than on studies of larger religious groups. Perhaps because the sect approximates to the anthropologist's tribe, many graduate students in sociology have come to regard the opportunity to study one as a form of doing field-work. Indeed, the sect presents many advantages to the would-be field-worker in sociology: it is restricted in size, sometimes limited in geographical dispersion, often lacking a long history, usually publishing ample literature, occasionally lacking the kind of professional leaders who might deter the less-than-intrepid researcher and being sufficiently restricted in the scope of its activities to facilitate overall judgements of its performance.

Monographs on the history, organization and ideology of the most important sectarian movements in Britain have now been completed and can serve as an invaluable springboard to either more intensive or more varied research. In our opinion, the fact that these studies outweigh the research on other types of religious group is not regrettable in itself. But what is regrettable is that relatively little work has been done within a *comparative* perspective on both sects and other types of groups.

One of the reasons for the undeveloped state of a comparative sociology of religious groups is that the analytical distinctions between the concepts of 'church', 'denomination', 'sect', and 'cult' have encouraged hermetic cloistering of groups of specialist scholars who may be unaware of the work being done in other groups. Nor is the situation made easier by typologies or classifications of sects because, while they may serve an important function in stimulating comparison between *sects*, they reinforce the tendency to keep this type of group analytically distinct from the others. It may be that the large-scale changes that have taken place in

modern societies in recent decades have called in question the usefulness
of maintaining the conceptual distinctions in their original sharpness.

In particular, we felt the 'blinkering' effects of the conventional concepts in our attempts to compare the Watch Tower movement—a collective title for the organization of Jehovah's witnesses—with groups that
bore marked similarities to it but that also happened to fall outside the
class of sects in other respects. Existing concepts, theories and even methods
in the sociology of religion are just not geared towards the kind of comparative research which was required to bring out the interesting pattern
of similarities and dissimilarities between the Witnesses and non-sectarian
religious groups.

There was, however, immense scope within the available conceptual
apparatus for a study of the social morphology of the Watch Tower
movement in Britain. For reliable and objective knowledge of Jehovah's
witnesses' beliefs, practices and social characteristics was, to say the least,
limited. This books sets out, therefore, to augment the stock of knowledge
by firstly describing the movement's social composition, its organization,
and its ideology. It examines closely and for the first time the complex
process whereby it 'sounds out' the market for recruits and attempts to
fashion them into full-fledged members. This analysis of the contemporary
situation is firmly located in the context of the sociological factors that
have influenced the movement's development since its beginning in the
1870s. These tasks were particularly pressing as far as Britain is concerned
because most of the sociological literature on Jehovah's witnesses relates
almost exclusively to their situation in the USA. Some factors will be shown
to apply in both countries, but important differences and their consequences also warranted close examination.

Both the contemporary and the historical analyses were conducted
against a background of existing theories (or, at least, theoretical ideas)
which provided the opportunity to make judgements about their potential
to explain various facets of this particular religious movement. Yet, perhaps a more important and, in some ways, exciting consequence of our
deliberate focus on theoretical issues was the occasion that it afforded for
comparison between the Witnesses and other social groups. The ground-
work for more extensive and more specific comparative studies was therefore prepared in the process of clarifying the sociological distinctiveness of
one particular religious sect.

Two theoretical problems that exercised us greatly in thinking compara-
tively about religious movements concerned, on the one hand, the conceptualizations and typifications that sociologists have customarily used
for dealing with such groups and, on the other, the association that is
widely believed to hold between types of religious ideology and particular
social strata. The anomalous status of the Watch Tower movement in

relation to the concepts 'church' and 'sect' or in the context of schemes for classifying different types of sects obliged us to amend current usages and to shift the emphasis of our analysis on to theoretical explanation rather than classification. Our solution to the second problem was to expose the invalidity of much current thinking on the Sociology of Knowledge and to argue in favour of a more empirical and a less sweeping, generalizing approach to it.

Our methods of studying the Witnesses were of four principal kinds:

(i) Information on the historical development of the Watch Tower movement's doctrines, organization, ideology and material fortunes was extracted from extensive reading of its published literature. A welter of Watch Tower magazines, pamphlets and books provided ample data for sociological analysis, although the volume of independent evidence about the group fell far short of the ideal. To some extent the handful of sociological studies that had already been made of the Witnesses were a source of information of this kind, but as they concentrated almost exclusively on Witnesses in other countries and in earlier periods of history, their relevance was only tangential to our requirements.

(ii) Wide-ranging interviews, each lasting several hours and following a schedule of open-ended questions, were conducted with a large proportion of the adult Witnesses in one of the two congregations in a central southern English town. The answers to our queries gave clear insights into the sort of questions that could be profitably put to a larger and more representative group of Witnesses.

(iii) On personal visits to ten congregations representing the major geographical divisions of England, Wales and the Scottish Lowlands questionnaire schedules were distributed to adult Witnesses in proportion to the apparent distribution in each congregation of age, sex and social status categories. In the absence of a sampling-frame there was no means of securing a random sample, and the hazards of our procedure are all too obvious to us. But the opportunity of conducting *any* kind of methodical survey for the first time among Jehovah's witnesses was too valuable to miss. In the event 78.2 per cent of the completed schedules, each containing twenty-six questions, were analysable and provided the bulk of our data on the social profile of British Witnesses.

(iv) Further information was collected from informal conversations with both practising and defected Witnesses. They supplied invaluable insights into the subjective experiences of Watch Tower converts and were often able to cast explanatory light on other inexplicable phenomena. In this respect the published testimonies of ex-Jehovah's witnesses were also useful, but the fact that they had bothered to write up their experiences made us suspicious of their motives. Similarly, the literature published by groups which had seceded from the main Watch Tower movement was

coloured by ideological interests that probably distorted their accounts of
the history and present practices of Jehovah's witnesses.

Journalists' accounts of the Witnesses' activities are barely more credible.

Finally, four years of personal observations of Jehovah's witnesses in
their homes, in congregations, in large assemblies and in public evangelism were an irreplaceable source of both questions and answers about their
background, activities and outlook. No attempt was made to conceal the
purpose of our observations, although conversation frequently and naturally centred around topics that were only incidental to this study.

However diverse and flexible our methods were, it still proved difficult
to secure reliable information about a number of important issues. The
precise workings of the administrative agencies in the highest echelons of
the Witnesses' governing body—the Watch Tower Society—remain largely
obscure; full details of the Society's financial state are kept absolutely
secret; the rationale and mechanics of the Society's international missionary enterprise are known only to a minute elite; and the Society's methods
of maintaining contact with Witnesses in hostile territories are never
divulged. These and other issues which might throw light on some aspects
of the Watch Tower Movement's sociological structure and dynamics
must await further investigation. But the design of our research was such
that it would facilitate replication and testing of the available results as
well as application in comparative studies.

Our first debt of gratitude to be acknowledged must be in an impersonal
and blanket fashion to the authors of all the studies from which the
present work has derived its *raison d'être*, its stimulus and in some cases
substantive guidance. To be able to follow a long line of predecessors is a
great advantage to the student embarking on a new project, and the
'pedigree' of this study reflects, albeit unworthily, the influence of some
outstanding forebears.

More particularly, it is a pleasure to record personal gratitude to Dr
Bryan R. Wilson of All Souls College, Oxford, for his unstintingly
generous interest in this book. His firm guidance during the hazardous
process of reducing an unruly doctoral thesis to a more manageable format
for publication was only the last of his many helpful contributions. He
had earlier provided moral support in the data-gathering stage and had
then given the benefit of his commanding knowledge of sectarian studies
in encouraging a comparative perspective. Dr A. T. Rogerson of Wolfson
College, Oxford, was not only an invaluable source of information on the
history of the Watch Tower Movement but was also a highly esteemed
and useful critic of factual errors. The willing co-operation of countless
Jehovah's witnesses made this study possible, and we are grateful to them
for their forebearance and kindness. Family, friends and colleagues are
thanked for listening so patiently for so long to the same story.

CHAPTER 1

ADVENTISM AND EVANGELISM

RUSSELL: THE EVANGELICAL ENTREPRENEUR

The history of the religious movement whose followers came to be known as Jehovah's witnesses extends over one hundred years and is marked by a rich variety of controversial incidents. From its obscure origins in the industrial city of Pittsburgh to its present-day status as a world-wide organization of immense complexity and power the Watch Tower movement has excited the curiosity, the anger, the compassion and the hatred of many commentators. This study aims at analysing the movement dispassionately from a sociological perspective, that is to say, by focusing narrowly on the patterns of human relationships between Jehovah's witnesses both as individuals and as members of groups.

If it seems strange that the name of one man, Charles Taze Russell, recurs so frequently in what purports to be a sociological investigation of the origins of the Watch Tower movement, this is because he was its founder, its chief apologist, its most powerful executive officer, its figurehead and its major benefactor for almost forty-five years. This chapter will therefore try to demonstrate the importance of sociological factors in influencing the ways in which Russell conceived of and cultivated a distinctive type of religious group.

Russell's contribution to the formative stages of the Watch Tower movement is clearly of the greatest significance for its later development, but reliable information on his background and early life in Pittsburgh is surprisingly sparse. On the one hand, his autobiographical statements[1] disclose that he inherited from parents of Scots–Irish descent a set of Presbyterian beliefs which he later abandoned in favour of a less harsh Congregationalist outlook. But even his commitment to Congregationalism was said to have been eventually eroded by the arguments of a

I

sceptical friend who persuaded him that the notion of an omnipresent, omniscient and omnipotent God was incompatible with the evident suffering that His creatures would have to endure in Hell. On the other hand, Russell's sister described his quest for an acceptable theology as the result of a prophetic dream that he had had about his calling to save men from doctrinal error at the time of his withdrawal from Presbyterianism.[2] It seems certain, however, that the solution to Russell's problem emerged from a chance encounter with a group of Second Adventists.

In accordance with deep-rooted eirenic convictions, Russell discarded the Adventists' predictions of a fiery destruction of human institutions as a preliminary to the closing stages of God's plan for the world, but he eagerly accepted their belief that human history represented the progressive unfolding of a divine plan. Furthermore, he wholeheartedly embraced the view that Christ's death had served as a ransom-price for the potential restoration to a state of Adamic perfection of all people of all generations. These beliefs served as the framework within which Russell and a small group of sympathizers undertook an informal study of the Bible around 1870. He published a pamphlet in 1873, *The Object and Manner of Our Lord's Return*, as a brief summary of their progressively crystallizing ideas, but important accretions took place following conversations in 1875 between Russell and an experienced Adventist preacher called N. H. Barbour. He convinced Russell that since Christ had descended from heaven in 1874 and had begun to prepare for the millennium on earth, it was imperative to disseminate their shared ideas as widely and as quickly as possible.

For several years Russell collaborated with Barbour in co-editing an Adventist magazine, *The Herald of the Morning*, and in publishing a book entitled *The Three Worlds or Plan of Redemption*. Despite Russell's investment in Barbour's schemes of some of the private wealth that he had derived from co-managing his father's haberdashery and clothing business, he still retained sufficient independence to break with Barbour's small organization in 1879 in order to begin production of his own magazine, *Zion's Watch Tower and Herald of Christ's Presence*, in the following year. Russell's own account of the break[3] was that he could not brook Barbour's alleged abandonment of the idea that Christ's ransom had been paid for *all* mankind, whereas later critics[4] have argued that selfish pride was Russell's sole motivating force.

Russell's small group of followers and his own magazine immediately began to convey a novel synthesis of ideas about God's direction of human history and about its chronological details which had long been current in Adventist teachings in a variety of separate forms. At this time Russell's Adventist beliefs were still unsettled and subject to influences internal and external to his group of supporters in Pittsburgh. In spite of the disturbances that subsequent revisions caused among the Russellites doctrinal flexibility probably secured more advantages than disadvantages during the group's formative stages. Certainly, the volume of Russell's evangelical work quickly outstripped Barbour's and in this he was undoubtedly helped by the fact that he had access from the very beginning to the circulation list of Barbour's magazine and to that of a Californian Adventist journal, *The Last Trump*. His personal wealth also enabled him to distribute effectively a large amount of free promotional literature at a time when the income from literature sales would not have been sufficient to cover production costs.

The theological ideas that gradually crystallized in Russell's mind during the 1880s may be profitably understood in their relation to the contemporary intellectual context.[5] In brief, Calvinistic Protestantism, a democratic social ideology and a popularized scientific philosophy represented the main strands of 'the intellectual matrix of the modern age' (Persons, 1961, p. 370) in the USA to which religious organizations demonstrated widely varying modes of adaption. On a superficial level they seemed to be prospering, but dissatisfaction was growing within some churches at the kind of adjustment to, and compromises with, 'modernism' that were becoming common (Goen, 1970). Russell chose precisely to oppose modernist philosophy, theology and ecclesiology by restating what he understood to be the unchanging principles of Christianity and by organizing a religious movement with the explicit goal of propagating those principles.

His proposed solution to the twin problems of 'infidelity' and 'modernism' was to restore faith in the 'principle (that) seems to be disappearing in respect to religious matters',[6] and his own set of teachings crystallized in the attempt to oppose error with truth and liberalism with 'principle'.

The writings of William Miller, George Stetson and George Storrs probably exerted the most formative influence on Russell's conservative religious beliefs, but the living influence of such Second Adventists as N. H. Barbour, J. H. Paton and Jonas Wendell is also detectable in certain aspects of Russell's general outlook. But, whereas millennial beliefs had occasionally erupted into prominence throughout the course of Christianity's history, and although Second Adventist preachers had enjoyed immense vogue in the first half of the nineteenth century in America (see Froom, 1946–54), the vitality of Second Adventism was already in decline when Russell began to propagate his own ideas. The fact that he managed to stimulate widespread interest in a type of religious belief that was being eclipsed in popularity by individual-oriented

Arminianism testifies to the originality of his version of millennialism, and to the vitality of his religious organization.

More concrete stimuli to a systematic defence of what Russell considered to be fundamental religious truths included the accusation that the formation of the Evangelical Alliance of 1846 had been the beginnings of a campaign by professional clergymen to protect their interests by cartelization. Moreover, the growing unease amongst some sections of the American clergy about unsatisfactory social conditions also convinced Russell that churches were neglecting their God-given responsibilities for the sake of allegedly short-sighted reformism. The Social Gospel movement that stemmed largely from the influence of Walter Rauschenbusch's *Christianity and the Social Crisis* (1907) attracted nothing but righteous scorn from Russell because it presented the dual threat of obscuring the primacy of Scripture over purely secular issues and of diverting attention away from God's promised resolution of all social ills. Finally, Russell found it essential to his 'restoring function' to criticize and ridicule the development of what he called 'social club churches' where congregations had to be attracted by the offer of such ancillary provisions as youth clubs, gymnasia and nurseries.

The set of ideas about God, man and history that initially underlay Russell's attacks on contemporary religious phenomena can be briefly summarized under eight headings. Further elaboration will be reserved for Chapter 5.

1. *God*

The existence of an omniscient Designer and Creator of the universe was believed to be proven by the rationality of Nature and by the reasonableness of the expectation that such a being should exist. Similarly, the belief that God was wise, just, loving, providential and powerful was assumed to be evident in the light of the potential for such attributes that His creatures displayed.

2. *The Bible*

On the grounds of internal consistency, conformity with reason, archaeological evidence, lasting popularity, signs of honourable motivation on the part of its contributors and uniqueness of its message Russell argued, *ex pede Herculem*, that the Bible must be an authentic revelation from God. Its purpose was believed to be the progressive communication of information about God's plan for mankind's development.

3. *History*

In response to the disloyalty that Satan had induced in Adam and Eve, according to Russell, God devised a plan for punishing mankind equitably and for eventually restoring it to the state of perfection forfeited in 'the Fall'. Human history was therefore believed to be the outworking of a plan which covers three distinct epochs: 'The World That Was', ending in the Flood; 'The Present Evil World' and 'The World To Come'.

4. *The Ransom*

Russell taught that mankind's perfection could only be redeemed by the sacrifice of a man who matched Adam's original state of perfection. Jesus Christ was said to have fulfilled that role and to have prepared the way by His death for the restoration of mankind's perfection in the World To Come.

5. *The Mystery*

It was an essential part of Russell's scheme that the full import of God's plan had not previously been revealed, because that would have altered the course of history and frustrated God's purposes. Accordingly, those who were aware of the plan (i.e. Russellites) were believed to be in a uniquely privileged position which would be shared by others only when 'The World To Come' was about to be established on earth.

6. *The Second Coming*

In contrast to the dominant tradition in nineteenth-century millennialism Russell held that Jesus Christ's Second Coming had occurred invisibly before He had completed the foundation for the Kingdom of God on earth and that the years leading up to 1914 were to mark the progressive diffusion of knowledge about the event.

7. *Resurrection and Judgement*

Russell believed that the process whereby the dead of all generations would be resurrected and given the opportunity to display faith in Christ's redemptive powers would begin as soon as the Millennium had been instigated. This would be prefaced by the 'translation' (i.e. death and immediate resurrection in heaven) of the 'peculiar people' who, in full awareness of God's plan and in perfect understanding of the Mystery, would be virtually exempt from the judgement and would proceed directly to everlasting life in heaven. The resurrection of the dead and the judgement of the rest of mankind would be spread over a long period of time in order to give everybody an equal opportunity to learn about Christ's ransom-sacrifice and thereby to exercise faith in its salvific power.

8. *The Millennium*

The 1,000 year period of peace and prosperity was envisaged by Russell as an event on earth, but it would be governed from heaven by Christ and the 'translated' saints. Each resurrected person would enjoy the experience of at least 100 years of perfection before being judged by Christ, but if anybody thereafter began to fall short of perfection in their behaviour they would be immediately consigned to an everlasting oblivion from which there would be no release.

ORGANIZING FOR EVANGELISM

The social organization of the group of people who supported Russell during the first decade of independent Adventist publishing was no less flexible than were the doctrines to which they held. Yet, just as Russell's doctrines progressively crystallized into a fairly permanent body of specific teachings, so a parallel process of structuring took place among the group of people who may be conveniently labelled 'Russellites'. (Incidentally, Russell was reluctant to allow them any special name and insisted that 'we call ourselves simply Christians',[7] but the term 'Russellite' was widely used to refer to them during his lifetime. We shall follow this convention and reserve the more acceptable term 'Bible Student' for referring to Russell's followers after his death.) Thus, the original Bible-study group in Pittsburgh was soon eclipsed in importance by the number of magazine subscribers which reached 10,000 within ten years of *Zion's Watch Tower*'s first appearance.

The unexpected achievement of early success in these matters ironically entailed the necessity to safeguard the commitment of existing sympathizers by creating more congregations. Disconfirmation of the widespread expectation that the millennium would have been instituted soon after 1879 had also rendered necessary a series of *ad hoc* adjustments in both doctrine and social organization.

Doctrinal changes were largely associated with a growing sense of Russell's personal uniqueness and with increasingly confident claims to exclusive truth on behalf of his teachings. The new outlook partly represented an adjustment to the unexpected failure of a crucial prophecy for 1881: contrary to Russell's expectations, Christ did not 'translate into a heavenly condition' all His faithful servants on earth at that time. Instead, Russell interpreted the continuing expansion of his work as a sign that the prophetic significance of 1881 had been God's 'casting off' of the 'nominal Christian churches' as agents of His plan. In addition, he predicted that the close of the Harvest Period for the identification of God's faithful 'saints' would not come before 1914 and that the Russellites had been divinely ordained to ensure that knowledge of God's plans was widely distributed in the interim.

The social organization of Russellites underwent changes consonant with the doctrinal revisions of the mid-1880s which, in turn, had reflected prophetic disconfirmations and unexpected opportunities to spread the knowledge of God's plan. In the face of continually expanding numbers at regular meetings in the Curry Institute Hall in Pittsburgh and of magazine subscribers in many parts of the United States, Russell was obliged to relax his earlier prohibitions against local gatherings of Russellites and to provide guidance about appropriate ways of organizing such occasions. But admonitions against the danger that local groups might develop into 'social club churches' continued to appear frequently in *Zion's Watch Tower*. At the same time, Russell personally supervised the organization and administration of the work of officially appointed colporteurs who hawked Russellite literature over large areas of the USA and of Britain. Indeed, the continuing success of Russell's early evangelism was reflected in decisions to move twice to larger premises, to incorporate Zion's Watch Tower Tract Society as a legal organization and to instigate a formal division of labour among the office workers.

In the later 1880s Russell's leadership became simultaneously more purposive and more personalized. For example, he published *The Divine Plan of the Ages* in 1886 in both book-form and as serialized articles and immediately instructed the colporteurs to concentrate on selling it more forcefully than any other item of literature.

If it was true, as Russell claimed in the Foreword to the 1916 edition, that secular bookshops had been prevented from selling it by the threat of boycott from 'religious zealots', he was quick to turn necessity into a virtue, for when subsequent volumes were incorporated into a series under the general title of *Millennial Dawn*,[8] Russell made vast funds available to help colporteurs to sell them, and the prestige of the colporteur division received frequent boosts from him at public meetings. Yet, he steadfastly refused to allow colporteurs any personal initiative in the presentation of Russellite teachings. For example, Russell dealt extremely harshly with

S. D. Rogers, a colporteur working in England who had successfully augmented sales promotions with public speaking between 1893 and 1894. Rogers was recalled to Allegheny, roundly rebuked and finally villified in a document circulated among Russellites for the purpose of countering Rogers' arguments against Russell's judgement and for exposing his attempts to undermine Russell's authority. In a manner characteristic of many Adventist leaders and portentous of many subsequent crises in the history of the Watch Tower movement, Russell's *ex post facto* explanation of Rogers' disloyalty and defection was that the Great Adversary had been 'concocting a dark conspiracy in the hearts of some who should be "true yoke fellows"'. (z.W.T., 15 April 1894) His remedy for this problem was to ask all faithful Russellites to inform his office immediately if they suspected that any of the salesmen were deviating from doctrinal or procedural norms.

Further prestige and importance were added to the colporteur division in 1895 when it was decided to encourage local groups of Russellites to devote one of their weekly meetings to the programmatic study of the *Millennial Dawn* books. As well as increasing the size of the colporteurs' market, Russell reduced the potential competition from other salesmen by restricting the availability of volumes on credit to full-time, accredited workers. The colporteurs' effectiveness as the main agents for Russell's religious views was reflected in the uninterruptedly upward trend of literature sales between 1890 and 1914 and in the steady increase in magazine subscriptions during the same period.

Not long after Russell had sanctioned the formation of local 'ecclesias' for his followers, he began to exercise increasingly effective control over their structure and functions. This began with the encouragement of a rudimentary liturgy,[9] a regular mid-week meeting that was 'devotional in character, not doctrinal' and that could include 'brotherly exhortation, conference and counsel'; (z.W.T., 15 September 1895) and a simple ceremony of adult baptism by total immersion.

The second indication that ecclesias were growing in importance was the official decision to encourage them to arrange their own version of the annual Memorial meeting in 1894. Previously Russell had conducted this approximation to a celebration of the Lord's Supper[10] in the Allegheny headquarters, but in the face of greatly increased numbers and of their wider geographical dispersion he preferred to encourage a degree of decentralization and, incidentally, a small measure of local autonomy. Nevertheless, there was no hint of any relaxation in the precise regulation of the manner of conducting the Memorial, and the leaders of all ecclesias were strongly urged to send attendance reports to headquarters. Yet, the idea of holding large assemblies of Russellites was not entirely abandoned:

it was merely reorganized in 1893. Large-scale meetings at regional and national levels continued to take place but only under the increasingly close surveillance of high-ranking officials from Russell's staff.

The final stage of the process whereby ecclesias came to assume functions that had previously been performed or directed by Russell's Allegheny office was heralded by the implementation in 1899 of a scheme whereby volunteer Russellites would undertake the distribution of pamphlets outside churches in the vicinity of their local meeting place. This required for the first time a degree of co-ordination among ecclesias that depended for its success upon regional supervision by a representative agent. The representativeness of the agent's position *vis-à-vis* ecclesias was eroded in 1903 when it became the practice for 'volunteer captains' to receive their appointments directly from headquarters and to submit their reports on each area's activities to a special office in Allegheny. At the same time, the strategy controlling group distribution of literature was modified: thenceforth, Russellites would cease to hand out pamphlets outside churches on Sundays only and would undertake house-to-house canvassing on all days of the week. What is more, they were provided with free copies of the *Millennial Dawn* books to be loaned to householders who clearly showed an interest in Russell's ideas. These schemes precipitated a feeling of collective identity among Russellites which, in turn, was a measure of the increasing responsibility for them that Zion's Watch Tower Tract Society was assuming: it had ceased to function merely as a publishing enterprise.

Two further evangelical initiatives from Russell's office during his lifetime cemented the collective relationship among Russellites and served to reinforce the growing dependence of many ecclesias on headquarters. In 1911 a Class Extension scheme was put into operation requiring local groups to arrange, advertise and execute meetings for the promotion of Russell's ideas in areas lacking a Russellite ecclesia. The headquarters supplied all the necessary equipment and advice in return for dictating the precise manner in which the meetings should be conducted. The fact that the scheme did not remain in operation for more than a few years indicates that it did not produce worthwhile gains in literature sales or ecclesial membership.

The second of Russell's later evangelical initiatives was also an attempt to draw attention to Russellite teachings through the medium of public meetings, but the novelty of the scheme and its less overtly missionary character probably accounted for its greater impact than that of the Class Extension scheme. It involved a lavish presentation of coloured lantern slides and a recorded phonograph commentary of Russell's ideas about God's plan for mankind beginning with the Creation and concluding with the Millennium on earth. At a cost of at least $300,000 the programme was first staged in a few American cities in 1914, but, as more copies became available, continuous performances were given in all parts of the country and in many European cities as well. The scheme attracted very large numbers of people and helped to sell enormous numbers of incidental publications but more significant than the amount of publicity that the Photo-Drama attracted were some of its long-term implications for the development of the Russellite movement's internal social structure. It accentuated the high degree of co-ordination between ecclesias that had made the scheme possible. This, in turn, reflected the power of Russell's headquarters staff to manipulate the majority of Russellites in the pursuit of the Watch Tower Bible and Tract Society's[11] own goals. It also evinced the growing dependence of ecclesias as evangelical bodies on Russell and on his fellow-Directors as distributors of the vast funds necessary to support a programme like the Photo-Drama.

Figure 1 (see p. 11) shows that the economic development of the Watch Tower Society under Russell's presidency falls into two fairly distinct periods. Until 1893 the volume of voluntary contributions and magazine revenue increased slowly but then remained static until 1898. At this juncture annual receipts and expenditure were in the region of $10,000, but a sudden improvement occurred after 1898 as a result of the transfer of printing plant worth $160,000 from one of Russell's privately owned companies, The Tower Publishing Company.[12] This facilitated a large reduction in printing costs, thereby freeing money for expanding the scale of operations in all fields of evangelism. It also allowed Russell to exploit overseas markets more efficiently than had thus far been possible.

FOREIGN OUTREACH AND SOCIAL CLASS

Beginning almost simultaneously with the dispatch of a missionary to Britain in 1881 and with the publication of some foreign language editions of *Zion's Watch Tower* in the United States, the foreign outreach of Russell's organization expanded only slowly until he made a number of personal tours of foreign centres of interest in the 1890s.

Missionary work began in Denmark in 1895 and was already under way in South Africa, Switzerland, the West Indies and Colombia. By the time that French and Italian missions had opened in 1903, the annual missionary budget was approaching $14,000, but thereafter Russell sanctioned even more generous budgets for overseas missions and was rewarded by a steady increase in the number of people committing themselves to his movement or, at least, purchasing his literature. Indeed, there were signs

FIGURE I

Watch Tower Bible and Tract Society. Income 1884–1917

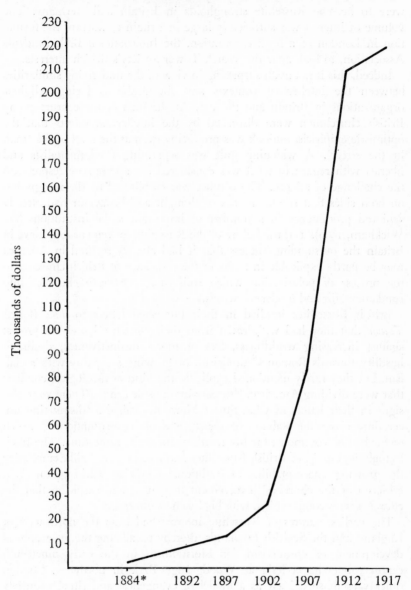

*This is a cumulative figure for the period 1881–1884

that Russell shrewdly foresaw the immense potential of at least the European 'market', and in consequence he spared little expense in the first decade of the twentieth century in sinking the foundations for what were to become Russellite strongholds in Britain and Germany. The volume of interest was sufficiently large in Britain to warrant the formation in London of a legal corporation, the International Bible Students Association, to look after the Watch Tower Society's British interests.

Indeed, this is not at all surprising in view of the underlying similarities between the intellectual contexts and the problems facing religious organizations in Britain and the USA. At the turn of the century many British churchmen were disturbed by the intellectual effects that the optimistic empiricist outlook was producing even at the level of the 'man in the street'. A widening gulf was separating fundamentalists and liberals with regard to what was considered the appropriate response to the challenge of science. The conflict was embittered by the recognition on both sides that secular modes of thought and behaviour had already achieved prominence in a number of important social institutions (see Wickham, 1969). Yet, the failure of the Russellite movement to achieve in Britain the outstanding success that it had already secured in America may be partly explicable in terms of the resistance of British churches to the process of polarization which split most American churches into fundamentalist and modernist wings.

British Russellites implied in their published letters to *The Watch Tower* that they had withdrawn from their churches largely in protest against increasing worldliness, loss of moral distinctiveness, declining hostility towards Roman Catholicism, or growing sympathy with socialism, but they rarely mentioned explicitly the kind of theological conflicts that were dividing American churches into hostile camps. There were also signs in their letters of what Stuart Mews has called a 'disquieting uncertainty about the stability of society and of its assumptions'[13] which seemed to be common to many freethinkers at the same time. The intellectual biographies of British Russellites and freethinkers[14] alike emphasize the growing unacceptability of traditional Christian teachings on Hell, criticism of the churches' involvement in politics and suspicion that the churches were compromised with big business interests.

The earliest centres of Russellite interest had been the north-west of England and the Scottish Lowlands, thereby paralleling the geographical development of enthusiasm for Mormonism in the early nineteenth century, but the ecclesia at Woodgrange Park in north-east London quickly established itself as a model of evangelical and ritual propriety for all nascent Russellite groups. Reliable evidence about ecclesial growth in Britain is unfortunately sparse, but the irregular statistical returns for

Memorial attendance suggest that in the first few years of the twentieth century groups of more than 100 Russellites were meeting regularly in London and Glasgow, while groups of more than twenty were also functioning in most of the large provincial towns. The output of Russellite literature in Britain increased slowly but steadily from 1900 to 1908—the latest date for which records are complete in Russell's presidency—but still amounted to only a small fraction of the American branch's output.

Between 1908 and 1913 Russell visited Europe and the Near East every year, addressing ever larger audiences wherever he spoke and supervising the administration of Watch Tower affairs. In particular he was eager to detect and punish signs of doctrinal deviation or independence of initiative, but he was nevertheless unable to prevent the eventual defection of such prominent Russellites as S. D. Rogers and W. Henninges. Serious disturbance was also reported in the Swiss and Irish branches, but nowhere were the problems of long-range missionary enterprise more acute than in Africa[15] where Joseph Booth, a Seventh Day Adventist missionary in Nyasaland, had introduced Watch Tower literature in 1906. Before reverting to his original Baptist affiliation, Booth had stimulated a widespread, albeit rudimentary, awareness of Russell's teachings in large sections of the native population, and the colonial authorities attributed a large proportion of the blame for the Nyasaland riots of 1915 to the diffusion of half-understood ideas about the millennial significance of 1914. Russell's immediate reaction was to sever all links with the 'unofficial' Watch Tower movement in Africa which has subsequently prospered, and to forbid the promulgation of his own teachings in the absence of 'official' agents of the Watch Tower Society.

Russell was greatly helped in the task of centralizing the administration of American and foreign affairs by the fact that towards the end of his presidency a large proportion of his followers in both Europe and the usa were drawn from the lower social classes (i.e. from all kinds of manual occupations, positions of personal service and minor clerical posts) and were readily submissive to their middle-class leaders. Evidence about the precise social class composition of the early Russellite movement is sadly lacking, but a patchwork picture can be composed from the tiny shreds that are available.[16] On the one hand, statements in the Society's literature make it plain that lower-middle and middle-class Russellites were not uncommon in the ecclesias and that 'people from the middle walks of life'[17] patronized the Watch Tower Society's public exhibitions and meetings. Moreover, the movement's cultural 'style' was clearly middle class in the sense that closely reasoned arguments on abstruse theological and scriptural themes formed the backbone of the Society's literature, and ecclesial meetings centred around the discussion of written works rather than oral teaching. The kind of religious emotionality and the simplification of Scripture that were hallmarks of contemporary religious movements among the working class were anathema to Russell, and the life-style demanded of his followers bore many signs of middle-class influence.

On the other hand, however, we know that working-class Russellites became increasingly numerous in many countries in the period immediately before, during and after the First World War, for schemes for exempting poor Russelites from some of the financial burdens of active participation in the Society's affairs were put into operation; criticism of capitalist businessmen increased in frequency in Watch Tower literature, while denunciation of socialist principles became less common; and the material deprivations of the lower classes received greatly increased sympathy.[18]

In sum, the Watch Tower movement received the cultural imprint of its middle-class founders and leaders during its formative decades and was culturally inappropriate to people from lower social classes, but changes in its internal constitution and its external situation at the time of the First World War heightened its appeal to some working-class people and prepared the way for a massive disturbance in the patterns of social class dominance after the war.

ELDERS AND AUTHORITY PROBLEMS

Not surprisingly, however, Russell's attempts to manipulate ecclesias for his own aims met with resistance in some quarters, more particularly among the middle-class Russellites. The struggle of local leaders to retain their independence of thought and action constitutes a major theme in the history of the Watch Tower movement until the mid-1930s. The earliest groups of Russellites were *informal* in the sense of lacking a written constitution, and *autonomous* in so far as decisions were made without necessary consultation with Russell's headquarters, and there was no written contract linking them. The progressive mobilization of Russellite ecclesias in the pursuit of Russell's own ends was therefore an eloquent testimony to his personal talent for influencing and manipulating people, for he lacked completely any rational-legal authority to control them. (See Beckford, 1972a)

Nevertheless, a small number of ecclesia leaders (or Elders, as they were usually called) persistently refused to collaborate with Russell's staff in evangelical programmes, and remained content merely to subscribe to Russellite ideas. The notion of partial co-operation from ecclesias became increasingly unacceptable to Russell in the 1890s, and he exerted immense pressure on their recalcitrant leaders to conform with his directives. Basically, sources of dissatisfaction among Elders were of four types, but each concerned their anomalous position in those ecclesias that were subject to Russell's efforts to control their internal activities.

In the first place, Elders were systematically discouraged from claiming and, *a fortiori*, exercising what they considered to be personal gifts for independent interpretation of Scripture or for preaching. In rejection of any particular Elder's advancement of special privilege Russell's dismissive reply was always, 'We never did advocate that the church should recognize a leader merely because he said he thought himself divinely appointed.' (z.W.T., 15 March 1906).

A second, and allied, point of conflict between Russell and the Elders concerned his attempts to substitute study of his own writings for study of Scripture. Thus, the establishment of Millennial Dawn discussion groups, Class Extension meetings and Berean Studies[19] seriously undermined the Elders' traditional grounds for their authority and prepared the way for the assertion of the principle that, 'It is not for the Elders, but for the class to determine what meetings it wishes to hold.' (W.T., 15 October 1912)

The third source of dissatisfaction was the method of their appointment to office. Originally, leaders of Russellite groups had emerged 'naturally' through the exercise of personal talents, but Russell became dissatisfied with this arrangement because he suspected that 'natural leaders' imposed their will too forcibly on the group, thereby frustrating his own plans for ecclesial development. Consequently, he argued that leaders should be elected democratically and for only a limited period of time. By the beginning of the First World War 'elective Elders' were common throughout the Watch Tower movement.

Finally, the position of Elders was disturbed by the rise to prominence in the Russellite movement of a body of itinerant representatives known as Pilgrims. From a very small group of part-time public speakers with the general brief to 'build up new congregations or ecclesias',[20] the Pilgrims eventually developed into a highly trained and mobile cohort of trusted executives who supervised many aspects of ecclesial administration and activity. Russellites associated Pilgrims closely with Russell, from whom they undoubtedly received reflected glory, and this largely accounts for the esteem in which they were widely held. The ascendancy of Pilgrims over Elders is also understandable in terms of the material and social advantages that they characteristically enjoyed as middle-class leaders in a movement with strong working-class support. Russell had initially chosen his Pilgrims from those followers whose secular occupations or private wealth enabled them to travel widely in the United States without requiring remuneration from the Watch Tower Society.

The Pilgrims' level of formal education was higher than that of most Russellites, and their preaching assignments undoubtedly gave scope for a display of intellectual superiority. Indeed, they maintained considerable social distance between themselves and the Russellites whom they visited because it made it easier for them to be critical and objective about their hosts and thereby to instill very high standards in congregational leaders. Thus, although they were small in number (rising from four in the 1890s to ninety-three in 1917), their influence over Russellites was enormous, and they were generally successful in ensuring that Russell's directives from headquarters were implemented at the grass-roots level.

It should, of course, be added that the special structural position of Pilgrims in Russell's movement rendered them potentially very powerful manipulators of public opinion. Consequently, those who defected from Russell were able to stimulate extensive support for their deviant views among Russellites.

In spite of (or, in some cases, because of) Russell's efforts to weld his followers into a uniform band of like-minded evangelists, a small number of collective secessions and a large number of individual withdrawals from the Russellite movement occurred before 1916. The immediate cause of disagreement usually concerned doctrinal and organizational matters, but there was an increasingly personal element in the issues that divided Russellites after 1900. On the one hand Russell seemed to become more dogmatically assertive and less tolerant of dissenting opinions, and on the other the public image of his private life was marred by a series of scandals which lent further weight to the criticisms of his detractors. These two aspects of Russell's highly controversial style of leadership were inter-related through common origin in certain personal characteristics.

At the outset of his career as an evangelical publisher and exegete Russell seemed to be heavily dependent for practical advice and moral support on his wife to whom he was married from 1879 until 1906. She had an extremely forceful personality[21] and had been active in stimulating the rapid growth of public interest in Russell's writings, but at the time of their separation in 1897 he was becoming far more self-confident and self-reliant. It appears that Russell's relationship with colleagues and friends could remain amicable only if they declined to challenge his exegetical superiority and his primacy in the Russellite movement. Much of the animosity surrounding the charges of immorality and cruelty levelled at him also derived from personal antagonism generated in the course of communal living in the Bible House at Allegheny and later in the Brooklyn Bethel. In these circumstances it was common for relatively trivial matters to grow into divisive issues out of all proportion to their significance for the Watch Tower movement. Russell's firm belief that the Great Pyramid of Gizeh was a prophetic symbol[22] and his vegetarianism, for example, both served to antagonize some members of the Bethel 'family'. His patriarchal manner, stentorian voice and starchily correct manner of dress also aggravated social relations with all but his most devoted followers and certainly did not endear him to people unacquainted with American middle-class piety.

Russell's growing personal sensitivity to suspected plots for undermining his authority was reflected in a drastic measure taken to test his followers' loyalty and to minimize the possibility of strife among them. In 1908 he asked all his followers to make a formal and public vow which contained the following clause:

> I further vow that, with the exceptions below, I will at all times and at all places, conduct myself towards those of the opposite sex in private exactly as I would do with them in public—in the presence of a congregation of the Lord's people and so far as reasonably possible I will avoid being in the same room with any of the opposite sex alone, unless the door to the room stand wide-open: In the case of a brother—wife, children, mother and sisters excepted. In the case of a sister—husband, children, father and brothers excepted.[23]

The virtual imposition of the Vow produced at least two anticipated results in precipitating the immediate secession of a group of Russellites hostile to Russell's increasingly personal style of leadership and, by contrast, in reinforcing the commitment of large numbers of people loyal to him. The Vow also contributed to the ideological justification for what has remained a distinctive feature of the Watch Tower movement—the inferior status of women. Russell's unhappy marriage and his alleged involvement in several scandalous incidents with young women undoubtedly strengthened his anti-feminism and made him even more sensitive to personal criticism. He had been accused of making sexual advances towards two young women of his housefold, and part of the evidence against him in the divorce court rested on allegations that he had made amatory suggestions to one of the girls. (See Toupin, 1958) The court rejected this evidence, however, on the grounds that the incident had allegedly taken place before the time that Russell was said to have inflicted mental cruelty on his wife, but the whole business clearly aggravated his distrust of women.

In symbolic rejection of the divorce that was granted to his wife in 1906 Russell refused to pay the alimony and preferred to suffer the indignity of seeing his shares in the Watch Tower Society and the United States Investment Company confiscated at a nominal value of $67. Russell had already donated all his shares in the Tower Publishing Company to the Watch Tower Society in 1898, but it is not clear whether this had been an attempt to forestall what he had predicted as the likely result of the divorce proceedings or whether, as Zygmunt suggests, he had disposed of the company because it was no longer economically viable. (See Zygmunt, 1967, p. 360) His fellow-Directors of the Watch Tower Bible and Tract Society saved him from arrest and further humiliation in 1909 by collecting a sum of $9,000 on his behalf in payment of the alimony until 1913 while he was absent in Europe.

But these experiences did not deter him from engaging in law-suits on his own initiative, for he laid charges of defamatory libel against *The Washington Post* in 1908, *The Brooklyn Eagle* in 1911 and the Rev. J. J. Ross in 1912. Only in the first case did Russell successfully defend his interests, but at least he established the important precedent of having recourse to law courts, for this practice has ultimately proved beneficial to latter-day Jehovah's witnesses.

SUCCESS AND SURVIVAL

The virulence of some journalists' and clergymen's attacks on Russell's integrity may become understandable in the light of the impressive statistics of Watch Tower growth in the period 1898–1914. Subscriptions to *The Watch Tower and Herald of Christ's Presence*, as the principal magazine was entitled after 1907, increased from about 10,000 to 45,000; sales of *Millennial Dawn* books, or *Studies in the Scriptures*, as the complete series was renamed in 1906, rose from 85,000 in 1891 (when only three of the six volumes had been written) to 728,474 in 1908; and the number of Memorial attendances grew from at least 6,267 in 1906 to 10,710 in 1911. None of these separate sets of figures gives an accurate picture of the rate at which the Russellite movement expanded in the years preceding the First World War, but in combination they suggest that Russellites were beginning to attract both public attention and its attendant problems.

The growth of effective organizational structures in the Russellite movement and the continual expansion in the volume of its evangelical work during Russell's lifetime are in themselves sufficiently impressive and interesting to warrant close study, but they also have a heuristic significance in the explanation of events occurring between 1914 and 1918. In particularly, they help to account for the Russellite movement's ability to survive a number of serious internal crises and threatening external contingencies that would almost certainly have destroyed any religious groups lacking such a resilient constitution. To these events we now turn.

Russell's prediction in 1886 that 1914 would mark 'the end of the time of the Gentiles' had served both to preserve the commitment to his ideas of those Russellites who might have been discouraged by the non-materialization of prophecies relating to 1881 and to maintain at a high level the evangelistic enthusiasm of those who participated in all the concerted programmes of evangelism prior to 1914. The prophetic signifi-cance of that year had received so much publicity and reinforcement that only an unequivocal sign that the millennium had begun could have averted widespread confusion and disaffection among Russellites. Yet, in the event, what must have seemed like a disconfirmation of their most fervent expectations entailed surprisingly little disturbance in their relationship with the Russellite movement.

In part, the persistence of at least the outward appearance of normality in the Russellite movement was due to Russell's efforts in the years immediately preceding 1914 to warn against the dangers of investing excessive faith in his personal interpretation of biblical prophecy.[24] Simi-larly, Russell was quick to publish articles in the early months of 1915 arguing for the wisdom of suspending judgement on what had (or had not) happened and urging his followers to remain in a state of readiness for an imminent 'translation' of the saints. When, however, it became clear in 1916 that fresh converts were still joining the movement and that it was therefore still possible to achieve success in evangelism, Russell was able to sound even more convincing in his arguments to revive the flag-ging interest of Russellites. Thus, by the time of his death at the end of October in 1916 the Russellite movement had already begun to recover from the traumatic disappointment of 1914 and was gathering numerical strength again.

Russell's sometimes ingenious *ex post facto* rationalizations of events in 1914 undoubtedly contributed towards the survival of the Russellite move-ment through the most potentially disruptive period of its short history, but it cannot be stressed too much that it was only when empirical evidence of continuing evangelistic success became available that the rate of recovery began to improve. In other words, the 'momentum' of the Russellite movement, stemming largely from its efficiently articulated organization, was an immensely important factor in helping it to survive a taxing crisis.

In this respect the apparent failure of prophecy to materialize in the anticipated form led to neither the disintegration nor to the strengthening of the Russellite group, thereby departing from the pattern of well-documented reactions to prophetic failure,[25] but it left the group in an ideological vacuum. Many people were sufficiently disheartened to withdraw from the movement between 1915 and 1916, and the shock of disappointment heightened the remainder's susceptibility to the kind of ideological rationalizations that Russell eventually produced. But these would have been ineffective in the absence of empirical evidence about the movement's *actual* survival and continuity. Furthermore, the fact that the Russellites were scattered over an enormous geographical area (in contrast to the situation of the groups studied by Lofland and Festinger, Riecken and Schachter) and were not therefore in constant communication with the brethren outside their local ecclesia helped to depress the level of overt anxiety and to prevent destructive forces from jeopardizing the movement's existence. Finally, their utter reliance on *The Watch Tower* as the movement's major vehicle for information increased the Editor's responsibility at this juncture for holding Russellites together by publishing highly selected items of news and ideologically appropriate doctrinal pronouncements.

NOTES TO CHAPTER 1

1. *The Watch Tower*, 1 January 1912.
2. Anon (1923), p. 179.
3. *Zion's Watch Tower*, 1 January 1909.
4. *The Bible Student*, vol. 8, no. 3, 1923.
5. For an extended examination of this topic see Beckford (1972b), pp. 360–80.
6. *The Watch Tower*, 15 June 1900. (Henceforward abbreviated to *W.T.*)
7. *Zion's Watch Tower*, February 1884. (Henceforward abbreviated to *Z.W.T.*)
8. The full title of the series was changed in 1904 to *Studies in the Scriptures* when the complete set was as follows:

> Vol. 1. *The Divine Plan of the Ages* (1886)
> Vol. 2. *The Time is at Hand* (1889)
> Vol. 3. *Thy Kingdom Come* (1891)
> Vol. 4. *The Battle of Armageddon* (1897) (originally *The Day of Vengeance*)
> Vol. 5. *The Atonement between God and Man* (1899)
> Vol. 6. *The New Creation* (1904).

9. *Poems and Hymns of Millennial Dawn* (1890).
10. The form of the ceremony was based on Christ's injunction to the Disciples in I Corinthians 11:25 and was timed to coincide with the Jewish Passover on Nisan 14.
11. Zion's Watch Tower Tract Society ceased to be the organization's official title after revisions to its charter in 1896.
12. According to Hébert (1961) the Tower Publishing Co. and the U.S. Invest-

ment Co. were holding companies for Zion's Watch Tower Tract Society and were a source of income for it. In return, the Tower Publishing Co. allegedly supplied the Zion's Watch Tower Tract Society's publishing needs, thereby keeping costs to a minimum.

13. Mews (1966), p. 76. Supporting evidence is also found in Masterman (1909).

14. See Budd (1967); and Minna Edgar (1918a) and 1918b).

15. More detailed accounts are available in Kaufmann (1964); Shepperson (1962); and Shepperson and Price (1958).

16. Extensive interpretation of the evidence, direct and indirect, is available in Beckford (1972b), pp. 518–44.

17. *W.T.*, 1 May 1915. See also Shepperson (1962), pp. 49–50.

18. For information on the predominance of the lower classes among German Bible Students, see Schnell (1957), p. 25.

19. Berean Study meetings, precursors of the present-day Watch Tower meeting, consisted principally of questions and answers based on the *Millennial Dawn* books.

20. *Jehovah's Witnesses in the Divine Purpose* (1959), p. 33. (Henceforward abbreviated to *Divine Purpose*.)

21. There may be grounds for questioning the unfavourable image that Watch Tower literature has always created of Mrs Russell's personality. See Rogerson (1972).

22. *Studies in the Scriptures*, vol. 3, pp. 314–15. Russell's knowledge of the pyramids was drawn largely from Smyth (1864). He was also in communication with the Scottish eccentric, Morton Edgar, who wrote *Great Pyramid Passages and Chambers*, London, 1910.

23. The full text was published in *The Watch Tower*, 15 March 1909.

24. For evidence on the Bible Students who ignored Russell's cautions, see Mac-Millan (1957), p. 47.

25. See, for example, Lofland (1966); Festinger, Riecken and Schachter (1964); and Sears (1924).

CHAPTER 2

CONTINUITY, CONFLICT AND CHANGE

THE SUCCESSION CRISIS

Russell's death on 31 October 1916 during a public-speaking tour of the mid-western United States left the Watch Tower movement in a perilous position, for, although the seriousness of his illness had been known to leading Russellites for a long time, there had been no agreement amongst them on the way in which the movement was to continue in his absence. Indeed, some Russellites even believed that Russell's death would signal the end of organizational developments and the beginning of a period of waiting for the next phase of God's plan to resolve their problems. But others were prepared to work for the movement's continued development, albeit within the framework established by Russell in both precedent and precept. In the event, a conflict between these parties was virtually inevitable and was actually complicated by an additional struggle among factions sharing the view that further development was desirable. The inevitability of a succession crisis was increased by the peculiar nature of Russell's position in the Watch Tower Society,[1] by the increasingly anomalous relationship between Russellites and the wider society and by the variability of the links between ecclesias and the Watch Tower headquarters.

The fact that Russell did not nominate a personal successor to his office of Editor of *The Watch Tower* and President of the Watch Tower Bible and Tract Society suggests that he understood the peculiar nature and locus of the paternalistic authority that he had exercised for nearly forty years. It was inconceivable that anybody should have expected to assume the leadership of the Watch Tower movement in Russell's own fashion, and that was why he had entrusted in his will all his voting rights in the Society to a group of women who, by reason of their sex, were disqualified from holding any office in the Society and were therefore unlikely to arrogate for themselves a monopoly of power. Similarly, he had nominated a committee of five people as joint successors to the office of Editor of the magazine, thereby separating the two major sources of his own power and endeavouring to prevent anybody else from reunifying them. Finally, he had instructed the seven Directors of the Watch Tower Bible and Tract Society to form an Executive Committee for the purpose of supervising day-to-day business. But these tentative moves towards a separation of presidential powers were soon rescinded by the man who was elected President at the Annual General Meeting early in 1917.

The new President, Joseph Franklin Rutherford, had been born into a Missouri farming family in 1869, trained as a lawyer and baptized at a Russellite convention in 1906. He had quickly risen to posts of responsibility in Russell's headquarters on the combined strength of his usefulness as a legal adviser and of his talent for efficient administration, and he became one of Russell's closest associates. Yet, his election to the presidency in January 1917 provoked some vigorous opposition on grounds related both to his personality and to his early actions as President. For, whereas Russell had usually been gentle and friendly with fellowreligionists (in public at least), Rutherford was often rude and brusque; his temperament was moody and his manner withdrawn.

The first incident of concerted resistance to his exercise of presidential power occurred when four Directors of the Watch Tower Bible and Tract Society who evidently disliked Rutherford's overbearing manner, resisted his exercise of executive power. By invoking an article in the Society's charter which demanded that every Director should be elected annually, Rurtherford expelled them from the board and thereby overrode the provisions of Russell's will according to which they should have held directorships for life. Since Rutherford and the other two Directors had been elected to executive positions in the Society at the recent Annual General Meeting, they could argue in their own defence, by implication at least, that they had been simultaneously re-elected to the board and were therefore holding their directorships legally. The struggle was largely conducted in the circulation of polemical documents,[2] but Rutherford's success in averting the threat of a 'palace revolution' was sealed at the Annual General Meeting of January 1918 with his own re-election to office and with the election to the board of Directors of all his personal nominees.

Although as many as fifty prominent Bible Students immediately seceded from the Watch Tower movement in protest against Rutherford's harsh autocracy, the incident left him in even closer control of Watch Tower affairs and more secure in the support of his entourage. His security was further reinforced at the 1920 Annual General Meeting when he persuaded shareholders to accept a charter amendment allowing Directors three years in office instead of only one. In this way, he obviated the threat that his rivals might have constituted for him at every annual gathering, but by 1923 active opposition within the Watch Tower Society had virtually died out. The incident is sociologically interesting for the light that it throws on the continuity of power and authority vested in the position of Editor of *The Watch Tower*. None of the 'opposition' broadsheets could have attained the wide distribution enjoyed by the Society's official organ which represented Rutherford's views exclusively.

The other major challenge to Rutherford's authority only resulted in a Pyrrhic victory for him, since it entailed a more protracted dispute and a serious drop in the numbers of active Bible Students. It centred around Rutherford's decision to commission two long-standing Bible Students to edit the notes left by Russell as a sketch for a seventh volume in the series *Studies in the Scriptures* and publish them in book form. When the book appeared in mid-1917 under the title *The Finished Mystery*, it was greeted by an outburst of indignation among Bible Students at Rutherford's audacity in suggesting that it was the conclusion to Russell's life-work. Prominent among the protestors were the four expelled Directors and P. S. L. Johnson who had formerly played important roles in Russell's administration but who had been virtually disfellowshipped by Rutherford for resisting his orders. The number of Bible Students remaining sufficiently loyal to Rutherford at least to carry on subscribing to *The Watch Tower* fell to less than 3,000. But it is clear that the violent opposition to publication of the alleged seventh volume of *Studies in the Scriptures* was not motivated solely by respect for Russell's memory but arose from a complex of different objections to Rutherford's personality, policies and practices.

The exaggerated, posthumous legitimations that the anti-Rutherfordites propounded for Russell's status as the exclusive inspiration and leader of the Watch Tower movement illustrate what A. Gouldner (1955), following Daphne du Maurier, termed the 'Rebecca myth'. Those Bible Students who remained convinced of Russell's unique status in God's plan refused to acknowledge the authority of his successor and actively plotted to remove Rutherford from office when it became clear that he was willing to depart from his predecessor's policies.

Yet, the effects of the crisis were still being felt long after the Watch Tower Society's internal upheaval had subsided, because publication of the infamous seventh volume had also triggered off external opposition to Rutherford's movement. Eight of the Society's top leaders (including Rutherford) were sentenced in the USA to long periods of imprisonment in 1918 on charges of publishing seditious material in *The Finished Mystery*, and their highly publicized trial attracted much public opprobrium to the Bible Student cause. Consequently, the Brooklyn Bethel was sold, the publishing programme was restricted to English language editions of *The Watch Tower* alone, and only minimal correspondence was maintained with Bible Student ecclesias. The fact that the leaders were released on appeal after less than one year in prison did not serve to restore Bible Student fortunes immediately, for it was not until the end of 1919 that full programmes of publishing and evangelism could be implemented from the new headquarters at Columbia Heights, Brooklyn. In a variety of ways, then, publication of *The Finished Mystery* had precipitated a two-year crisis for the Watch Tower movement from which it emerged both depleted in strength and discredited in many people's eyes—but perhaps more internally cohesive under Rutherford's assertive leadership. In part, the cohesion was a reaction against the agitation of ex-Russellites and ex-Bible Students for the downfall of Rutherford's regime, and awareness of enemies within the movement as well as outside it certainly incited Bible Students to a strenuous defence of their cause.

Reverberations of internal and external disruptions in the American branch of the Watch Tower movement were felt in the European branches, but their full force was tempered by the remoteness of overseas Bible Students from the intensely personal issues that were contributory to the struggle for power at the centre of the movement's administration. The core of active opposition to Rutherford could only be mobilized therefore by personal contact with people who had either witnessed events at Brooklyn or learnt of them from reliable first-hand sources, but for the majority, rumour offered the only antidote to official propaganda. In addition, European Bible Students were distracted from disruptions in the American branch by the relatively more pressing considerations of the World War. At the same time, Bible Students were still experiencing the depressing effects of the apparent disconfirmation of Russell's interpretation of prophecy relating to 1914, and in Britain, at least, schismatic Russellites were actively undermining support for the claims that the Watch Tower Society still enjoyed divine guidance.[3] Thus, it was only after 1920 that European Bible Student organizations began to regain their pre-war levels of activity, and even then the rates of growth remained low outside Germany.

IDEOLOGICAL AND ORGANIZATIONAL INNOVATIONS

In addition to the advantages that Rutherford derived from the withdrawal of his personal enemies from the Watch Tower Society, the enforced hiatus in normal administration allowed several hallowed traditions to fall into desuetude, thereby providing him with scope for comprehensive reform of existing arrangements. In particular, the two years of disruption were a breaking-in period for a radically new style of leadership which achieved outstanding results in the following two decades. Rutherford was well aware that he could not expect legitimation for his exercise of authority on the same charismatic grounds that his predecessor had enjoyed, and some of his earliest actions as President evinced the conscious desire to establish purely rational-legal grounds for the legitimation of his authority. This was clearly paralleled by a move towards greater standardization in the formal communication between Bible Students and the Watch Tower offices which, in turn, probably reflected Rutherford's ambition to stamp out the vestiges of personal influences bequeathed by Russell to the structure and style of his movement. Similarly, Rutherford advanced no claims to special divine guidance for himself but argued that, if God had used Pastor Russell as His agent on earth, then it was most unlikely that He would fail to make continuing use of the organization that Russell had founded. As soon as the activities of the Watch Tower movement showed signs of expansion, Rutherford tried to reinforce his position with the argument that God must still be favouring the Watch Tower Society and that Rutherford's leadership must, therefore, be acceptable to Him.

On the strength, therefore, of largely rational and pragmatic claims to legitimation for his authority Rurtherford undertook to reorganize and reinvigorate the Watch Tower movement[4] after the First World War. Ideological (as distinct from doctrinal) revision was clearly a necessary adjunct to his tasks, but it attracted a surprisingly small amount of his attention: in fact, the first few years of his presidency were marked by his failure to produce a different account of the prophetic significance of events after 1914 from the account offered by Russell in 1916. Following some of Russell's later hints, Rutherford suggested that the 'Harvest period' of forty years might have begun in 1878 and might therefore be expected to culminate in 1918 (*W.T.*, 1 October 1917), but his tentative reaction to the passing of 1918 was that the Harvest had indeed finished and that the full complement of the class of people destined for translation to heaven had been assembled. The further delay in the materialization of the millennium was therefore interpreted in 1919 as a sign that the loyalty and powers of endurance of the 'Kingdom class' were being tested, and Rutherford saw in the disruptions of the Society's work unmistakable evidence that God was indeed finding fault with some supposedly sanctified people. (*W.T.*, 15 August 1919)

Meanwhile, support for continued commitment to the Watch Tower movement was derived from his prediction that the year 1925 would be the date when the 'ills of humankind shall begin to be treated with divine remedy² (*W.T.*, 15 April 1920) and that, in consequence,

> Never before in the world's history has there been such a propitious time and opportunity for doing good to the people. All mankind is in distress; all are in perplexity; the panacea for these human ills can be found only in the message of the Kingdom, and the Lord's ambassadors are granted the privilege and opportunity of delivering this message of consolation. (*W.T.*, 15 September 1919)⁵

Yet, curiously, it was not until 1923 that Rutherford published an extended interpretation of the parable of the Ten Virgins as a coherent account of the scriptural significance of events occurring between 1916 and 1919. (*W.T.*, 1 October 1923) Thus, the initial and crucial phase of Rutherford's attempts to revitalize the Watch Tower movement in 1920 was lacking in strictly doctrinal justification.

Rutherford's most pressing objective in the early 1920s was to establish clearly, and to justify, a limited number of goals that Bible Students could agree on pursuing together, and in this concern he showed that he was continuing some of the policies of Russell. To argue, as did many of his critics, that Rutherford had deserted the traditions of Russellism is to overlook the considerable degree of continuity in purely *practical* matters between the two presidencies. The trend towards the attempted subordination of ecclesias to central agencies, the assertion of public evangelism as the primary responsibility of Bible Students and the interference of Watch Tower Society officials in ecclesial and regional administration had begun in the 1890s with Russell's approval. In fact, the early years of Rutherford's presidency paralleled in remarkable ways the developments of the 1880s: in both cases an important prophecy failed to be obviously confirmed by observable events; large numbers of sympathizers deserted the movement; *ex post facto* doctrinal interpretation was slow to crystallize; but the continuing conversion of newcomers evinced a continuity in the group's mission; and, finally, a new ideological understanding of the future crystallized around the central notion of unremitting evangelism.

Although Rutherford did not introduce ideological changes as soon as he had acquired presidential power, the changes that he did promote in the mid-1930s represented a significant reorientation of the Watch Tower movement's basic commitments and values. For, whereas he had considered the task of Bible Students in 1919 to be the delivery of a 'message of consolation', his views underwent severe modification in the following decade. In the conviction that since 1918 Bible Students had constituted a

New Nation under the active guidance of Jesus Christ, Rutherford first demanded that they 'advertize, advertize, advertize the King and his kingdom'. (*W.T.*, 1 November 1922) Then he chose to direct Bible Students' energies towards an aggressive attack on what he termed 'the unholy alliance of "Big Business" and big politicians supported by big preachers'. (Rutherford, 1927, p. 11) By the mid-1930s Rutherford had welded together the elements of a grand theory of Satan's conspiracy against the attempts of Bible Students to disseminate knowledge of God's strategy for saving people from the impending holocaust. In the process, of course, the 'tone' of his ideological writing was transformed into an abrasive and caustic demagoguery that alienated still further the few remaining middle-class Russellites.

Although the identity of cause and effect may be difficult to establish with precision, it is nonetheless clear that the changing ideological tone of Rutherford's propaganda coincided with the growth of lower-class support for the Watch Tower movement after the First World War. This would bear out the interesting comparative proposition of Peter Worsley:

> The aims, and the focus of interest, of the upper-class millenarists are normally anything but revolutionary. (But) . . . when alternative radical ideologies are lacking, these quite unrevolutionary creeds can be invested with quite different meaning, and can come to possess a different social and sociological significance when taken up by radicalized masses, whatever the initial mildness of the doctrines, and however unrevolutionary the original progenitors. (Worsley, 1957, pp. 316–17)

In order to achieve his evangelistic aims Rutherford had also antagonized many Bible Students by eventually mounting a two-fold attack on Russell fifteen years after his death.[6] On the one hand he denied that Russell, as an individual, had been foreshadowed in Scripture as 'the faithful and wise servant' depicted in *Matthew* 25:45 and 'the man with the writer's inkhorn' from *Ezekiel* 9:2 (thereby confounding two long-cherished items of Bible Student symbolism), but argued that the Watch Tower Society as a collectivity, was the correct referent of the symbols. (*W.T.*, 1 September 1931) On the other hand Rutherford openly criticized Russell for suggesting that Bible Students should pray for the sake of the allied war effort in 1916, for an allegedly incorrect interpretation of the Book of Ruth, for apparently favouring wealthy followers and for endorsing the elective Elder system.

Two important consequences followed from Rutherford's adoption of 'abrasive' tactics in confronting the world with his views of God's plans.

Firstly, leaders of organizations that recurrently received the thrust of Rutherford's incendiary polemics responded with equally aggressive campaigns to stifle his outbursts. The American government's decision to charge Watch Tower leaders with sedition for circulating copies of *The Finished Mystery* had been an omen of what was to come, and there is evidence that spontaneous acts of violence had been committed against Bible Students in Brooklyn at the same time. It is not altogether surprising, therefore, that ill-will towards Bible Students was widespread at the end of the war and was aggravated by the increasingly acerbic tone of Rutherford's public denunciations of major social institutions. Indeed, stories of violence and discrimination against them abounded in the columns of *The Golden Age*, a semi-monthly magazine introduced in 1919 to supplement the almost exclusively doctrinal contribution of *The Watch Tower*.

Secondly, the deterioration of relations between leaders of the Watch Tower movement and representatives of powerful social institutions and agencies in America and Europe alike had the effect of heightening the Bible Students' sense of belonging to a distinctive body which was in important respects at odds with its environing society. This was facilitated by the preparation of clear policies on conscientious objection, noncombatant status and appeals against conscription. The fact that Bible Students were among the estimated 6,000 (Sibley and Jacob, 1952) conscientious objectors imprisoned in Britain also helped to strengthen their own and their fellow religionists' consciousness of kind.

Unwittingly, Bible Student leaders found themselves representing the Watch Tower Society in quasi-official capacities, thereby formalizing the kind of relations with political and judicial agencies that had previously been disparaged. A comparison with Christadelphianism (B. R. Wilson, 1961, pp. 258–9), however, is instructive at this juncture since some prominent Christedelphians strove hard to induce uniformity into their followers' position *vis-à-vis* military conscription despite this movement's overriding concern for ecclesial autonomy. There was relatively little anxiety among Bible Students, by contrast, about their varied attitudes towards conscription and they would almost certainly have resented any attempt by their leaders to impose uniformity on them.[7] If the events of the First World War had helped to stimulate feelings of brotherhood among Bible Students, Rutherford's vitriolic attacks on a wide range of post-war social institutions sealed their unity by being directed on behalf of Bible Students at 'outside' groups and by precipitating retaliatory attacks from 'outsiders'. At the same time he emphasized the separateness of Bible Students from the rest of society by denying that 'character development' was the principal end of their religious life and by asserting that they constituted a 'peculiar people' having distinctive evangelical tasks to perform. This represents a sharp departure from Russell's views about relations with 'the world', and it is instructive to note that while Rutherford often used phrases that had been hallowed by Russell, he changed their meaning in accordance with the reorientation of Watch Tower ideology. Thus, 'peculiar people' in Russell's usage had referred to the unique privilege of life in heaven to be enjoyed exclusively by Russellites, but in Rutherford's usage the phrase referred rather to the uniqueness of the evangelical task facing Bible Students on earth. The switch of emphasis from the future to the present and from heaven to earth is indicative of Rutherford's determination to mobilize his followers in the pursuit of highly specific and practical goals.

The fact that the aggregate number of subscribers to Watch Tower magazines remained largely static from 1919 to the early 1930s probably conceals a high turn-over rate in actual personnel, for the evidence from groups of schismatic Bible Students (Rogerson, 1969, p. 200 and p. 218) indicates that there was a steady 'migration' of Bible Students out of Rutherford's movement and into groups proclaiming loyalty for the most part to the form and ideals of the Watch Tower movement during Russell's presidency. Nevertheless, the number of colporteurs grew from 507 in 1919 to about 2,000 in 1932, and in the same period, according to Alan Rogerson's estimate (1969, pp. 52–3), the number of Bible Students supporting Rutherford increased from 18,000 to 25,000. Probably more significant was the disproportionately large growth in the sheer volume of evangelical material distributed by the relatively constant number of Rutherford's Bible Students. Yet, apparent improvements in their *per capita* efficiency as evangelists undoubtedly mask a bi-polar distribution of effort between on the one hand relatively few but extremely active and enthusiastic 'field-workers' and on the other, the large mass of committed but inactive Bible Students.

A symbol of Rutherford's intention to mould Bible Students into a cohesive group of efficient evangelists was the official endowment in 1931 of the collective title 'Jehovah's witnesses' on his active supporters. The new title symbolized a break with the legacy of Russell's traditions, the instigation of new outlooks and the promotion of fresh methods of administering evangelism. The new title also heralded doctrinal changes whose main sociological consequence was clarification of the spiritual status and life prospects of various categories of supporters, members and non-members of the Watch Tower movement.

Whereas Russell had argued after 1881 that the boundaries of the group of 'saints' who were to form part of Christ's government of the impending Kingdom of God on earth had not been fully determined at that time,

Rutherford was obliged by the sheer numerical strength of people professing faith in Watch Tower beliefs and by the non-materialization of the
millennium to teach that the 'church class' or 'little flock' of 144,000
would not be the only people to survive Armageddon. (*W.T.*, 1 May
1929) But the 1930s witnessed a gradual narrowing of Rutherford's ideas
about the precise delimitation of the groups which would survive on
earth. The notion that only Jonadabs (i.e. people professing faith in the
divine nature of the Watch Tower Society's guidance) and 'saints' would
survive Armageddon became orthodox by 1932, and by the beginning of
the Second World War the distinction between the 'little flock' of 144,000
and Jonadabs also began to lose its significance. Thenceforth, *all* active
participants in the Watch Tower movement were considered to be the
exclusive beneficiaries of a covenant with God for their protection. By
contrast, of course, those who did not align themselves with the Watch
Tower Society were believed to have forfeited their chances of surviving
Armageddon and were implicitly excluded by categorization from enjoy-
ment of the envisaged millennial benefits.

The symbolic and doctrinal innovations of the early 1930s occurred
within a framework of organizational rearrangements designed to make
the Watch Tower movement more resistant to the internal and external
forces of disruption and, in a longer perspective, better equipped to
accomplish evangelism. Above all, it was essential to secure the loyal
co-operation of all ecclesial leaders in the increasingly standardized and
systematic organization of evangelism at the local level, for these men held
the key to the loyalty and mobilizability of their ecclesial members.
Rutherford's imposition of routines that accorded with his overall strategy
and that received constant ideological reinforcement in the Society's
publications gradually eroded ecclesial opposition to his schemes or at
least provoked outright dissent. Thus, unless Elders agreed to take and
to pass the *Verbi Dei Minister* test of doctrinal orthodoxy, they were
subject to immense social and ideological pressures either to revise their
views or to resign from positions of responsibility. The test consisted of
twenty-two questions dealing with topics from *Studies in the Scriptures*
and fulfilled some of the functions of a catechism in so far as the answers
could be learned rote-fashion. Their performance of leadership tasks was
scrutinized after 1928 by Regional Service Directors whose brief specifically included general responsibility for implementation at local level of
evangelistic schemes originating in the highest echelons of the Society's
administrative hierarchy. Furthermore, Elders in the same neighbour-
hood were forbidden to form 'speakers' circuits' in which, during
Russell's presidency, the more talented orators had enjoyed considerable
freedom of expression and public esteem. Finally, they were explicitly

discouraged from creating their own exegetical or liturgical styles in preference to the pattern of uniform ecclesial meetings that Rutherford was trying to establish.

Yet, the prospects for absolute control over local ecclesias were poor as long as Elders continued to be elected into office by members of their own groups. Russell had also tried to check the independence of 'natural leaders' in ecclesias, but in the 1930s the centralizing and standardizing thrust of Rutherford's schemes demanded an even greater measure of control over ecclesias (or 'companies' as they were called after 1936) and, *ipso facto*, over their leaders. Thus an article in *The Watch Tower* in 1932 (*W.T.*, 15 August 1932) announced that, in the absence of scriptural justification, the practice of electing Elders in companies should cease and should be replaced by the nomination of suitable candidates for actual appointment by officials of the Watch Tower Society. The demise of the elective Elder system represented a serious loss of the already dwindling autonomy of companies of Jehovah's witnesses, for the active involvement of the Society's full-time staff in selecting local leaders virtually ensured that only men who displayed complete dedication to the pursuit of the kind of goals that Rutherford had been promoting since 1919 would be appointed.

Rutherford's concern to gain control over Elders and thereby over whole companies was not dictated principally by considerations of doctrinal purity, as has frequently been the case with other religious movements,[8] but was largely rooted in the desire to achieve ever higher levels of evangelical 'output' by Jehovah's witnesses. This could only be accomplished, according to Rutherford, through unremitting striving to satisfy quotas for hours by individuals in door-to-door sales campaigns, and this, in turn, depended upon the ability of company Elders to stir their members to enthusiastic activity. Pressure on Elders to persuade their fellow Bible Students to engage in the officially sanctioned programmes of 'field-service' had been exerted as early as 1920, but they were greatly helped in later years by the provision of schemes under the direct supervision of Watch Tower headquarters. On the one hand, the Society established its own radio station in New York in 1924 and broadcast regular programmes to a progressively numerous audience until 1937, and on the other hand, the Society made available to volunteers portable phonographs and sound recordings of Rutherford's broadcast speeches as aids in door-to-door evangelism. Eventually, synchronization between broadcasts and distributions of Watch Tower literature produced a high degree of uniformity in the work of Jehovah's witnesses all over the USA, and the role of the Society's own agents in arranging such concerted action was far from negligible. Needless to say, many companies refused to participate in the 'service work', and as late as 1934 only 346 out of 371 British groups were actually engaged in official programmes. In the USA the proportion of 'dissenting' groups among the total number of groups affiliated to the Watch Tower movement was smaller, because schismatic groups had already siphoned off most disaffected Witnesses.

By the mid-1930s, therefore, Rutherford had succeeded in creating a high level of doctrinal orthodoxy among his followers, he had persuaded most of them of the need to be unselfishly energetic in centrally organized 'service work' and he had largely ensured that the leaders of companies complied with his plans for their development. At the same time, however, he had sullied the movement's public image and he had provoked the lasting anger of several important interest-groups in American and European societies. The costs of Rutherford's reorganization were also reflected in the steadily declining number of American subscribers to the Watch Tower magazines after 1928, in the lack of financial stability for the movement as a whole before the mid-1930s and in the stagnation of membership statistics in Britain.

EXTERNAL PERSECUTION

A new factor that came into operation in the mid-1930s was the necessity to confront systematic and ruthless persecution or suppression in many parts of the world, and it occasioned a wide variety of effects in the structure of the Watch Tower movement and in its material fortunes. But the overall result was probably a strengthening of internal cohesion and an improvement in evangelistic performance.

Many of Rutherford's followers were already accustomed to the view that Satan was intensifying his campaign of terror against the defenders of truth on earth. Consequently, the news that Adolph Hitler had begun to persecute Jehovah's witnesses in Germany came as little surprise but merely confirmed most of them in their conviction that the contemporary social order was showing signs of imminent collapse. Yet, the brutality and ruthlessness of persecution in Germany must have shocked even the most hardened veterans of Watch Tower clashes with civil, military and religious authorities. German Bible Students had been subject to periodic harassment since the First World War and were inured to being charged with alleged subversion or financial chicanery, but administrative tribunals usually found in their favour.[9] In February 1933, however, Hitler formally proscribed all Watch Tower activities and stipulated penalties for infraction of his edict ranging from fifteen months to five years in prison. Nazi ideologists accused them of sympathizing with the Jews, being implicated in international communism and showing disrespect for the *Führer*.

By 1939 at least 6,000 Jehovah's witnesses were living in prison-camps or mental institutions, and additional 'unofficial' persecution was commonly meted out by mobs of Nazi sympathizers. Jehovah's witnesses were sufficiently numerous in the camps to warrant special classification and identification, and some evidence suggests that they were often singled out for especially violent or degrading treatment.[10] But it is not known how many of them died either directly or indirectly as a result of their prison-camp experiences. Despite protests to the League of Nations, massive petitioning of Hitler personally and the active intervention of the American State Department, Hitler confiscated all Watch Tower property in Germany including the extensive buildings and effects of the large Branch headquarters at Magdeburg, which were retained after the war without compensation first by the Russian forces of the occupation and then by the German Democratic Republic.

Although the number of active Jehovah's witnesses in the solidly Roman Catholic countries of Italy and Spain was considerably lower than in Germany, the available evidence suggests that they were subjected to basically similar patterns of proscription and persecution. Indeed, their refusal to undertake military duties has remained the occasion of tenacious harassment and legal penalization in Spain, Italy, Portugal and France.

By cruel irony Jehovah's witnesses were simultaneously persecuted in Germany for allegedly communist or Jewish sympathies and in the USA for allegedly pro-Axis sympathies, but in the latter case the penalties were less harsh and the legal procedure more intricate. There were similarities, however, between these two countries in the pattern of discriminatory violence committed against the Witnesses before the 1930s. Several outbursts of indignant anger among some patriotic and religious groups had been directed at the Witnesses, but it was only in the early 1930s that aggressive and provocative Watch Tower activity sparked off widespread violence against Jehovah's witnesses. They had deliberately challenged local ordinances and laws in spreading their millennial message as effectively as possible and had therefore forced the opponents of the Watch Tower movement to adopt forceful counter-measures. Consequently, their legal tactics included invoking against Jehovah's witnesses both local and State laws requiring travelling salesmen to possess vending licences, forbidding certain kinds of work on Sundays and preventing salesmen from entering privately-owned housing estates. In 1936 alone, for example, 1,149 Jehovah's witnesses were arrested on charges relating to these ordinances and laws,[11] but a Supreme Court verdict of 1938 in the Witnesses' favour did not prevent their enemies from employing such 'extra-legal' tactics as harassing them in door-to-door evangelism, covertly blocking attempts of Watch Tower leaders to make radio broadcasts on commercial radio networks and occasional bouts of overt, physical violence or destruction of property.

The urgent need for Jehovah's witnesses to present a unified and organized resistance to hostile forces in the usa helped to reinforce their collective consciousness and the development of centralized agencies to protect their common interests. The bulk of their legal problems followed from the decision of a large number of American States to make it compulsory for schoolchildren to salute the national flag during the daily assembly.[12] A spate of expulsions of sectarians' children for refusing to salute the flag followed a District court verdict of 1935 supporting a Jehovah's witness named Gobitis in withdrawing his children from a school in which flag-saluting was compulsory. A loose coalition of patriotic associations appealed the decision at all levels of the judicial system until the Supreme Court reversed the lower courts' decisions and ruled in May 1940 that schools *did* have the right to impose the flag-saluting ceremony on all children in their charge. Until the verdict was reversed in the Supreme Court in 1943 the Witnesses suffered untold violence and discrimination.

The coincidence of a Supreme Court verdict that was inimical to Jehovah's witnesses' interests and the outbreak of the Second World War in Europe fanned the fires of anti-Watch Tower feeling that had been smouldering since 1917 in the usa. War-fever and heightened patriotism canalized widespread hostility towards several minority groups and in particular towards the Witnesses who were commonly accused of sympathizing with the German cause and of trying to undermine the potential American war-effort. Their widespread refusal to register for conscription, to bear arms or to undertake directed civilian work made them a convenient scapegoat for patriotic indignation. Thus, they constituted about 75 per cent of all people prosecuted in civil courts for conscription offences and, if convicted, they received average sentences of 30.6 months imprisonment. (See Sibley and Jacobs, 1952) As many as 2,000 Witnesses were thus imprisoned in the usa during the Second World War, and most of them served full sentences because they would not accept parole on the condition that they refrained from doing any public service-work.

The contrast between the haphazard way in which Watch Tower leaders had attempted to defend the interests of Bible Students in the First World War and their systematic, forceful strategy for coping with similar problems in the Second World War illustrates the extent of the Watch Tower's development over two decades. Similarly, the fact that

Bible Students had made their own decisions about an appropriate position *vis-à-vis* military conscription in the First World War, whereas Jehovah's witnesses relied heavily on directives and guidance from headquarters in the Second World War underlines the increasingly close and inclusive relationship that developed in the interim between the movement's centre and its periphery.

Outside the USA preparations for the Second World War brought serious disruptions to Watch Tower evangelism and to the private lives of Jehovah's witnesses. Nowhere was their plight as dire as in Germany and Austria, but they were widely harassed or suppressed in many countries. The suppression of Watch Tower activities occurred in Canada, New Zealand, Australia and in many smaller British dependencies, but in Britain itself there was no formal proscription on company meetings or service-work. British Jehovah's witnesses suffered mainly from the ban on imports of literature from the USA and from problems of classification under the National Service Act of 1939. Like their American brethren, those liable for enlistment also found it almost impossible to win the status of minister of religion and were consequently classified as conscientious objectors, but most of them refused to accept directed labour in the civilian sphere. By the end of the war at least 1,500 British Jehovah's witnesses had served prison sentences for infraction of conscription laws, and some notorious cases of successive imprisonments for repeatedly refusing directed civilian work had occurred. Yet, British Witnesses rarely suffered the kind of discriminatory violence that was widespread elsewhere.

The inability of the Watch Tower movement to resist governmental pressures for its suppression outside the USA was clearly illustrated during the Second World War in Germany, France, Italy, Spain, Australia, New Zealand, Canada, Japan and the majority of African colonial territories. The disruption of international communication networks proved an insurmountable obstacle to the maintenance of normal company activity in countries where Watch Tower literature had to be imported. Clearly the policy of imposing American control over Branch affairs had not been helpful in preparing Branch officials to take full responsibility for the Society's affairs in their own country. Nevertheless, the British Branch officials were sufficiently well prepared to accept a measure of autonomy from 1942 to 1945, and elsewhere in the world clandestine Watch Tower activity served to prevent a total collapse of the movement.

There was no parallel among Jehovah's witnesses of the kind of 'treating with the State for special privileges' that became the practice of Christadelphians, for example, whose 'hostility to temporal powers . . . was replaced by a greater emphasis on "rendering to Caesar"'. (B. R.

Wilson, 1961, p. 264) In contrast, Jehovah's witnesses refused categorically to agree to a compromise between their absolute refusal to obey enlistment orders and the temptation to accept directed civilian labour tasks from conscription tribunals. Thus, although Bryan Wilson was correct in observing that:

> Groups which seek to respond only to divine government find themselves involved in the secular purposes and arrangements of human governments. Sects must thus develop organs to function in accordance with the categories employed by the State and its bureaucratic structure of administration. (B. R. Wilson, 1961, p. 57)

the example of Jehovah's witnesses shows that the development of organs suitable for dealing with enlistment problems does not necessarily entail obedience to the State's directives. It also shows that neither persecution nor prosecution entailed any moderation of Rutherford's attacks on the state of contemporary society.

The relatively detached and retreatist tone of Rutherford's early observations on secular affairs yielded to a more caustic and bitter outlook in later years. Whereas his advice to Bible Students in 1925 had been to 'avoid controversies, keep away from mobs, do not participate in radical movements, live a peaceable and quiet life' (*W.T.*, 1 May 1933), he later encouraged American Jehovah's witnesses not simply to accept with resignation all the attempts of Catholic Action, Fascism and Nazism to prevent them from doing service-work but to fight back through deployment of large numbers of supporters and, if necessary, to answer violence with violence. Similarly at the outbreak of war he enjoined all loyal Witnesses to help unmask the alleged campaign of Roman Catholic forces to obstruct Watch Tower evangelism and to combat all attempts to besmirch the Society's public image.

Paradoxically, the period in which Jehovah's witnesses were most vociferous in their anathematization of external conditions in the late 1930s coincided with a move towards greater collective introversion in the Watch Tower movement. The term 'collective introversion' refers in this context to the predisposition of Jehovah's witnesses to look towards the Watch Tower Society for the provision of an increasingly large number of basic services and consciously to insulate themselves as a group against influences originating outside the group.

Firstly, Kingdom Schools were established to accommodate children expelled for refusing to salute the American flag. Despite repeated disclaimers of official Watch Tower involvement in the scheme, there is little doubt that the Society's leaders encouraged it. Secondly, Pioneer homes were established in Britain for accommodating small groups of young, full-time evangelists. Thirdly, and less deliberately, Witnesses who were evacuated from British cities turned for moral support to Witnesses in their new neighbourhoods, thereby creating an extensive network of social relations which still survives in some places. The material hardships of that period also helped to increase the extent of mutual obligations among members of all companies. Finally, the purely 'sacramental' functions of companies were accentuated at a time when supplies of American evangelistic materials were unavailable. The fact that such ideas had always been frowned upon in the past by Watch Tower leaders indicates how far-reaching these apparently trivial changes were in the Society's adaptation to perceived social change.[13] These findings are in line with B. R. Wilson's expectation that 'revolutionist sects, under circumstances of external duress, have altered their response to one of introversion' (B. R. Wilson, 1959), but we must emphasize that this change represents only a temporary shift of emphasis in the Watch Tower movement's response to prevailing conditions and does not indicate that it experienced a complete transformation of character.

THE THEOCRACY

The move towards greater collective introversion also reflected changes in the design of its internal organization, for the culmination of Rutherford's reforms was the declaration in June 1938 (*W.T.*, 1 and 15 June 1938) that Jehovah had assumed direct control of the Watch Tower Society and that the increasing intensity of anti-Watch Tower activity in all parts of the world was proof that the new 'theocratic' arrangements had provoked Satan to launch a last desperate campaign to suppress the forces of goodness and truth. Discussion and contemplation of theocratic reorganization therefore focused Jehovah's witnesses' attention on matters of relevance to the internal working of their movement. The detailed reorganization of the Theocracy provided for unmitigated central control over all Watch Tower activity, for the appointment of personnel to all posts of responsibility to be the prerogative of the Society's top leaders and for the requirement that all company members (including Jonadabs) should submit to headquarters regular accounts of their evangelical work. The ideological justification for theocratic reorganization was constructed on the major premise that since Jesus Christ was actually working at the head of the Society through the medium of its earthly leaders, it would thenceforth be blasphemous to disagree with their directives. In this way, Rutherford was able to supplement his earlier claims for rational-legal legitimation for his authority with the new claim for legitimation on grounds of 'mediated' or 'vicarious' charisma. Since the whole leadership was now claiming a sort of collective charisma of office, Rutherford was thereby able to avoid any obvious emulation of Russell's status as a divinely inspired leader, but he was no less successful than his predecessor in securing widespread agreement among Jehovah's witnesses on the reasons for granting him legitimation. Deviation from the Society's codes and programmes would thenceforth entail 'everlasting death' because loyalty to the theocratic Society had become a test of a person's spiritual merit and fitness to survive Armageddon.

Much potential opposition to the Theocracy was silenced by the effective web of ideological arguments supporting the new measures, and the final solution to certain recurrent problems was thereby achieved. The question of Elders' autonomy, for example, was unequivocally resolved in favour of regional surveillance of company affairs and of the abolition of the elective Elder system. Similarly, service-work was finally established as a matter between the individual Jehovah's witness and the Watch Tower Society's central leaders with only minimal scope for the interference of company officials.

A Jehovah's witness's status in the Society was reflected in the new titles adopted in 1939: 'Company Publishers' were expected to devote sixty hours per month to service-work, while 'Pioneers' faced a requirement to spend an average of 150 hours per month in door-to-door ministry, pavement witnessing or Home Bible Studies. The class of 'Special Pioneers' had been established two years earlier as full-time, salaried evangelists, managers and representatives of Watch Tower interests in areas of either outstanding potential for recruitment or of serious need for firm administration. In this way the nature of the relationship between the Watch Tower Society and its followers achieved greater precision and rigidity than had been the case at any previous point in history. But one of the side-effects, therefore, of Rutherford's reforms may have been to precipitate a sharper division between active Jehovah's witnesses and 'fellow-travellers' than had been necessary when many local congregations had tolerated greater variability in the strength of members' commitment. At the same time, the structure of authority relations within the Watch Tower movement was established in a form which has remained basically unaltered for thirty-five years and which has undoubtedly contributed to its ability not only to survive the extreme conditions of the Second World War but also to expand and to prosper. Certainly no major secession from the Watch Tower Society has occurred since the Theocracy was established.

An explanation of the Society's sudden improvement of its material fortunes in the late 1930s in terms of increasing tension in international relations, the growing threat of war and the heightening of anxiety about personal safety would be only partial if it overlooked the parallel systematization of Watch Tower evangelism and its explicit orientation towards problems of political instability. In other words, *improvement in the Watch Tower Society's fortunes resulted not only from growing anxiety and an associated interest in religious matters amongst the population 'at risk' to its evangelism but also from the greater effectiveness with which its agents were deployed following the declaration of the Theocracy.* Strikingly similar events occurred in the Japanese Soka Gakkai movement when a new president came to office in 1945 (see J. W. White, 1970). His thoroughgoing administrative reforms and the new-found aggressiveness of Soka Gakkai proselytism provoked not only a sharply disapproving public reaction but also a paradoxically impressive increase in the movement's recruitment rates. This similarity between ideologically dissimilar religious groups implies that the 'stance' of a group's organization is at least as important a factor in determining its numerical growth as the social situation of its recruits.

Yet, the improvements in the evangelical 'productivity' of Jehovah's witnesses were not achieved without concomitant disadvantages: the imposition of uniformity on the Witnesses' thought and behaviour had adverse effects on their spiritual creativity and individuality. They forfeited the (already slight) possibility of contributing to the development of Watch Tower doctrine by accepting the legitimacy of their subordination to the Society's leaders in all matters and by subjecting themselves to the authority of appointees to posts of responsibility in their own companies. Variability in liturgical forms gave way to uniformity, and differential rates of involvement in service-work among rank and file Witnesses ceased to be acceptable to their mentors. The strengthening of collective consciousness among Jehovah's witnesses has entailed the loss of congregational autonomy, and the very fact that the Watch Tower movement was able to survive the forces of oppression in the whole of the Second World War period indicates that its nature as a social movement had undergone extreme transformations.

Allowing for (a) the growth of widespread anxiety in all parts of the world at the prospect of a war in 1939 and for the presumptive[14] increase in public concern with religious matters, and (b) the orientation of the newly theocratic Watch Tower movement towards proselytism, the actual upswing in all branches of its activities is still surprising in its abruptness and its extent. Tables 1 and 2 (see pp. 42 and 43) illustrate the point clearly. In the USA the number of company publishers increased by 90 per cent, and the output of *The Watchtower* more than doubled between

1939 and 1942, whereas in the same period in Britain there was almost a four-fold increase in subscriptions to Watch Tower magazines. Wartime interference with Jehovah's witnesses' activities naturally prevented the British Branch from emulating the American example in all aspects of its growth, but it vindicated its efficiency after the war by maintaining a steady rate of increase in nearly all its activities.

Tables 1 and 2 illustrate the prodigious transformation in the levels of Watch Tower activity in the concluding years of Rutherford's presidency. The full significance of the upswing lies in its violent contrast to the pattern of instability then stagnation that had characterized nearly all branches of the Society's activity in the early and mid-1930s. The years between 1939 and 1942 therefore represented a major watershed in the history of the Watch Tower movement in the West because they witnessed a sudden world-wide upsurge in all aspects of its work to a level below which it has never again subsided. This period is analogous to the 'take-off' stage of economic development when the full potential for a nation's sustained and cumulative economic growth is first realized, but the analogy is imperfect because the Watch Tower Society's rates of growth have remained consistently higher than could be reasonably expected of any national economy.

One important feature of the Watch Tower Society's statistical development that will demand further examination in later chapters but that first became evident during Rutherford's presidency is the growing shortfall between annual rates of increase in baptized Publishers and annual rates of increase in new magazine subscriptions. In Britain, for example, there were 25,435 new subscriptions to the magazines in 1941, but the net increase in Publishers for 1942 was only 1,461. While the number of new subscriptions for each year since 1940 has ranged from 17,000 to as many as 77,000 the net annual increases in active Publishers have never shown comparable advances. The conclusion suggests itself that, as a result of Rutherford's success in training Jehovah's witnesses to be effective sales-men, the Watch Tower Society was selling a large amount of literature to people who did not subsequently play a more active role in the sect's affairs. The figures show that a very similar state of affairs has also existed in the United States since 1940. Unfortunately, the published statistics do not permit a comparison of the net annual increases in active Publishers with annual figures for baptisms into the Watch Tower faith during the Second World War period. It is not therefore possible to attempt a calculation of the 'turn-over' rate among Publishers, although, as we shall see below, such a calculation may be attempted for later years. One highly tentative interpretation of these facts is that from the late 1930s onwards Watch Tower salesmen became such a common sight in

TABLE 1   *Statistics of Development in the USA 1917–1942*

Year	Watch Tower Golden Age* (No. of copies printed in 000,000s)		Workers in Bethel‡	Full-time Colporteurs† and Pioneers	Active Classes or Companies	Publishers	Memorial Attendance	Memorial Partakers
	Watch Tower	Golden Age						
1917								
1918								
1920								
1921			107	350				
1922				319				
1923				269	980			
1924			170	921				
1925	1.42		172	439	901			
1926	1.50	1.80		414				
1927	1.57	1.86	180	398	866			
1928	1.99	1.47		1,183	931			
1929	1.96	1.34		1,339				
1930	1.33	1.84		1,751				
1931	1.24	2.04	200	1,685				
1932	1.29	2.16		1,997				
1933				1,976				
1934	1.33	2.40	196	437				
1935	1.42	2.65	195	1,829			32,495	26,826
1936	1.54	3.23	200	1,831			35,172	25,435
1937	1.56	3.32	200			21,451		
1938	1.60	4.26		1,910		23,013		
1939	4.44	4.92		2,176	2,425	33,290		
1940	7.21	5.49		2,686	2,815	45,076	58,874	15,873
1941	8.09	5.81	154	4,049	2,860	52,696	61,449	13,889
1942	9.92	6.64	213	4,204	3,421	62,179	83,894	13,131

† From October 6th 1937 onwards this magazine was entitled *Consolation*.

* The figures for the years 1928 to 1933 refer to the highest number of colporteurs at work in the course of each year: after 1934 they refer to the average number of colporteurs at work during the twelve-month period.

‡ Total includes workers in offices, factories and farms.

TABLE 2

Development of the Watch Tower Bible and Tract Society—British Branch—1935–1942

	Watch Tower Subscriptions	Golden Age Consolation* Subscriptions	Pioneers	Companies	Publishers	Bethel Staff	Memorial Attendance	Memorial Partakers
1935	244 increase		204	368	5,496			
1936	673 increase	724 increase	201	364	5,464			
1937			184	369	5,590			
1938			242	351	4,601		6,360	4,853
1939	3,493 increase		429			22	8,349	4,548
1940	9,284 combined increase		1,037	449	8,823	24	8,755	3,636
1941	25,935 combined increase		1,184	480	11,024	27		
1942	25,150 combined increase			582	12,436	27		

* From October 6th 1937 onwards this magazine was entitled *Consolation*.

American, British and German towns that the public accepted them as 'normal' and consented to purchase their literature out of a sense of duty, or rather, through a lack of deliberate motivation to refuse their offer. There are, however, ideological reasons why they have never attained the level of 'indifferent acceptance' enjoyed by Salvation Army salesmen, for example, but the two groups are at least similar in having benefited from becoming familiar and visible representatives of minority religious views.

The latter half of Rutherford's presidency is important for present-day Jehovah's witnesses because the idealized view of it that Watch Tower literature conveys to them stresses the point that loyalty and steadfastness in the face of adversity secured the movement's survival. The heroic events of the period serve as a useful framework within which the theo-cratic innovations can be all the more easily explained and legitimated. For the younger Jehovah's witnesses who have no personal recollection of the persecution meted out to their elders in the Second World War period, current harassment of their brethren in several African States serves the same purpose. The plight of their brethren in countries of the Communist bloc is a constant reminder to British Witnesses of all ages that the world is hostile to their work and to all that they represent. In the context, then, of their self-identity as an oppressed minority, the seeming harshness of theocratic discipline and the remoteness of Watch Tower administrative processes are both mitigated. Any account of the Watch Tower movement's present condition and future prospects must take cognizance of these factors, for they help to explain why its course of development has departed, and may continue to depart, from the pattern expected of comparable religious groups.

NOTES TO CHAPTER 2

1. For the view that Russell had virtually run the Society singlehanded, see Mac-Millan (1957), pp. 61–74.

2. See, for example, Anon (1917); and Rutherford's *Harvest Siftings* (1917).

3. Opposition to Rutherford was strongest from the Bible Students' Committee and from the separate, Edinburgh-based Bible Student Publishing Co., whose magazine *The Bible Student* carried an incessant stream of anti-Watch Tower invective. The Bible Students' Committee, in close association with the Pastoral Bible Institute of Chicago, maintained fraternal links among ex-Russellites in Britain by circulating literature and arranging occasional gatherings.

4. Rogerson (1972) argues strongly for the necessity to conceive of 'the Watch Tower movement' after about 1919 as an heterogeneous set of conflicting groups. But for reasons of convenience we shall continue to use the phrase as if it referred exclusively to Rutherford's organization. The other component groups will be

referred to by their proper titles. Similarly, 'Bible Students' refers to those who remained in association with Rutherford's organization, although the term could, strictly speaking, refer to the members of anti-Rutherford groups as well.

5. Quoted in Zygmunt (1967), p. 798.

6. For earlier criticism, see below, p. 112.

7. The Bible Students who left the Watch Tower Society in order to form the Standfast movement constituted an exception: they objected strongly to Rutherford's failure to advance hard-and-fast views on the question of conscription. See Rogerson (1969), p. 196.

8. Compare the account of the largely doctrinal bases for social divisions in the Christadelphian sect and the Brethren in B. R. Wilson (1961), pp. 242–5; and Embley (1967), pp. 227–8.

9. Extensive documentation on the plight of Jehovah's witnesses in Germany before 1938 is contained in Zuercher (1939).

10. The British Government White Paper, *Germany no. 2. Papers concerning the Treatment of German Nationals in Germany 1938–39*. Cmd. 6120, p. 35 alleges that Jehovah's witnesses were almost as badly treated as Jews.

11. *The Yearbook of Jehovah's Witnesses, 1937*. (Henceforward abbreviated to *Yearbook*.)

12. See the excellent analysis in Manwaring (1962).

13. There were signs of equally inward-looking and equally 'heterodox' behaviour among Christadelphians at the same time: youth circles were founded, and the Lecturing Society and the Benevolent Fund were restructured. See B. R. Wilson (1961), p. 265–6.

14. The evidence about religious groups similar in size and status to the Watch Tower movement renders dubious the strength of the putative correlation between widespread apprehension at the approach of, or during, a war and increased rates of participation in their activities. The Elim Foursquare Gospel Church, for example, did not achieve 'spectacular results' in its wartime evangelism, the rates of growth in various aspects of Christian Science slackened after 1930, and the gradual process of decline in the numerical strength of the Christadelphian movement after the First World War showed no sign of abating in the pre-Second World War period. See B. R. Wilson (1961), pp. 57, 152 and 262–3.

CHAPTER 3

POST-WAR EXPANSION AND REORIENTATION

The achievement of 'theocratic' reorganization was probably the last of Rutherford's major contributions to the movement's development, for he spent the few remaining years before his death in February 1942 in virtual retirement at the Society's mansion in California. Prominent among those officials who had been effectively running the Society during that time was Nathan Homer Knorr, vice-president of the Watch Tower Bible and Tract Society and a long-standing confidant of the President. His accession to the presidency in 1942 had been widely and favourably forecast among Jehovah's witnesses, and there was consequently no parallel of the succession crisis that had disrupted Watch Tower affairs following C. T. Russell's death in 1916. What is more, there has been no parallel of the process by which Rutherford gradually dissociated himself explicitly from the heritage of Russell's ideas and practices in the 1920s in order to assert his own independence: in fact, Rutherford's name has hardly appeared in Watch Tower literature since his death. This, of course, may indicate that the post-war Watch Tower leaders were embarrassed by memories of Rutherford's style of administration and simply wished to ignore him for fear of provoking a witch-hunt among Jehovah's witnesses.

N. H. Knorr had been converted to the Watch Tower faith as a teenager in his native Allentown (Pennsylvania) and almost immediately accepted a full-time post in the Bethel factory in Brooklyn. A reputation for efficiency and reliability gained him steady promotion in several aspects of factory supervision and in 1934 a seat on the Board of Directors of the Watch Tower Bible and Tract Society Inc. of New York. Before succeeding to Rutherford's position he had also been invited to join the Board of the Pennsylvania corporation and the London-based International Bible Students' Association. Apart from a brief period prior to working in Bethel, then, Knorr's work as a Jehovah's witness had been confined to productive, supervisory and managerial tasks at the movement's headquarters. His experience of the company Publisher's life is extremely limited, and there seems to be agreement among British Witnesses that he is an 'organisation man' rather than a spiritual leader.

Knorr has spent his whole adult life as a resident of Brooklyn's Bethel, apparently shunning the idea of extensive public appearances. He only appears in public in highly structured and formal situations, and even then he appears to be nervous and ill-at-ease. He does not attempt to emulate Russell as a popular father-figure nor does he imitate Rutherford's fiery panache, but his public speaking is carefully modulated and betrays meticulous preparation.

IDEOLOGICAL CHANGES AND PRACTICAL INNOVATIONS

Knorr's personality and administrative experience fitted him for the task of consolidating the gains made by the Watch Tower Society in many parts of the world in the early 1940s and for adapting the theocratic institution to a wide variety of wartime and post-war conditions. In the first place, it was becoming urgently necessary by 1942 to adjust the Watch Tower ideology to the inescapable fact that, at a time when persecution of Jehovah's witnesses might have been thought to presage the imminence of Armageddon, more and more people were actually joining the movement, and the prospects for even greater expansion of evangelism and recruitment were promising. In these circumstances Watch Tower literature began to advance a novel proposition: Jehovah's witnesses, as defenders and propagators of God's plan for the world, were responsible for *educating* the rest of mankind in the divine truth and for providing a collective example of the benefits deriving from theocratic living. The pre-First World War emphasis on character development and the pre-Second World War emphasis on vociferous denunciation of the secular world were skilfully obscured by the new focus for Witnesses' thought and activity.

Yet, since the educative task could only be accomplished if Jehovah's witnesses were persuaded to relax a little in their extreme hostility towards all non-Watch Tower aspects of life, a prior necessity was to inculcate *indifference* towards the world rather than outright rejection of it. Post-war Watch Tower literature, therefore, exalted the positive advantages of being able to communicate easily with prospective proselytes through well-mannered tactics and by setting a visible example of virtuous living. Whereas anathematizing all secular institutions and turning their minds away from external affairs may have been a rational response to the mounting threats against their collective survival before the war, it was equally rational for Jehovah's witnesses to adopt an outward-looking ideological position after the war in view of the sharp increases in membership and the slow decline of persecution.

The feasibility of Jehovah's witnesses' new educative functions was also conditional upon an improvement in the general standards of their evangelistic performance. For if the full benefits were to be derived from the methodical employment of all Publishers in service-work of a more subtle and persuasive nature than had been current before the war, then they had to acquire and to practise novel skills. Indeed, no time was lost after Rutherford's death in establishing the first of several educational institutions—the Theocratic Ministry School at the New York Bethel. After only one year's experiment among Bethel residents every company was encouraged to form its own School and thereby to raise the standards of its local witnessing. Uniformity of procedure was secured by the distribution of a standard textbook[1] and by the imposition of rules which have remained basically unchanged for thirty years: after a short talk about witnessing techniques and rationale a small number of 'students' delivers a prepared sermon which is publicly criticized and evaluated by the School Conductor who maintains a written record of each performance. The scheme undoubtedly contributes immeasurably towards the inculcation of good public-speaking habits in many people who would otherwise be incapable of such activity. It is also important in helping to create and to sustain a phatic community among Jehovah's witnesses which derives its solidarity partly from their voluntary participation in esoteric forms of language use and partly from the overt, positive reinforcement awarded by the Study Conductor for correct use of the shared language. (See Janis and King, 1954)

A roughly contemporary innovation in the printing of *The Watchtower* and in the conduct of the weekly Watch Tower meeting also seemed to be designed to improve Jehovah's witnesses' grasp of doctrine and their ability to articulate their beliefs. Beginning in May 1942 every paragraph in the leading doctrinal articles of *The Watchtower* bore a number corresponding to a relevant question at the foot of each page. In the Watch Tower Study each paragraph was read aloud to the congregation, and the Conductor then invited answers to the formal questions until he was satisfied that the doctrinal essence had been adequately propounded. The effectiveness of this arrangement may be reflected in its unbroken and unchanged persistence for thirty years; in essentials, of course, this meeting resembles closely the Berean Study groups that originated among Bible Students in 1902.

The decision (taken in the mid-1940s) to produce a translation of the Bible that was suited to the special needs of the sect was a further attempt to improve the Witnesses' grasp of doctrines. Beginning with the publication in 1950 of *the New Testament Translation of the Christian Greek Scriptures*, a committee of translators went on to produce a complete translation of the Bible in five more volumes published between 1953 and 1960. 'Outside' commentators have been highly critical of its allegedly biased and contorted representation of Christian concepts, but it cannot be denied that the work has been immensely valuable in increasing the Witnesses' consciousness of participating in an integrated religious movement. The language of the translation is the same as that of all Watch Tower literature, and this facilitates the exegete's task of persuading the reader of the intimate connection between the Bible and the sect's own doctrines.

Yet the most prestigious of Knorr's educational innovations was the establishment in a part of rural New York State of the Watch Tower Bible School of Gilead. The syllabus of the taught course was designed to equip missionaries and high-level administrators with advanced knowledge of scriptural studies, evangelistic techniques, law and foreign languages. Candidates for the course[2] must not only be nominated by their local Presiding Minister and regional representative of the Watch Tower Society but must also satisfy several stringent entrance requirements: extensive experience in Pioneer work, sound doctrinal knowledge, attainment of more than elementary levels of secular education and utter dedication to the Society's cause. Gilead's 'graduates' constitute an elite among Jehovah's witnesses and are revered by rank-and-file Publishers, for their apparently selfless devotion to the service of Jehovah is widely cited in Watch Tower literature as an ideal for others to aim at. They also constitute an elite in the sense of belonging, or being swiftly co-opted, to the swelling ranks of Branch administrators in all parts of the world. In this respect, their training probably contributes more directly in the long-term towards the administration, rather than the practice, of missionary work. But this displacement of tasks only increases the desirability from the Society's point of view of advanced training for some Jehovah's witnesses in all aspects of its work.

The only major changes that have occurred in the running of Gilead were connected with its adaptation in 1961 to the purpose of training high-level Branch officials in advanced administrative methods. By 1966 the programme had reverted to the former pattern of two courses each year for missionary training only. Gilead graduates are therefore still being trained to stimulate and to harness the massive expansion of Watch Tower activities that occurred during or immediately after the Second World War, and their work unquestionably reflects Knorr's two-edged policy of improving the standard of professional preparation for Watch Tower personnel and of increasing the efficiency of the witness that they give to the world.

A further consideration may have been the determination to keep a close check on development in countries where American military 'presence' had abruptly stimulated the growth-rate in the number of indigenous Jehovah's witnesses, for several earlier missionary enterprises (especially in Africa) had ended in the establishment of dissident Watch Tower groups. The function of Gilead graduates would have been partly to ensure that the post-war 'boom' in recruitment to the Watch Tower movement was carefully supervised and canalized along orthodox lines. For this reason they concentrated in some underdeveloped areas on teaching literacy at the same time as Watch Tower doctrines in order to build up the kind of stable and efficient indigenous leadership that would remain loyel to the American-run Society.

In the modern Watch Tower movement it is no longer necessary for high-level administrators to possess material or social privileges in order to rise to prominence, but the possession of largely intellectual gifts has become a basic prerequisite. Formalization of training is nowadays matched by formalized methods of examining candidates for important positions and by the award of official qualifications to the successful, thereby removing much of the confusion about authority that had hindered Russell's Pilgrims in the exercise of their tasks. But a corollary of these developments has been the progressive restriction of administrators' responsibilities to highly specific areas of competence. The division of administrative labour has therefore entailed changes in the grounds on which administrators' authority can be legitimated. One major consequence has been the virtual elimination of the possibility that a section of the elite could realistically expect to take over control of the Society against the President's wishes.

Both of Knorr's predecessors had toured foreign outposts of interest, or potential interest, in Watch Tower affairs and both had recommended the expansion of schemes to service the growing number of Jehovah's witnesses outside the USA, but Knorr's concern was rather to intensify the *consciousness* among all Jehovah's witnesses of participating in an international organization. Whereas earlier manifestations of internationalism had taken the form of such practical matters as radio links and distribution of relief supplies, a more indicative sign of the new outlook was reflected in the revised terms of the charter of the Pennsylvania corporation which allowed for each Branch of the movement to provide at least one representative to act as a full member of the Society and, in theory, to influence its programmes. While the revision may not have seriously undermined American hegemony in the Brooklyn headquarters, it was nevertheless an important symbol of the intention to recognize the growing numerical strength of the non-American Watch Tower followers.

Finally, the new-found orientation towards internationalism was embodied in the post-war elevation of international assemblies of Jehovah's witnesses to the status of major ritual and evangelistic occasions. But when the New York public authorities complained in 1958 that the disruption to basic services caused by a gathering of as many as 190,000 people could not be tolerated again, a decision was taken to conduct future assemblies in the form of either a travelling show which is staged consecutively in a large number of different countries or a simultaneous performance of an identical show in different national locations. Yet, the change in format has clearly not depressed the enthusiasm of Jehovah's witnesses for these immense gatherings, lasting usually six days in capital cities all over the world, for the aggregate attendances are still impressively high.

The value of international assemblies as evangelistic devices is probably insignificant compared with their importance as a means of stimulating high levels of morale among existing Witnesses. It is doubtful whether many 'outsiders' attend these gatherings, and the programmes of lectures, demonstrations, baptisms, dramatic performances and songs do not seem to be designed to arouse the curiosity of newly interested people so much as to reinforce the convictions of initiates. But in the light of what is known about the contemporary Watch Tower Society's skill in using its resources in the rational pursuit of maximum gain, one is forced to conclude that the costs of international assemblies are likely to be justified in terms of their positive contribution towards the maintenance of good morale among Jehovah's witnesses and the creation of an internationalist outlook which, in turn, stimulates recruitment rates outside and inside the USA.

Knorr's policy of methodically exploiting the market for conversions to the Watch Tower faith in all parts of the world and of encouraging Jehovah's witnesses to think of themselves collectively as an international movement has helped to swell the numbers of Watch Tower followers, but it has proved difficult to maintain a consistently high rate of recruitment. Furthermore, there are marked contrasts between the growth-rates in different countries, and the return on resources varies widely. But it seems to be Watch Tower policy to persist with missionary work in even the least 'responsive' areas and to resist the temptation to deploy resources only where the gains would be easily won.

The last of Knorr's attempts to increase the efficiency of senior regional and congregational officials was the creation in the late 1950s of an intensive programme of doctrinal, pedagogical and administrative instruction under the title of The Kingdom Ministry School. Each course for Congregation Servants in Britain lasted for four weeks and entailed not only extensive study and discussion but also regular periods of manual work in the printing-plant or on the dairy farm. In the course of the next decade virtually all District, Circuit, Congregation and Assistant Congregation Servants in Britain were required to devote at least one annual holiday to a residential course at the Mill Hill Bethel. Thus, the day-to-day administration of Jehovah's witnesses' affairs in this country is now conducted very largely in accordance with official Watch Tower policies and betrays no obvious signs of local variability.

ETHICAL RE-ORIENTATION

Since the Second World War, Watch Tower propaganda has concentrated on issues relating to the personal qualities and life-style of Jehovah's witnesses in a manner reminiscent of the 'character development' campaign that Russell conducted until roughly 1900. The approach of the supposedly critical year 1914, then the tribulations of the succession crisis and finally the persecution of the 1930s contributed towards the eclipse of Russell's moralizing proclivities behind the rival ideological orientations towards prophetic protest and rationalized evangelism. But the frenzied Watch Tower propaganda of the inter-war years has given way to an encouragement to cultivate the virtues of moderation and mildness and to 'put away moral badness' for the sake of 'putting on a new personality'. The exclusive focus on evil conditions in the world has changed into a more optimistic celebration of the joys of 'harmonious living' in the New World Society, and Jehovah's witnesses are urged to cultivate the 'fruitage of the spirit' which means to strive for the ideals of love, joy, peace, faith and kindness. The end-state of the moral striving is 'right heart condition' —but not in isolation from the Watch Tower Society, for participation in a 'clean organisation' is said to be a condition of personal moral integrity. The new ideological orientation does not, therefore, disturb the centripetal tendency of the Society's functioning, but merely clothes it in more subtle language that gives the appearance at least of fostering moral individualism.

Perhaps the appearance of a reversion to 'character development' was created by the reintroduction in the 1950s of the distinctly Russellite practice of giving explicit guidance on how Jehovah's witnesses should behave in a wide variety of situations. Timothy White has gone so far as to argue that

> Since [1953] *The Watch Tower* has added regulation upon regulation. The Witnesses are specifically forbidden to practise gambling, hunt or fish for sport, tell lies among themselves, laugh at dirty jokes, wear mourning clothes for long after the death of a relative, justify themselves, masturbate, become an officer in a union or picket, go out on a date without a chaperone, throw rice at weddings, display affection in public except for momentarily at greetings and partings, become a member of, or frequent, a nudist colony, participate in prayer led by one not dedicated to Jehovah, give free rein to unbridled passion whilst having allowed sexual intercourse, use profanity, or do the twist. (1967, pp. 384–5)

But what he ignores is the pattern that underlies the apparent randomness of the moral injunctions imposed on Jehovah's witnesses nowadays. Linking a wide variety of moral rules is the general premium placed on the sanctity of the *family* unit as the major source of stability and strength for individuals and societies alike. In addition to celebrating the Watch Tower movement's claim to be 'the one family on earth today that is supremely happy' (*W.T.*, 15 January 1960) its literature has recently begun to advocate the practical benefits and virtues of life in conjugal units.

Whole chapters of two books recently published by the Society[3] examine in detail the ideal structure of family groups, and the more general topic of sexual relations has also received no less attention from Watch Tower propagandists. Again, this is in sharp contrast to the reticence that the Society maintained on sexual matters into the mid-1950s, but not surprisingly, of course, the tenor of its injunctions is far from radical, for they endorse the high value of chastity and the virtue of extreme moderation in sexual relations between husband and wife. Indeed, it is often suggested that married couples should abstain completely from sexual activity during times when field-ministry or assembly-preparation are expected to occupy a Jehovah's witness's undivided attention. But the conservatism of the Watch Tower code of sex ethics contrasts curiously with the outspoken way in which articles in the Society's magazines treat such subjects as adultery (*W.T.*, 1 October 1956), masturbation (*W.T.*, 1 September 1959), sodomy and homosexuality (*W.T.*, 1 October 1956 and 15 May 1970).

The Society's views on sex are perfectly congruent with its new-found enthusiasm for the family-institution as the basic unit of theocratic society, and the two topics are both closely connected with a third feature of its ethical orientation, namely, *paternalism*. This term refers to the predominant position that Watch Tower ideology has always accorded to men in general and to heads of families in particular. The justification for paternalism is based solely on Scriptural statements and takes no account of prevailing social ethics but rather rejoices in its old-fashioned flavour. If it seems quaint that Russell should have warned his followers in 1914 that 'The very womanliness of woman renders her peculiarly liable, not only herself to stumble in her attempt to shine, but liable also to stumble others' (1960, vol. 6, p. 267), it is almost incredible that in 1951 a *Watchtower* article should have defended the traditional proscription against short hair for women on the grounds that they would otherwise 'remove this natural, God-given sign of a woman's subjection to man' (*W.T.*, 15 February 1951) or that in 1960 a similar article should have insisted that women must wear a hat when leading congregational activities because it 'alerts Christian men against succombing to female influence' (*W.T.*, 15 March 1960). Watch Tower ideologists are so committed to this principle that they are prepared to recognize the duty of a female Witness to submit to the commands of her non-Witness husband even if he thereby prevents her from fulfilling her religious obligations.

The underlying paternalistic assumption also helps to explain the Society's egregiously fierce antipathy towards homosexuality and artificial insemination by donor, since both practices could be seen to constitute a threat to traditional views about the necessity for men to guard their privileged position of superiority over women. A second reason for the antipathy is that it has become fashionable in the USA in recent years for some clergymen to defend the interests of homosexuals, and it therefore provides a valuable illustration for the argument of Watch Tower writers that Christian churches are actively condoning the collapse of general moral standards. The reasoning against artificial insemination by donor is more complex and relates to what Jehovah's witnesses consider to be the sanctity of male reproductive organs. (*W.T.*, 1 July 1959)

The acceptability of male contraception and the abhorrence of artificial insemination by donor and vasectomy are dictated by the need for the Watch Tower ideology to preserve the sacred mystique of male superiority, and this explains why divorce is only regarded as justifiable for a female if the husband is guilty of adultery and vice versa. Thus, paternalism, as a distinctive feature not only of the Watch Tower movement's social organization but also of its ideology and code of ethics, promotes the importance of the conjugal family for contemporary Jehovah's witnesses and evinces the unrelenting concern of the Society's leaders for the moral quality of their followers' lives.

Whereas before the Second World War the vast majority of offences punishable by disfellowshipment concerned infractions of rules governing theocratic practice, disfellowshipment since the war has more commonly resulted from offences against the Society's code of personal morality.[4] The change reflects partly a change in the type of post-war recruit but more importantly a new-found commitment by the Society's leaders to maintain a high standard of morality among its members. Consequently, the procedure for disfellowshipment has been extensively revised in order to standardize it and to make it appropriate for handling moral, rather than doctrinal or procedural offences. Disciplinary hearings now take place, therefore, in a small committee comprising only a few of the congregation's leading officers.

There has, of course, been no relaxation of the Watch Tower tradition of vilifying what are perceived to be the continuing decline of moral standards in general and the imminent approach of total collapse in some advanced societies. A common theme is that

Today is a time when the most firmly established institutions are falling or changing their principles and structures radically to avoid complete fall. (*W.T.*, 15 December 1964)

'Popular religion' is frequently blamed for failing to function as a 'moulding force' in people's lives (*W.T.*, 15 January 1959), and the spread of communism is often cited as a lamentable, but deserved, punishment for a society's moral laxity. Thus, although anti-communism is not a dominant theme in Watch Tower ideology, it is certainly important as a focus for more general criticisms of present-day morality, and its spread is undoubtedly regarded as a sign that Armageddon is close. But in recent years this largely negative outlook has been supplemented with the kind of positive ethical thinking that was outlined at the beginning of this section.

The Watch Tower Society is far from unique in condemning communism and liberalism as catalysts or indicators of decline. In fact, it shares a highly critical stance towards contemporary moral standards with many conservative, evangelical religious bodies in the USA and elsewhere. (See McLoughlin, 1967, p. 59)

But the similarities and parallels with other groups should not obscure the underlying differences: Watch Tower teachings do not hold out any hope that progressive moral reform of individuals will result in collective improvements in the human situation. But a fairly new feature of the teachings is that the Society believes that individual Jehovah's witnesses should now strive to improve the quality of their own lives whilst awaiting Armageddon and that the family unit can play a major part in assisting the improvement. There is no truth in the view that Jehovah's witnesses are being encouraged to regard the cultivation of moral propriety as more important than relentless evangelism. But it could be true that the new-found value of the family might be functioning as a device for strengthening the Watch Tower Society's grip on its followers. A third interpretation is probably closer to the truth, namely, that what we have termed an 'ethical reorientation' is undoubtedly being manifested in Jehovah's witnesses' lives but is largely the result of deliberate Watch Tower propaganda.

'IN THE WORLD, BUT NOT OF IT'?

This account of post-war changes in the Watch Tower Society has included only aspects of its internal reorientation, but there has been a no less striking process of change at the same time in the 'tone' of its relations with institutions and agencies of the 'outside' world. Indeed, it is in the latter respect that the most significant effects of the ideological reorientation towards 'world-indifference' have been achieved, for the history of the Watch Tower Society's recent relations with secular governments, military authorities and social welfare agencies has demonstrated the decreasing appropriateness to Jehovah's witnesses of the label 'world-denying'. This is not necessarily to argue that they have ceased to maintain the classic sectarian position of being 'in the world, but not of it', but it is to suggest that there has been a diminution in their sense of opposition to secular institutions and a growing readiness to make selective use of those outside agencies that help promote their interests. This can be illustrated by reference to three principal sources of persisting conflict between Jehovah's witnesses and the institutions of the societies in which they conduct their evangelism.

(1) Programmes of compulsory military conscription have been adopted by many countries in the twentieth century, and, as we showed in Chapters 1 and 2, Jehovah's witnesses have consistently refused to undertake military duties on the grounds that fighting for Jehovah would be the only situation in which the Scriptures could justify their enlistment. But a Supreme Court decision of 1953 to grant full-time Pioneers exemption from the draft as ministers of religion heralded a gradual improvement in their relationship with the American government. In 1958, Congregation Servants were included in the ministerial classification, and draft boards have recently shown great reluctance to enlist even Congregation Publishers. The situation in Britain, however, remained difficult for all Jehovah's witnesses until the termination of National Service in 1960, but it is interesting to note that the Watch Tower Society had been prepared

as early as 1953 to argue that it constituted a religious denomination in order to secure exemption for its officials. This argument was advanced in a test case on behalf of a Scottish Congregation Servant, but ironically, the Lords of Appeal (All England Law Reports, 1956) seized upon the claim that the Watch Tower movement constituted a religious denomination and rejected it explicitly on the grounds that (a) its so-called ministers lacked formal ordination and (b) there was very little distinction between ministers and laity. The failure of this test case entailed continuing hardship for male Jehovah's witnesses whose unconditional refusal to comply with conscription laws usually led to their imprisonment, and the situation of their fellow-religionists in other parts of the Commonwealth was basically the same. On the other hand, the fact that Jehovah's witnesses had pleaded for comparability with other religious groups symbolized a reorientation in the Society's collective self-image and in its relations with the State which was to be eventually reinforced in Britain by the repeal of National Service regulations.

(2) Just as the immensely complicated litigation that resulted from attempts to prevent Jehovah's witnesses from proselytizing in the USA in the 1930s and 1940s unintentionally helped to clarify several points of constitutional law (see Waite (1944) and Mulder & Komisky (1942)), so the present-day attempts by Jehovah's witnesses to secure the right to self-determination in the matter of medical treatment are also raising fundamental issues of law and ethics. The end-product of much of Jehovah's witnesses' voluntary litigation, for example, has been the clarification and protection of individual rights in respect of such things as religious belief, publication, free speech and political opinions, but paradoxically it is no part of the Watch Tower movement's ideology to value highly the abstract notion of individual rights.

Blood transfusions, in particular, are the subject of an on-going controversy in many parts of the world because Jehovah's witnesses regard them as unscriptural and dangerous, whereas medical authorities commonly regard them as not only necessary in certain circumstances but also obligatory according to the terms of the Hippocratic oath.[5] For present purposes, however, the significance of the controversy lies in the tactics that Jehovah's witnesses have adopted to defend their interests, for they reveal a further modification in the Watch Tower movement's collective attitude towards civil authorities.

The legal and ethical problems following from Jehovah's witnesses' refusal to sanction blood transfusions are complex and varied, but a general pattern can be discerned in the course that events now commonly take. In the case of adult Witnesses who are in possession of their reasoning faculties, medical authorities in Britain are becoming increasingly reluctant to impose transfusions in disregard of the patients' express wishes even if it is thought that by so doing they can save life. The provision of small cards indicating the bearer's 'Refusal to Permit Blood Transfusion', the availability of medical personnel sympathetic to Jehovah's witnesses' convictions, the repeal in 1961 of earlier laws regarding suicide and the common understanding that a physician may adopt what he considers to be the second best course of treatment if the patient has refused the most advisable course, have all reduced much of the controversy with regard to this type of case in Britain. In the USA, by contrast, there is still perplexing variation in both the readiness of hospital administrators to override Jehovah's witnesses' wishes and the response of judges to applications for court orders to sanction transfusions for them. Courts of appeal have also given conflicting decisions on this matter: on the one hand the Illinois Supreme Court ruled in 1958 that a circuit judge who had ordered a blood transfusion for a Witness had interfered with basic constitutional rights (*Awake!*, 18 May 1965), but, on the other hand the United States Supreme Court twice denied Jehovah's witnesses the right of appeal in 1968 against adverse decisions in lower courts on precisely the same issue. (*Awake!*, 8 July 1965)

In the case of minors or of people deemed incapable of making decisions for themselves, medical and legal authorities have been increasing their powers to override the wishes of Jehovah's witness parents or guardians. In Britain it became common practice for hospital administrators to call for a special session of the juvenile court in order to seek an order making the child a ward of court (see *The Times*, 14–17 March 1960); if the application succeeded, the court was likely to sanction blood transfusion. If it proved impracticable to convene a special court, a physician who proceeded with blood transfusion without the parents' permission would have been liable to prosecution on a charge of wilful neglect, but such a case has never reached the courts. In fact, the climate of legal opinion seems to have changed recently, for the Minister of Health issued a statement in the House of Commons in 1966[6] to the effect that recourse to hastily convened courts of law by hospital authorities was not considered advisable and that physicians should exercise professional discretion in proceeding with transfusions against parental wishes. The fact that British Jehovah's witnesses have never prosecuted medical personnel for overriding their express parental wishes and have never formally challenged the use of the Children's and Young Persons' Act of 1933 for this purpose indicates that they are not completely lacking sympathy for the authority vested in the country's medical and legal institutions.

By contrast, Australian, Canadian and American Jehovah's witnesses are less conformist in this respect and have repeatedly defied and challenged both medical and legal authorities. Significantly, it is in these countries that legal proceedings are not infrequently taken against Jehovah's witnesses whose refusal to sanction blood transfusion for a dependant results in his or her death or permanent injury.[7] The general conclusion suggests itself that the differential severity of legal measures to override the wishes of Jehovah's witnesses in a given country is directly related to the intensity of Jehovah's witnesses' overt scorn for the law.

One of the intriguing questions arising from the idea that the degree of State interference in the activities of Jehovah's witnesses has a reciprocal relationship with the sect's own attitude towards the sovereignty of law is whether its opposition to such things as flag-saluting, conscription, vasectomy, artificial insemination by donor and blood transfusion has been dictated more by considerations of tactics than of principle. In each case the evidence shows that the Watch Tower Society's initial position was unclear and that it formulated doctrinally justified arguments only after a lengthy period of deliberation and in response to requests for assistance from individual Jehovah's witnesses. Only a complete analysis of the precise way in which the decisions were taken at Brooklyn could provide satisfactory answers to these questions, and in the absence of the necessary information three interpretations are possible. (a) The decisions may have been taken with a view to optimizing the Society's chances of defending and promoting its interests. (b) They may have been *ad hoc* responses to immediate problems without an underlying rationale. (c) They may have reflected sincere attempts to translate certain abstract scriptural principles into rules for practical conduct. Whatever the answer (and the truth probably embraces all three possibilities) it is interesting to note that in each case the Watch Tower Society provided legal, moral and material assistance to its members in their struggle to implement its decisions in the face of stern opposition. In this way, the ensuing hardships have not been a strongly divisive factor among Jehovah's witnesses but have contributed in part towards a greater sense of solidarity, for on balance, the positive advantages of public distinctiveness probably outweigh the depressing effects on recruitment rates.

(3) The last major cause of acerbic denunciations by the Watch Tower Society of a Western nation-state was the protracted campaign by Roman Catholics in Quebec to prevent Jehovah's witnesses from carrying out door-to-door evangelism in the 1940s. Only after hundreds of arrests, extensive damage to property, much verbal aggression and dubious political manoeuvring did the Canadian Supreme Court offer legal protection to the embattled Witnesses in 1950. (See *Divine Purpose*, pp. 241–9) Elsewhere in the world, however, there remain outstanding problems in the relationship between Jehovah's witnesses and the governments of some

nations. Yet, it is consistent with our interpretation of the Watch Tower Society's recent ideological evolution that even when Jehovah's witnesses are subject to evident persecution, its propagandists do not nowadays react in the violently indignant and abusive way that was characteristic of their predecessors in the 1920s and 1930s. This fact is all the more significant in view of the immense difficulties, hardships and penalties that are still imposed on Jehovah's witnesses in some countries: the Iron Curtain countries, Spain, Greece, Portugal, the Dominican Republic, the United Arab Republic, Turkey, Uganda, Malawi and Zambia are notorious centres of occasionally brutal anti-Watch Tower activity. But the contemporary Society's response often takes the form of tempered protest in the magazines, formal declarations of concern at mass-meetings, attempts at reconciliation through diplomatic channels or relief-work through international agencies. Similarly, vitriolic attacks on the United Nations organization no longer feature quite so prominently in Watch Tower literature, nor do the Society's propagandists attempt to make so much capital out of the alleged Communist plot to subvert world politics as did their predecessors in the 1930s.

The situation of Jehovah's witnesses in some newly independent African States is particularly delicate because their numerical strength and high levels of commitment are one of the causes of their present hardships. In Zambia and Malawi,[8] for example, the harassment of Jehovah's witnesses by State authorities began only when Watch Tower groups became common and when Jehovah's witnesses threatened to constitute a considerable proportion of the total population. The official charge that Jehovah's witnesses display disloyalty to the State by refusing to join the ruling political party (or any other) and to show requisite respect for symbols of national honour reflects not only the insecurity of such States but also the dilemma facing the Watch Tower Society: should it curtail its promotional work for the sake of relieving the pressure, or the threat of persecution, on its existing members or should it attempt to secure their safety through acquiring even greater numbers of new followers? On balance, its principal tactic nowadays seems to be to conduct negotiations with its oppressors with the minimum of publicity and in the real hope of thereby securing protection for its members. An instructive instance of this tactic occurred recently in Malawi when as many as 21,000 Jehovah's witnesses were reported (*Sunday Telegraph*, 14 January 1973) to have fled from persecution into neighbouring Zambia. A high-level Watch Tower administrator immediately visited the area and, working in conjunction with Zambian government officials and the United Nations High Commission for Refugees, tried to persuade the refugees to return to their own country.

It is tempting to see in this tactic a sign that the Watch Tower movement has acquired sufficient 'momentum', stability and self-confidence to dispense with aggressive measures of self-defence and to be able to wait more or less patiently until the situation improves. Certainly, this is consistent with our interpretation of changes in the orientation of the Society's post-war propaganda towards an increasingly spiritual, ethical and educative outlook. The post-war emphasis on internationalism may also have a bearing on these events. Whereas in Rutherford's era the international bond amongst Jehovah's witnesses was a shared burden of persecution, post-war propagandists have tried to supplement it with evidence of more positive and more pleasant aspects of the Watch Tower movement's international structure.

MATERIAL DEVELOPMENT

In Britain the Watch Tower movement's post-war ideological reorientation and practical innovations have coincided with gentle rates of increase in most branches of its personnel and activities. Rather than attempt to unravel the direction and strength of causation in this particular relationship, we shall simply emphasize the probability that it is one of mutual reinforcement between the two sets of factors. The actual rates of increase have never emulated the spectacular gains made in some other parts of the world, and there are signs that Watch Tower leaders are dissatisfied with several aspects of the British Branch's achievements. But the general state of the movement, as indicated in Table 3 (see p. 62) has unquestionably improved since 1942.

In particular, the number of active Publishers has increased more than five-fold, but the rate of growth in each decade since 1942 has slowed considerably from about 100 per cent in the years 1943–52, to 80 per cent in the years 1953–62, and to about 40 per cent in the last decade. The declining rate of growth is seriously affected by a high drop-out rate among Publishers, and this has provoked stern warnings from the Branch Servant. In 1964 alone, for example, he reported that 3,500 Publishers had become inactive (*Yearbook*, 1965), thereby reducing the net increase for the year to 1,796. Since the current drop-out rate has been estimated by a Branch official to have reached about 18 per cent per annum, it is not unlikely that, all other things being equal, the British Watch Tower movement may soon enter a period of stagnation in the size of its following which would in fact conceal a high turn-over rate in personnel. The scanty evidence about annual numbers of baptisms confirms this general interpretation, for in the four years between 1969 and 1972 the shortfall

TABLE 3   *Summary of development of the British Branch of the Watch Tower Society: 1943–72*

	Kingdom Publishers	Regular Pioneers	New subscriptions to *Watch Tower* and *Awake!*	Number of Congregations	Baptisms	Ratio of one Publisher: population
1943	11,174	376	1,580	593		
1944	11,227	311		612		
1945	11,622	268	15,000	610		
1946	11,395	274	58,383	602		
1947	12,149		77,232	601		
1948	14,676		56,387	612		
1949	17,239		66,191	613	2,283	
1950	20,842	1,126	73,683	624		
1951	23,080	1,238	55,544	631		
1952	24,847	1,161	51,800	695	2,850	
1953	26,104	1,000	60,953	729		
1954	27,145	939	55,744	718		
1955	28,073	836	51,883	716		
1956	30,342	933	56,688	733		
1957	34,004	1,192	58,598	755		
1958	37,416	1,298	54,691	825		
1959	40,884	1,479	44,021	893		1,167
1960	43,650	1,577	58,859	924		1,106
1961	44,974	1,423	55,556	932		1,064
1962	46,842	1,610	56,641	935	3,444	1,057
1963	47,053	1,903	58,214	930	3,079	1,030
1964	48,849	2,291	62,558	905		1,017
1965	48,942	2,779	60,329	900		1,031
1966	49,073	2,806	41,316	896	4,586	1,076
1967	50,154	3,230	60,995	876		1,007
1968	52,805	3,881	48,632	875		981
1969	55,876	4,263	44,655	883	5,563	929
1970	59,705	4,640	46,560	891	5,273	875
1971	62,813	4,369		895	5,177	844
1972	64,434	3,870		905	5,228	822

between the number of baptisms and the net increase in active Publishers has been 2,492 (roughly 4.4 per cent of the aggregate of Publishers), 1,444 (1.5 per cent), 2,069 (3.1 per cent) and 3,607 (5.6 per cent). Thus, taking the four year period as one unit, the discrepancy between the cumulative total of baptisms and the net increase in Publisher strength amounted to about 13 per cent of the Publishers' total in 1972. Given that some newly-baptized people may already have been enumerated as active Publishers before their baptism, the actual shortfall might appear to be even higher, but this distortion is more than corrected when account is taken of the loss of Publishers through natural causes. Thus, a crude interpretation of the statistics is that in very recent years the gain of three new members has been matched by the loss, for a variety of reasons, of two existing members.

While no official statistics for service-work have been issued since 1953 when 69 per cent of Publishers were regularly engaged in field-service, successive reports of the Branch Servant have indicated that the percentage has been dropping slowly. Furthermore, a personal scrutiny of the records of a dozen congregations in different parts of the country confirmed that even those Witnesses who were working regularly were falling short of the monthly target of ten hours per Publisher. It seems more difficult nowadays to elicit consistent application to public evangelism from Publishers but this is not entirely unexpected since the quality of the individual Publisher's spiritual life is now considered no less important than his service record.

The upward trend in the number of *Pioneer* Publishers since the Second World War suggests, however, that there is at least a solid core of Jehovah's witnesses in Britain who are highly committed to the Watch Tower Society's values and goals, and this augurs well for future development because the majority of Pioneers are young people, most of whom will eventually graduate to positions of responsibility in the organization. The growth of Pioneer ranks could be seen as a sign of the distinction that is developing within the Society between its more and its less mobilizable followers. The notion of a uniformly activist following may no longer be fully applicable to the contemporary movement and may be in process of eclipse by that of a more highly differentiated body of, on the one hand, professional and semi-professional workers and, on the other, largely passive 'parishioners'. The formalization of training for Branch administrators and missionaries could also be seen as a mark of the trend towards a greater differentiation of elites from the mass of Jehovah's witnesses.

The stagnation in the number of new subscriptions to magazines since the late 1940s evinces the failure of Branch and congregation leaders to

TABLE 4   *Summary of development of the United States Branch of the Watch Tower Society: 1943–72*

	Kingdom Publishers	Regular Pioneers	New subscriptions to *Watch Tower* and *Awake!*	Number of magazines printed *The Watch Tower* (in millions)	*Awake!*	Number of Congregations	Baptisms	Ratio of one Publisher: population
1943*	56,484	4,788	157,748	9.12	6.65	3,227		
1944	56,126	3,834	208,166	10.43	7.46	3,056		
1945	57,869	3,178	229,524	11.57	7.75	2,871		
1946	58,399	2,684	285,020	14.55	10.68	2,858		
1947	67,680	2,322	308,618	15.55	13.12	2,879		
1948	72,945	4,143	230,278	14.70	12.43	2,901		
1949	82,958	4,637	291,296	15.70	14.70	2,905		
1950	98,468	5,273	322,805	18.03	16.49	2,941		
1951	118,462	6,966	389,793	21.73	18.03	3,015		
1952	126,626	7,110	424,715	26.13	19.99	3,103		
1953	139,966	6,921	552,594	29.03	19.95	3,195		
1954	153,969	6,379	618,975	33.85	23.53	3,350		
1955	163,875	5,809	609,403	39.06	27.59	3,484		
1956	169,835	5,957	687,596	49.30	34.42	3,597		
1957	187,762	7,467	777,856	59.70	46.90	3,718	15,275	
1958	202,141	7,724	755,315	68.40	55.52	3,848		
1959	221,240	8,970	743,176	63.95	48.61	4,020	21,951	727
1960	232,632	8,664	782,673	57.40	47.93	4,170	20,220	702
1961	248,681	8,353	779,769	61.07	54.04	4,333		653
1962	267,436	10,006	818,064	64.39	55.75	4,564	22,023	635
1963	280,052	11,806	877,705	65.12	57.20	4,777	15,960	600
1964	292,318	13,295	937,158	69.44	61.91	4,943		594
1965	302,450	14,680	983,908	74.68	66.72	5,099		581
1966	305,481	14,332	877,643	74.20	67.38	5,242		605
1967	311,378	16,101	1,061,110	79.75	74.92	5,317	18,582	587
1968	323,688	18,287	1,149,316	88.07	81.07	5,341		590
1969	343,673	20,943	1,215,357	100.27	96.45	5,384	29,730	554
1970	371,561	24,448	1,459,786	109.90	102.60	5,492	38,790	524
1971	402,893	25,740				5,676	40,336	485
1972	418,239	23,330				5,794	47,953	476

* Changes in the methods of collecting statistical data were introduced in 1943. The report for that year covers only eleven months.

extract from the growing numbers of Publishers at least a constant level of application to the task of selling subscriptions. Instead, there seems to be an inverse relationship between the aggregate number of Publishers and their average success-rate in selling new subscriptions which bears out our earlier interpretation of the changing importance of service-work to contemporary British Witnesses. This finding is in sharp contrast to the situation in the USA where Jehovah's witnesses have managed to double the sales of new magazine subscriptions in each decade since 1941. Similarly, the Brooklyn presses have maintained very high rates of increase in the annual number of magazines printed, although in recent years the rate has dropped well below that of the immediate post-war period. Thus, there would seem to have been no change in the Watch Tower Society's *policies* which might account for the declining success of British Jehovah's witnesses to sell new subscriptions.

Table 4 (see p. 64) shows that in most branches of their work American Witnesses have performed with more conspicuous enthusiasm and success than their British brethren, although it is interesting to note that a general decline in the rate of all aspects of growth occurred in both countries in the 1960s. Thus, rates of expansion in the total of native American Publishers in the decade 1963–72 sank to about half of the 100 per cent level to which the two previous decades had approximated. But there has been no concomitant decline in the annual rates of increase in sales of new magazine subscriptions, and the Pioneer ranks have swollen more quickly than in Britain. Similarly, the shortfall between the number of baptisms for the past few years and the net annual increase in Publishers has never exceeded 3 per cent of each year's aggregate of Publishers, so that the ratio between new recruits and drop-outs is probably in the region of 3:1.

The disparity in social and cultural conditions between the different national Branches of the international Watch Tower movement calls in question the usefulness for analytical purposes of world-wide aggregate statistics, but Table 5 (see p. 66) at least serves to present an overview of the trends in world-wide development since 1947.

With a few minor set-backs in the number of Pioneers and baptisms the figures display a consistently upward trend in the strength of the Society's personnel, but the annual percentage increase in Publishers has fluctuated quite markedly. Perhaps more significant, however, is the finding that for the period 1963–71 the net increase in Publishers fell short of the cumulative total of baptisms in roughly the same way as in Britain and the USA: expressed as a percentage of the Publisher aggregate for 1971, the shortfall over the nine-year span amounted to about 19 per cent. This is consistent with Knorr's report in 1956 (*Yearbook*, 1957) that the shortfall for the previous seven years had amounted to 80,000 Publishers or about 13·5 per cent of the Publisher total for 1956. For the reasons given on page 65 we would refrain from reading into these findings anything more significant than an indication that the turn-over in Publishers on grounds other than natural loss has probably not fallen below 10 per cent for the last twenty years.

TABLE 5

World-Wide Development of the Watch Tower Society: 1947–72

	Monthly average Publishers	Attendance at the Memorial	Monthly average Pioneers	Baptisms
1947	181,071			
1948	230,532	376,393		
1949	279,421	453,274		42,524
1950	328,572	511,203	14,093	
1951	384,894		17,995	
1952	426,704	667,099	18,181	
1953	468,106		17,443	50,665
1954	525,924	829,836	17,265	57,369
1955	570,694	878,303	17,011	63,642
1956	591,556	919,994	16,783	
1957	653,273	1,075,163	20,912	
1958	717,688	1,171,789	23,772	62,666
1959	803,482	1,283,603	28,688	86,345
1960	851,378	1,519,821	30,584	69,027
1961	884,587	1,553,909	29,844	
1962	920,920	1,639,681	33,560	
1963	956,648	1,693,752	38,573	62,798
1964	1,001,870	1,809,476	42,938	68,236
1965	1,034,268	1,933,089	47,853	64,393
1966	1,058,675	1,971,107	47,092	58,904
1967	1,094,280	2,195,612	53,764	74,981
1968	1,155,826	2,493,519	63,871	82,842
1969	1,256,784	2,719,860	76,515	120,905
1970	1,384,782	3,226,168	88,871	164,193
1971	1,510,245	3,453,542	95,501	149,808
1972	1,596,442	3,662,407	92,026	163,123

One plausible interpretation of this phenomenon is that it is becoming increasingly common for Jehovah's witnesses to remain active for only a short time and then to 'retire' into a form of 'associate' or 'peripheral' membership, thereby forming a penumbra around each congregation which is activated only occasionally. A case could be made for arguing that the ideological orientation towards spirituality and brotherly love in congregations has partly legitimated the notion of 'peripheral' membership by removing the former emphasis on the necessity of achieving service-work targets and by condoning relative laxness in this branch of work.

Although the Watch Tower Society steadfastly refuses to reveal the extent of its financial resources, we may infer from the fact that in Brooklyn alone it owns four complete city blocks of ten storey buildings that it has acquired considerable assets; it also owns three blocks of offices and residences on Columbia Heights and the former headquarters of the Squibb Pharmaceutical Company at Brooklyn Bridge. Furthermore, the Society owns much property overseas either directly or through its associated Branch organizations which are controlled by means of directorships overlapping with the directorships of the American corporations.

Until the late 1940s the International Bible Students' Association (the legal holder of the Society's property in Britain) regularly incurred a deficit in its annual income and expenditure account that was always underwritten by the Watch Tower Bible and Tract Society, but, in return the British Branch was never sufficiently solvent to repay the debts. The post-war expansion in all aspects of its activity boosted the IBSA's finances to the point where it became more or less self-sufficient, but in 1957 it moved into debt again by issuing £37,875 of unsecured loan notes at 2 per cent per annum in a campaign to raise money for building a new Branch headquarters at Mill Hill, London. For its part the Watch Tower Bible and Tract Society contributed a sum in excess of £200,000 between 1958 and 1963 to the building fund, and as Table 6 indicates, donations since then have increased still further the IBSA's indebtedness to it.

One of the reasons for the IBSA's failure to capitalize on its new buildings and achieve financial viability is that it derives no income from the sale of Watch Tower literature and does not benefit directly therefore from increases in Jehovah's witnesses' productivity at either the productive or the distributive stage. Rather, the Watch Tower Bible and Tract Society buys at cost-price the literature that the British organization produces at Mill Hill and sells it at an economical rate to other Branches. The IBSA can only expect to improve its financial position by attracting new members, but the policy of its parent organization is not directly conducive to this end. Consequently, as Table 7 demonstrates, it is largely dependent on gifts and on receipts from assemblies for financing its own operations.

TABLE 6

*Debts, Donations and General Fund
of the International Bible Students' Association: 1958–69**

	Loan notes outstanding	Donations from the Watch Tower Bible & Tract Society	General Fund
	£	£	£
1958	26,925	86,000	34,786
1959	37,875		14,354
1960	33,375	55,000	28,989
1961	29,975	20,500	18,502
1962	23,950	40,000	18,503
1963	20,300	10,000†	12,703
1964	19,925		37,208
1965	18,150		57,690
1966	10,475		60,752
1967	10,425	11,000	53,045
1968	10,375	6,000	51,747
1969	10,325		50,978

* Source: Annual Returns of the International Bible Students Association deposited with the Registrar of Companies, Board of Trade.
† Approximate figure.

TABLE 7

*Sources of the International Bible Students' Association's Income:
1958–69**

	Legacies and bequests	Assembly receipts
	£	£
1958	2,155	2,070
1959	5,750	2,790
1960	10,096	2,759
1961	5,243	11,972
1962		
1963		
1964	29,637	7,214
1965	13,679	7,421
1966	7,549	5,071
1967	10,486	5,687
1968	13,594	7,940
1969	22,574	4,708

* Source: Annual Returns of the International Bible Students Association deposited with the Registrar of Companies, Board of Trade.

Thus the financial state of the IBSA is not an accurate reflection of its strength as the organization of Jehovah's witnesses in Britain but is largely an indicator of the Watch Tower Society's policies with regard to overseas expansion and to the rationalization of its publishing programme. It is wiser to think of the factory at Mill Hill as American property and of the offices and Bethel Home as legal and practical necessities which also happen incidentally to benefit the British Branch. There can be no question, however, that the Watch Tower movement in Britain would never have attained its present-day strength if it had not received enormous gifts and subsidies from the parent organization in America, and this fact reinforces the argument at the end of Chapter 2 that a sociological explanation of the collective fortunes of Jehovah's witnesses in Britain cannot be meaningfully constructed without taking into account the 'stance' of its organization and the way in which it puts its resources to proselytizing use.

NOTES TO CHAPTER 3

1. *A course in Theocratic Ministry* (1943). This was followed by *Theocratic Aid to Kingdom Publishers* (1945), *Equipped for Every Good Work* (1946), and *Qualified to be Ministers* (1955).

2. Since 1946 the students have been drawn from a wide range of countries.

3. *Life Everlasting in Freedom of the Sons of God* (1966), chapters 8 and 9; and *The Truth that Leads to Eternal Life* (1968) chapter 20. (Henceforward abbreviated respectively to *Life Everlasting* and *The Truth*.)

4. The Assistant Branch Servant in Britain estimated in a private communication that between 1 per cent and 2 per cent of all British Jehovah's witnesses were disfellowshipped each year.

5. Much of the technical information in the following section is drawn from Farr's (1972) valuable study. The views of the Watch Tower Society are clearly stated in *Blood, Medicine and the Law of God* (1961).

6. See *Parliamentary Debates: Hansard, House of Commons Official Report*, 724, 47, Monday, 14 February 1966, quoted in Farr (1972).

7. See, for example, the reports in *The Times*, 19 May 1959 and 30 March 1960 of the trial and conviction for manslaughter of an Australian Jehovah's witness whose refusal to sanction a blood transfusion for his new-born child was held to have resulted in its death.

8. Newspaper reports are the principal source of information on the situation of African Witnesses at the moment. See *The Times*, 24 October 1967; 16 January 1968, 6, 10, 26 March 1968. For an overview of their plight in very recent times, see B. R. Wilson (1973), pp. 73–5.

CHAPTER 4

WATCH TOWER ORGANIZATION

To understand the structural relationships that hold present-day Jehovah's witnesses together in something that can justifiably be called a religious movement we must examine the development of its organizational rationale, the distribution of authority, the forces of integration and disintegration and the internal factors affecting growth and change. But none of this will make sense unless it is prefaced by a brief description of the activities in which British Jehovah's witnesses participate and which serve to give precision to their relgious self-identity as a group. This will be followed by a sociological account of the division of labour and of status and role divisions among them.

The principal self-defining characteristics of the Jehovah's witness in Britain include being a student of Watch Tower literature, learning official doctrines, showing willingness to proselytize actively, undergoing baptism by total immersion into the Watch Tower faith as a symbol of 'dedication to Jehovah God' and participating regularly in all the congregation's meetings. These characteristics hold good regardless of considerations such as old age, infirmity or family obligations which, in other religious organizations, would probably warrant dispensation from at least some of the obligations. By contrast with some other modes of religious sociation, then, it is theoretically impossible to be a Jehovah's witness without joining a local congregation and without remaining firmly in association with it. The congregation participates as a group in five meetings each week: a Public Talk on Sunday, an hour-long study of *The Watchtower*, an evening study in small groups of one of the Watch Tower Society's recently published books, a Service Meeting for improving the standard of the congregation's collective evangelism and a

Theocratic Ministry School where individuals methodically practice all aspects of personal evangelism. Attendance at all meetings is theoretically *de rigueur* but in practice the congregation's leader, the Presiding Minister, castigates laxity in only those Witnesses whose attendance is very irregular. But his treatment of those who fail to submit a weekly analysis of the hours spent in field-service, magazine sales, making back-calls and conducting Bible Studies with newly interested people is likely to be much more severe. The targets for service-work[1] are carefully and precisely defined, and each congregation is expected to ensure that its average rates of work approximate closely to them.

The congregation comprises not only 'ordinary' Jehovah's witnesses or 'Kingdom Publishers', but also two other grades of member. *Pioneer Publishers* (usually young people who can supplement their very meagre earnings from sales of Watch Tower literature with part-time secular employment or with subsidies from their parents) are expected to achieve monthly averages of 100 hours in service-work. *Special Pioneers* are full-time, salaried evangelists who are entirely at the disposal of Branch administrators and who aim to achieve 150 hours per month in service-work. They are typically mature adults, often married couples, whose extensive experience in the Pioneer division and/or in administrative positions has fitted them to tackle evangelism in 'difficult' or remote areas. Alternatively, they may be drafted as Presiding Ministers of congregations either lacking suitable internal leaders or suffering from internal disruption. Thus, their contribution to the stability and continuity of the Watch Tower movement at 'grass roots' level is out of all proportion to their numerical strength, for in addition to setting and embodying ideal standards of dedication to the Watch Tower Society's goals and values, they are also invaluable agents in recruiting and training new members.

Special Pioneers are not therefore unlike the trained cadres of the Bolshevik party at the time of the 1917 revolution in Russia (see Selznick, 1960). They could not have succeeded in this task unless they had been efficiently trained and instantly mobilizable, and with the major exception that the Bolsheviks worked in secrecy, Special Pioneers have adopted very similar strategies in their campaigns to establish congregations in new territory or to revitalize congregations falling short of required standards. Perhaps an even closer functional analogy could be drawn with the Jesuits whose contributions to the stability and development of the Roman Catholic Church have been of a similar order of importance, and whose unique loyalty to the office of the Pope is paralleled by the failure of Special Pioneers to arrogate to themselves any kind of autonomous authority. (See McKenzie, 1969) Their geographical dispersion and high rates of mobility conspire to prevent them from constituting a 'horizontal' interest-group within the Watch Tower movement which might threaten to cross-cut and to subvert the dominantly 'vertical' pattern of authority relations. Special Pioneers have not, therefore, realized their full power in the Watch Tower movement, nor is there evidence that, since their formation in 1937, they have even sought to achieve it.

Responsibility for the day-to-day running of a congregation and for planning its long-term objectives resides nowadays in the hands of a *Presiding Minister* who is selected from the congregation's Elders to hold office for a term of one year. The *Elders* are mature male Publishers who must be able to teach Watch Tower doctrines competently and who are adjudged to have the congregation's interests at heart. Their appointment came from regional and Branch officials when these arrangements were first instituted in 1972, but subsequent recommendations for appointment must now originate in the body of existing Elders within each congregation. Yet, Branch officials have retained the power to confirm or to reject all nominations for the eldership, thereby keeping check on the quality of local leaders and, ultimately, on the conformity of congregations with Branch directives. The present scheme provides for an annual review by the Branch office in September of all appointments to the eldership and of all nominations to posts of responsibility. This represents the logical outcome of J. F. Rutherford's attempts to eliminate the 'elective Elder system' and of post-war moves to prevent inactive men from retaining authority in congregations. For, until 1972 Congregation Overseers (or Congregation Servants) were expected to hold office for as long as they proved acceptable to members of the congregation, and it was peculiarly difficult for Branch officials to remove an incumbent without creating much ill-will. The responsibilities of the incumbent have not, however, changed for they still include oversight of the congregation's administrative, material and spiritual welfare, and he continues to be regarded as the appropriate conductor of major ritual functions.

Major executive positions in the congregation are filled by those Elders who have evinced doctrinal correctness, enthusiasm for service-work and administrative competence. The *Assistant Presiding Minister* deputizes for the Presiding Minister in his absence and is responsible principally for collecting and collating Publishers' service-work records. The *Bible Study Servant* looks after all aspects of collective and individual evangelism, including the 'in service' training of Publishers. These two Servants join with the Presiding Minister to form a *Congregation Committee* which acts as an occasional forum for discussion of strategy, an advisory body on decision-making and a judicial agency for hearing cases of complaint against congregation members. The importance of this 'inner cabinet' itself has suffered no diminution since the 1972 rearrangement, because it will still be held collectively responsible to regional and Branch officials for the congregation's welfare and will continue to be the source of most local initiatives in practical matters. Moreover, from the point of view of local Publishers it will remain important as a court of first instance for charges of immorality, heterodoxy and inactivity. If anything, it has grown in importance at the expense of the Presiding Minister's personal authority.

On a second level of status other Elders are appointed to positions of responsibility for the Watch Tower Study and the Theocratic Ministry School. The method of appointing them is the same as for the senior positions: recommendations are made by the whole body of Elders in each congregation to regional and Branch officials who then make what they consider to be an appropriate appointment. One of the intentions of the 1972 rearrangements was that these posts would all be held in rotation for one year periods, but it remains to be seen whether there will in fact be much 'job mobility' at the end of each year of operation.

A third stratum of congregation functionaries is composed of male Publishers whose characters, experience and abilities are expected to fit them for less onerously responsible positions than those open to Elders. *Ministerial Assistants*, as they have been called since 1972, are nominated and appointed in the same way as Elders and are also intended to hold their positions in rotation, but they are excluded from the congregation's inner councils and are not held collectively responsible for its progress. They supervise the distribution of literature, congregation accounts and congregational property and on occasions they may be allowed to perform some Elders' functions. Appointment to this stratum is consequent upon nomination by Elders and is usually awarded either to younger men showing leadership potential or to older men who are no longer capable of more exacting tasks.

Until 1972 each congregation's affairs were administered by a number of Servants working under the direction of an Overseer or Congregation Servant and they shared their duties in more or less the same way as Elders and Ministerial Assistants now do, but the crucial difference between the two schemes are in (a) the method of selection and (b) tenure of office. Formerly, Servants were recommended by the Congregation Committee to the regional officer of the Watch Tower Society, and their appointment was announced from Branch headquarters, but the new arrangements theoretically allow greater freedom to the whole body of Elders in nominating men for appointment. On the other hand, the decision still rests ultimately with Branch officials, and since it was they who appointed each congregation's constituent body of Elders in 1972, it is unlikely that their appointees will nominate unacceptable colleagues. It is therefore unclear whether the new method of selection will result in greater congregational autonomy. Similarly, with the new scheme for rotating tenures of office, it was officially justified on the grounds of promoting a stronger sense of self-determination at congregational level, and indeed this would be true if it entailed the removal of Servants who had consistently furthered Branch aims rather than local interests. But in other circumstances the new scheme could result in a relative loss of local autonomy if annual changes of leadership diminished the congregation's corporate strength to resist Branch injunctions, but it seems improbable at the moment that the replacement of Servants by Elders will seriously disrupt the pattern of relations between the Watch Tower movement's centre and periphery that had crystallized following the declaration of a Theocracy in 1938.

The recent introduction of government by Elders is compatible in various ways with the movement's post-Second World War ethical re-orientation. In particular, the qualifications for appointment to the status of Elder reflect the post-war premium on moral integrity and correct behaviour in the home: consistent adherence to 'the highest moral standard' (*Yearbook*, 1972, p. 12), moderation in habits, hospitality, 'a fine testimony from people on the outside' (*Yearbook*, 1972, p. 18) and 'a man presiding over his own household in a fine manner, having children in subjection with all seriousness'. (*Yearbook*, 1972, pp. 16–17) The pre-war emphasis was, by way of contrast, on such characteristics as 'organization mindedness' and 'loyalty to Jehovah's organization'. C. T. Russell, on the other hand, would probably have endorsed the new order of priorities, and this would be congruent with our argument that the last two decades have witnessed at least a superficial reversion in some aspects of the Watch Tower movement to its pre-1914 condition. Nevertheless, we must repeat our misgivings about the motives behind the reorganization and about the intended consequences, for there is evidence to indicate that promises of greater congregational autonomy may be no more than an ideological carrot for inducing higher rates of service-work from Jehovah's witnesses in the West. If this is the case, then the recent reforms of ideology and organization represent tactical adaptations to the changed circumstances of the post-war West rather than a strategic re-orientation of the movement's whole ethos and response to the world.

The case for the above interpretation of recent changes is strengthened when the developments at regional and Branch levels of the national organization are taken into account, for our principal thesis is that the role of leaders at these levels is crucial for the recruitment, socialization and evangelistic career of grass-roots Jehovah's witnesses. It is significant, for example, that the role of the salaried *Circuit Servants* in Britain who each have charge of about fifteen congregations has hardly altered since 1972 nor have the qualifications for the post. A Circuit Servant will probably have served as a Special Pioneer and have given proof of his abilities as a public speaker, administrator and evangelist, but above all he must have acquired a thorough understanding of the organizational complexities of the Watch Tower movement. Not surprisingly, Circuit Servants usually display a higher level of educational attainment than the average Jehovah's witness, and their life-style is unquestionably middle class. The introduction of government by Elders in congregations has not seriously affected the Circuit Servant's responsibilities for paying six-monthly visits to congregations in order to check on their progress in detail, for arranging Circuit Assemblies, for checking on nominees for the Pioneer branch or for positions of responsibility and for arbitrating in those judicial cases which present grave problems for Congregation Committees. In short, he has retained the position of mediator or link between congregations and the higher echelons of the Watch Tower Society.

The Circuit Servant is undoubtedly identified with 'the Society' rather than with particular groups of Witnesses. His only point of personal contact with Publishers is when he accompanies them in the door-to-door ministry in order to study their methods and offer advice, but the situation is so fraught with anxiety for most Publishers that they can only perceive it as an official inspection. Similarly for Pioneers and Elders, the principal reason for his visit is a scrutiny of their service-work records and of the congregation's collective condition, for one of his responsibilities is to make recommendations to Branch office for future appointments which are eventually made on the basis of findings from a questionnaire that he administers to each aspirant. (See Stevenson, 1967, pp. 105–6)

Thus, since their official establishment in 1946[2] Circuit Servants have been particularly attentive to improving Publishers' evangelistic efficiency and to ensuring that congregations function correctly as productive, liturgical and social units. The reforms of 1972 are reflected in the Circuit Servant's role only to the extent that he is now expected to show greater concern for the spiritual welfare and moral integrity of the Jehovah's witnesses in his charge. But we take the view that as long as he continues to be a kind of official inspector of local personnel, the expressive aspects of his role will fail to be taken seriously. Moreover, we interpret the issue of explicit directives to Circuit Servants to become spiritual guides as an ideological device for cloaking less disinterested concerns with Publishers' evangelical productivity and dedication to the Watch Tower Society's goals.

The four *District Servants* of Britain who each have responsibility for about two hundred congregations or twelve Circuits are unquestionably seen by Jehovah's witnesses as representatives of the Watch Tower Society because they have very little personal contact with the everyday life of Publishers. On the other hand, they will all have served as Special Pioneers and as Circuit Servants and will therefore have acquired many acquaintances among Publishers. Indeed, many rank-and-file Jehovah's witnesses seem to pride themselves on their personal relationships with high-ranking officials, but further questioning usually reveals that there has been no contact between them since the other person's appointment to an important position. In this way the Watch Tower movement in Britain can be partially understood as a myriad of criss-crossing 'potential' relationships that are only actualized at large social gatherings or when patronage of superiors is required for purposes of advancement. The situation is largely brought about by the high rates of geographical mobility among Special Pioneers, Circuit Servants and, to a lesser extent, District Servants.

The District Servant's isolation is only broken on the occasion of (a) his attendance *ex officio* at all Circuit Assemblies where he delivers an hortatory/doctrinal talk and a 'state of the District' message, (b) his more intrusive participation in the infrequent District Assemblies and (c) twice-yearly visits to Circuit Servants. But an indication of his structural import-ance in other than administrative affairs is his privilege of announcing on behalf of the Society any significant changes in doctrine or organization. His position is therefore much more clearly defined than that of the Circuit Servant and is best understood as being on the lowest fringes of the Society's elite. The recent reforms in congregational government have not impinged on his role at all, and there has been no revision of his tasks since the post was officially established.

Other representatives of the lowest stratum of the elite in Britain include the *Branch Servant* and the executive heads of the seven departments at national headquarters. Like the District Servant, most of these officers will have formed countless relationships with individual Jehovah's wit-nesses in the course of their progress through various organizational grades, and those who graduated from the Gilead Bible School will also have acquired relationships with brethren in overseas missionary territory. They therefore constitute an elite not solely on the basis of their adminis-trative responsibilities but also on the grounds that they are probably amongst the most widely known British Witnesses and are powerful sources of personal influence. From the viewpoint of communication theory their situation at the nodal points of intersection between many different networks enables them to exercise enormous power through control, or threat of control, over the flow of communication inside and outside the Branch territory. Their potential for exercising power is further enhanced by the fact that most of their tasks are accomplished invisibly and that they are not accountable to any higher or more representative body of Witnesses in Britain.

Nevertheless, the other executives make themselves available to Jehovah's witnesses who seek advice or assistance at Branch headquarters and they often accept invitations to participate in assembly programmes as guest speakers, but they never discuss administrative policy or the details of their work in public. Rather, they talk exclusively on topics relating to either doctrine, evangelism or personal life in an apparent attempt to stress that their administrative functions have not removed them from the ordinary concerns of Jehovah's witnesses.[3] They frequently make it known that they are under the same obligations as all other members of the Watch Tower movement to satisfy service-work quotas.

Critical decisions affecting the movement's goals and strategies are reserved for the top stratum of the elite residing in Brooklyn, but much routine decision-making on issues of purely local interest takes place at Branch level. Most communications to or from the parent body in the USA pass through the Branch office, and in the eyes of Jehovah's witnesses it derives considerable prestige from its exclusive association with the movement's charismatic leadership. But the importance of the Branch office is undoubtedly felt more strongly by the Pioneers and Special Pioneers than by rank-and-file Publishers because the former receive their orders, their training and their remuneration directly from the responsible executive at headquarters. Kingdom Publishers, on the other hand, identify themselves more readily with a congregation and have only slight consciousness of belonging to a particular Branch, although it must be stressed that membership of the world-wide movement is probably their most salient point of reference. They do, however, enjoy a kind of vicarious association with Branch office through the mediation of personal contact with workers in the Bethel printing factory and hostel which happen to share buildings at Mill Hill with the national leaders.

The factory and office are linked through the intermediary of the Factory Manager, but the two units are functionally independent of each other. The factory staff is composed very largely of young male volunteers who sign four-year contracts imposing stringent working conditions, a miserably low salary and a strict regimentation of their non-working lives, but there is always a waiting list of applicants. For among Jehovah's witnesses it is felt that a job in the Bethel factory confers great honour on the incumbent and on his family, and their style of life is often applauded as a model of industriousness, virtue and loyalty to Jehovah's organization. For this reason they are attached individually or in pairs to a large number of separate congregations in north London so that they may set a public example of 'New World' living and thereby avoid an unhealthy concentration of piety in the Mill Hill congregation. This arrangement parallels the dispersion of Branch officials' talents over many congregations outside Mill Hill and may be part of the scheme to prevent the overlapping of spiritual and administrative excellence within one particular congregation.

However, the *de facto* concentration of spiritual, evangelical and administrative excellence in the Branch's headquarters is one of the distinguishing characteristics of the Watch Tower movement and it follows from the group's theology in the following way: it is believed to be impossible for a Jehovah's witness to develop religious excellence in independence from the Watch Tower Society, and the more an individual aspires to such a condition, the closer should be his attachment to 'God's visible organization'. This view naturally produces a centripetal effect on the true believers and virtually precludes the possibility that 'legitimate' excellence could be cultivated outside the core of full-time workers in close association with the Branch office. Once a Jehovah's witness accepts the Watch Tower Society's own definition of excellence, he or she can no longer aspire to the highest status among fellow-religionists without abandoning purely local attachments and gravitating towards the theocratic centre.

The formal methods and channels of promotion in the Watch Tower movement are well-known to most Jehovah's witnesses, and there is no mystery surrounding the process whereby people are appointed to positions of higher status and responsibility.[4] It is no secret, for example, that appointments within the congregation are made almost exclusively on the basis of the relevant Circuit Servant's recommendation and that candidates for entry to the Gilead Bible School must have the backing of their District Servant. There can also be little doubt that patronage from superiors adds valuable strength to a Witness's claims for promotion. The pattern is set out on p. 79.

The use of three columns in Figure 2 is designed to emphasize the distinctions between three different types of promotion: (a) promotion resulting from an application to join a group of limited size, e.g. Bethel workers or missionaries, (b) promotion resulting from an application to be considered for inclusion within a status group of theoretically unlimited size, e.g. Special Pioneer or Pioneer, and (c) promotion resulting from appointment by superiors to a specific position in the administrative hierarchy, e.g. Presiding Minister or Circuit Servant. Strictly speaking, being classed as a Pioneer or Special Pioneer is not an accurate description of a particular position but is rather an indication of general status which, in turn, can be a qualification for certain appointments, but we have included it

under the rubric 'promotion' because it looks like becoming a necessary
precondition of all forms of upward mobility in the present-day Watch
Tower movement.

FIGURE 2

Channels of promotion in the IBSA

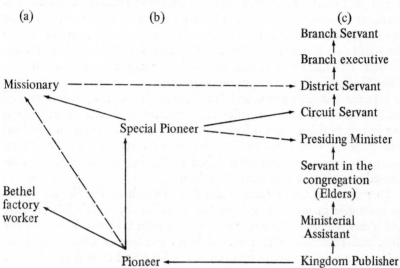

(Unbroken lines indicate normal channels of promotion; dotted lines indicate
unusual channels.)

Passage through the Pioneer and Special Pioneer divisions is now
virtually a precondition for promotion above the level of Presiding
Minister. This means that even the regional representatives of the Society
must nowadays prove their utter loyalty to the organization by first
making themselves totally mobilizable at their leaders' behest and by
undergoing formal training in the skills of Watch Tower administration
and evangelism. They must therefore be 'organization men' whose
attachment is undoubtedly to the Society as a whole rather than to any
local grouping. A growing number of responsibility posts in congregations
are also becoming the prerogative of active or ex-Pioneers, and the situation may soon develop in which promotion within the congregation is
available only to those men who volunteer to display the kind of selfless
dedication to the Society that is expected of Pioneers. If this does happen,
it will be the full realization of Rutherford's scheme to break the resistance
of congregational personnel to the overriding interests of the Watch

Tower Society as perceived by its own elite. Finally, these changes could be interpreted as a step in the direction of the professionalization of local leadership and of a sharper differentiation between 'lay' and 'clerical' Jehovah's witnesses.

What Figure 2 cannot conveniently convey is the very high degree of alternating mobility between some positions which is partly due to changing organizational needs and partly to changing personal circumstances. It is fairly common, for example, for a Publisher to work as a Pioneer for as long as his material and family situations permit and then to revert to the status of Kingdom Publisher. Later in life he may be able to resume Pioneer duties again or at least to perform 'vacation pioneering' in holidays. Similarly, alternations between Special Pioneers and Circuit Servant or between District Servant and Branch executive are not uncommon and are related to the Society's policy of preventing all officials from remaining in one position for too long. Of course, this can create antagonisms and personal bitterness, but the long-term costs of such impersonal rationality are more than outweighed by the benefits derived from increased efficiency in sales and evangelism.

To repeat an earlier point, the British Branch of the Watch Tower movement is in no sense independent of either the Watch Tower Bible and Tract Society of Pennsylvania or of its sister body the Watch Tower Bible and Tract Society Inc. of New York. The former, which dates from 1884, has a membership of between 300 and 500 and must legally include at least seven residents of each of the States of the USA; the other members are mainly prominent Jehovah's witnesses from nearly all the countries where the Watch Tower movement is presently active. The New York corporation was founded in 1909 as The People's Pulpit Association for the purpose of holding legal title to real estate in New York State and it has continued to function largely as an administrative convenience. Its membership includes about fifty prominent Jehovah's witnesses who serve as informal policy advisers to the Board of Directors. The senior Directors of the Pennsylvania corporation, who are the most powerful men in the Watch Tower movement, have always held seats simultaneously on the board of the New York corporation and of the other corporations that have been established in many parts of the world to take legal responsibility for the Society's local interests.

American domination has been assured since Russell's day by the device of overlapping directorships between the three principal corporations. In the case of the IBSA, its Board of five Directors has always contained at least two representatives of the American bodies. From its origins in 1914 until 1958 it functioned theoretically as a share-capital business for 'promoting Christian knowledge', but only 25 shares at a nominal value of £1 each were ever issued, and they were held by leading members of the Bible Students movement in Britain and the USA. Alterations to the Articles of Association in 1958 extinguished the nominal share capital, renamed the former share-holders 'members' and empowered the Council of the Association to appoint or to expel as many members as it saw fit. In its new form, therefore, the IBSA is slightly more flexible as an organization because its leaders do not have to worry about the possibility that voting shares could be inherited by troublesome relatives of shareholders, and its Council has greater control over the voting membership: but it has gained no measure of independence from American surveillance.

What is absolutely crucial in both the British and American cases is that the voting members can in no sense be considered as representatives of the mass of Jehovah's witnesses and are in no safe position to challenge the actions or the authority of the Directors; their status is purely symbolic and has no firm roots in a real power base.

The danger that the British Branch Servant might find himself in the difficult position of being responsible for the affairs of Jehovah's witnesses in Britain to two distinct governing bodies does not arise because the IBSA is only a satellite of the Watch Tower Bible and Tract Society. The fact that all editorial facilities are concentrated in Brooklyn, critical decisions are taken there and economic resources are distributed from there accentuates the complete dependence of all Branch organizations, including the IBSA, on the international centre of the movement. It is from Brooklyn that the unitary ideological thread is produced that links all the diverse parts of this vast organization and that suppresses most opportunities for the production and circulation of deviationist views. Following the example of his two predecessors in office, N. H. Knorr has not failed to realize the immense importance of retaining absolute control over the Watch Tower Society's organs of communication, for, while the President no longer writes most Watch Tower literature himself, he does still preside over the committee which commissions and supervises the contributions of Watch Tower writers.

A potential source of disruption to the on-going process of centralization of all aspects of Watch Tower administration is the increasingly common practice in Britain of congregations buying their own permanent buildings and furnishings. In some cases the Branch office has made loans available at a low rate of interest or has helped a congregation to obtain a mortgage for accommodation, but in each case the freehold title is in the name of the congregation's trustees and not of the Branch office. If therefore, a congregation seceded from the Watch Tower movement, the Society would have no legal claim to the congregation's property, although it would obviously have a very strong interest in it. Such a case has never arisen in Britain, but the hypothetical example underlines the rather precarious nature of the structure within which congregations are linked with the IBSA and the Watch Tower Bible and Tract Society: there is deceptively little *formal* linkage.

STRUCTURAL PATTERNS

The Watch Tower movement, as we have described it, can be schematically analysed in at least three different ways, for there is no single set of relationships that could be said to constitute its basic organizational framework. There are, in fact, several latent structures, each of which is based on a distinct set of relationships and each of which may, in the appropriate circumstances, emerge as the dominant one. Our account of the movement's historical development stressed the changing nature of its underlying structures and the strains that undoubtedly grew up between them. It is now appropriate to examine closely the present-day constellation of patterned relationships that make up the Watch Tower movement in Britain.

(a) The hierarchy of authority relationships descending from the President of the Watch Tower Bible and Tract Society, through the other Directors, its executive officers in Brooklyn, the Branch Servants, their executive officers, District Servants, Circuit Servants, and Presiding Ministers serves as the backbone for the organization of most of Jehovah's witnesses' activities. Legitimation for this authority structure is claimed and granted principally on the grounds that the Watch Tower Society acts as God's agent on earth and as Christ's instrument for ruling the impending millennial Kingdom of God and is thus a charismatic community. There is also a secondary kind of legitimation for the specific articulation of roles and statuses within the Society which rests on legal-rational grounds in so far as it stems from a formal charter and from a consciously designed organizational schema. Finally, low-level officials make claims to legitimation for their authority on the pragmatic grounds that they have specialized knowledge about ways of efficiently achieving the Society's stated goals in evangelism and proselytism.[5]

This plurality of differing claims to the legitimate exercise of authority by different actors within the same organization does not normally lead to structural disintegration or to excessive malfunctioning, because the group's ideology leaves no doubt that the Society's self-definition as a charismatic community is the dominant source of legitimation and is unquestionably a powerful force for integration. In addition, a certain amount of personal charisma attaches to the President, although it must

be stressed that N. H. Knorr adopts a distinctly 'low profile' in comparison with his two predecessors and therefore benefits more from charisma
of office than from purely personal qualities. Legitimation for presidential
authority is grounded in the notion that he is head of 'God's visible
organization on earth' and consequently not only the representative of all
Jehovah's witnesses in a democratic sense, but also their 'appointed'
leader. When he issues edicts, for example, he speaks *for* the Society
rather than on its behalf, and public announcements of major policy
decisions are stage-managed in such a way as to give the impression that
consultation with colleagues forms no essential part of the decision-
making process.

Knorr develops the potential of his charismatically legitimated position
principally by maintaining considerable social distance between himself
and the mass of Jehovah's witnesses and by shrouding in a veil of mystery
the precise workings of his inner councils. In this way he can claim credit
for the Society's successes but can always disclaim responsibility for failure
by imputing the blame to his subordinates. This tactic also lends strength
to the claim that it is God who actually directs the Society's interests but
that He must necessarily rely on fallible humans to carry out His directives. The variety of grounds for legitimating authority within an integrated organization like the Watch Tower Society lends it short-term
flexibility and long-term stability.

(b) Even in the present-day Watch Tower movement it is theoretically
possible for an individual Jehovah's witness to feel that he or she has a
direct, unmediated relationship with the Watch Tower Bible and Tract
Society by virtue of subscription to its magazines and to its set of doctrines.
But it is unlikely that this relationship would be actualized unless the
Witness felt aggrieved by the unresponsiveness of local officials to his
needs or requests. If a Witness tried to make direct contact with the
Society's leading officers, they would refer the matter automatically to the
local congregational officials, because the idea that the Watch Tower
movement consists simply of mass and elite is unpalatable to them. It is
significant, for example, that Russell's original conception of the Bible
Student movement as a loose aggregation of individuals in separate
relationships with the Watch Tower office proved both unworkable and
undesirably inefficient as a base for large-scale evangelism. The subsequent
history of the Watch Tower movement has been largely characterized on
the one hand by a strengthening of the links between local groups and
the central organization and on the other by a weakening of the local
groups' sense of independent identity.

There are, nevertheless, aspects of the organization of the Watch Tower
movement which are characteristic of 'mass movements' and which help

to account for some features of its structure and dynamics. For present purposes we shall assume that a mass-movement consists of a small elite manipulating and mobilizing a large mass of individuals in the pursuit of specific goals.[6] The Watch Tower movement fits the definition because it lacks both autonomous sources of authority below the elite level and intermediary agencies representing the 'mass' over against the 'elite'. Moreover, the policy of agitating people by direct and recurrent propagandizing reflects the elite's intention of using the mass to achieve its own goals; and the absence of opportunities for the mass to influence policy-decisions indicates that it is definitely the elite's goals for which the mass is mobilized. The intended function of the Special Pioneer cadres is to police the mass and safeguard the elite's interests.

The peculiar effectiveness of the Watch Tower movement as an evangelical agency is largely derived from the rare combination of 'mass' features and more conventional features of religious groups. Thus, from the individual Jehovah's witness' point of view, the congregation is an important point of attachment, but from the point of view of the elite, the congregation has very little importance except as a convenient 'retail outlet' for its propaganda. The elite's policy is reflected in the curious fact that the ratio of congregations to Jehovah's witnesses has remained fairly constant, whereas the ratio of elite members to Jehovah's witnesses has dropped steadily since the First World War. The apparent stability of local structures of authority therefore conceals a widening gap between a small elite group and a rapidly expanding mass of followers. The ability of the elite to maintain its isolation and cohesion is crucial for its power to manipulate the mass. In this respect, it is important to observe that mobility from the mass into the elite takes place very rarely, and since 1917 there has never, for example, been a wholesale purge of elite members.

(c) The third latent structure of relationships making up the Watch Tower movement is one that has threatened to become dominant on only a handful of occasions but that is potentially most damaging to the ascendancy of the elite. It consists of close ties between Jehovah's witnesses in congregations *and* of federal links between congregations. This type of structure has characterized a large number of Protestant religious groups such as the Baptists, (Harrison, 1959) the Christadelphians (B. R. Wilson, 1961) and the Brethren (B. R. Wilson, 1967; and Embley, 1967) all of which are founded on the principle that, in the absence of a clear-cut scriptural justification for a thoroughgoing distinction between clergy and laity, either the individual believer or the local congregation is believed to be an autonomous source of authority in spiritual and material matters.

In Russell's presidency and in the early years of Rutherford's regime, the problems of locating and legitimating authority were posed in personal terms, since both men chose to adopt a 'high profile' in administrative matters, but in the later 1930s the problems were finding expression in more objective terms of competing organizational rationales. Subscribers to the view that sovereignty was an emergent property of groups of Bible Students gathering in conformity with scriptural standards rejected or at least resisted the Watch Tower Bible and Tract Society's claims to sovereignty as an organization independent of Bible Student companies. Post-War modifications of the Theocracy have been mainly designed to reinforce the sovereignty of the Watch Tower Bible and Tract Society and to prevent congregations from either reasserting claims to independent status or forming 'horizontal' links with other congregations. The potential for federalism has thus been defused by the persistent centralization of all editing and publishing functions, by the central control over communication channels, by the subservience of worship to personal evangelism and by the elite's policy of encouraging congregations to check on their neighbours and report any signs of deviance. Significantly, groups that seceded from the Watch Tower movement before the Second World War (see Rogerson, 1972) and seceding groups in contemporary Africa have usually joined an inter-congregational federal organization and have subsequently developed in ways commonly associated with religious groups.

The 'mass' and the 'federal' types of structure have each enjoyed short periods of threatened ascendancy, but the 'normal' situation has been the formal imposition of the hierarchical structure on the Watch Tower movement with minor incursions from the other two. Further anomolies in the movement's organizational structure can be briefly demonstrated by reference to A. Etzioni's typology of organizations which takes the structural location of charisma as its basic criterion. (Etzioni, 1961) In organizations where the reasons for compliance with orders are normative rather than coercive or utilitarian, it is common for charisma to be distributed among all incumbents of positions in a hierarchy (L-structure), but in the Watch Tower movement charisma ('the ability of an actor to exercise diffuse and intense influence over the normative orientations of other actors' [Etzioni, 1961, p. 203]) is concentrated in the top positions of the hierarchy only and in a way that is more characteristic of utilitarian types of organization (T-structure). Thus, this religious group is organized in roughly the same way as are commercial, industrial and administrative bodies in which,

The lower ranks are instrumental performers; decisions about means are made by middle-ranks of the line personnel and by the middle-ranking staff; decisions about ends are concentrated at the top. This division suggests that the highest need for legitimation occurs at the top, where indeed charisma is concentrated. (Etzioni, 1961, p. 214)

Yet, the Watch Tower movement is also anomalous in comparison with purely utilitarian organizations on the grounds that its members comply with orders for largely normative reasons. The intensity of their commitment to its goals and values is therefore sufficiently high to explain their compliance, and the utilitarian style of organization helps to account for their equally high levels of evangelical productivity.

GOALS AND STRAINS

Our suggestion that the Watch Tower movement could be fruitfully considered as a utilitarian organization should not obscure the equally important point that it is also a value-oriented movement (see Parsons and Shils, 1962) in the sense that its stated goals include the promotion of certain notions of ultimate goodness and truth. The propagation of these notions and the development of efficient means of evangelism have served as general aims of the vast majority of participants since the First World War, but this is not to say that other, incidental or indirect, goals have not been pursued by Bible Students and Jehovah's witnesses. In part, this has resulted from the conscious limitation of expressive or affective aspects of the religious life that might have relegated doctrines and evangelism to second place behind pure sociability. An indirect consequence of this policy has been the reduction of the number of occasions when activities or caucuses which would fall outside the normal channels of communication might develop into competition with evangelism for Jehovah's witnesses' time and interest.

A second consequence of the Watch Tower Society's distrust of activities smacking of 'social club churches' has been the complaint frequently voiced by ex-Jehovah's witnesses that congregations are rarely warm or friendly enough to prevent some members from feeling lonely and dispirited.[7] They attribute lack of friendliness to the unremitting pressure to achieve service-work targets which, in turn, is related to the top leaders' fears that strong friendship bonds might detract from organization-mindedness. The highly affective quality of the bonds uniting members of other minority religious groups is patently lacking in the Watch Tower movement.

A third consequence of the overriding pre-eminence of formal structures of organization and 'official' goals has been the failure of informal structures to develop within the movement as a source of 'unofficial' goals. Contrary to P. Selznick's view that 'All formal organizations are moulded by forces tangential to their rationally ordered structures and stated goals . . .' (Selznick, 1948, p. 250) the Watch Tower movement has not lost sight of its original goals nor has it spawned and retained sub-groups with 'sub-goals'. The reasons for its departure from the common pattern include the careful testing and selection of all new members to ensure their intense dedication to the movement's 'official' goals and values; the incessant training and in-service testing of practising Publishers; the rigid control over 'horizontal' information-flow between congregations; and the hierarchical principle whereby each officer is responsible to his superiors for the conduct of those in his charge without enjoying what is normally thought of as concomitant authority over them.

It would be incorrect, however, to argue that the movement does not contain *any* informal structures, for we have discovered that at least two such organizational complexities are represented in the British Branch, but they do not present any sort of threat to the Society's hierarchy. Firstly, kinship relations at all levels of the Watch Tower movement's organizational structure facilitate a flow of information that is outside the Society's official channels and that links sections having no formal contact. We shall see later how obtrusive are family links in helping the movement to expand and to remain united, but there is no evidence to suggest that they constitute, or are even perceived to constitute, a threat to the efficient pursuit of the Society's goals. Secondly, the set of mature male Publishers who have held important posts of responsibility in the Branch and who are now more or less in retirement from full-time Watch Tower work can be considered to constitute another kind of informal structure within the movement. The disparity between their lack of formal authority and their exercise of considerable informal influence (if not authority) points to a potential source of problems for the Branch hierarchy which is aggravated by the fact that some of these men are still loosely attached to Bethel. In practice, however, their influence on regional and Branch affairs amounts to nothing more sinister than a conservative restraint on policy change which is born of long experience in handling delicate relations between Jehovah's witnesses and secular agencies in the 1930s and 1940s. Indeed, 'Elder statesmen' of the Watch Tower movement can only hope to exercise influence through informal channels, because they have very little bargaining power either as individuals or as a group.

If the principal sources of potential dissidence or factionalism in the movement do not, in fact, seriously disrupt its pursuit of goals chosen by the Society's elite, there are nevertheless other causes of strain between different parts of the whole structure. Orderly and efficient pursuit of the 'charter goals' is impeded by five major obstacles, all of which are associated with the overwhelming problem of adapting a value-oriented movement to the achievement of practical, quantitative goals.

(a) In the first place, as we saw in Chapter 3, the Watch Tower Society's officials at all hierarchical levels are becoming increasingly anxious about the continuing high rates of membership turn-over among Publishers. The combination of pressure to evangelize and restrictions on pure sociability prove unbearable for a growing proportion of contemporary Witnesses. These problems seem particularly acute during the first two years of association with the movement, for those who survive this critical period can usually tolerate the pressure successfully for a long time. The problem is especially severe for a movement relying for its vitality on continuing high rates of practical work on the part of its members, and the present-day condonation of relatively low work-rates may be the first sign that the Society is becoming resigned to a better balance between the expressive needs of Jehovah's witnesses and its own instrumental demands.

(b) A slightly different problem for the Society is presented by those Publishers who continue in membership and who adhere to orthodox beliefs but who fail to remain enthusiastic about service-work. Until recently the Book Study Servant and the Congregation Committee were usually mobilized to counter such laxity, but nowadays there seems to be some reluctance on the part of congregational officials even to issue formal admonitions to backsliders; imposing sanctions on them is now a rare event. Disfellowshipping occurs only when it can be proved that the individual was guilty of committing a serious breach of moral norms, subscribing to deviant doctrines or harming the Society's wider interests.

Concomitant with the high drop-out rate among Jehovah's witnesses, the declining rates of service-work practice have produced a novel effect on the social structure of Watch Tower congregations—they have swollen the size of the peripheral group of lapsed and inactive Publishers who make only occasional appearances at Kingdom Hall. So strong were the internal discipline and consistency of pre-war congregations that backsliders were not tolerated at meetings, but changes in the post-war situation of Western Jehovah's witnesses have gradually eroded the formerly strict boundaries around each congregation and have facilitated the formation of a kind of 'associate membership'. The 'associates' rarely lose faith in Watch Tower doctrines and they remain convinced of the unique status allegedly enjoyed by the Watch Tower Society in God's plan for the world. Despite, therefore, the operation of mechanisms to ensure that the Society's allegedly divine mandate is indissolubly equated in Jehovah's witnesses' minds with the obligation to pursue its objectives, there are signs that loyalty to 'the *objectives* of the organization' is being partially eclipsed by loyalty to the *organization* itself. (Simon, 1957, p. 118) The waning of some Jehovah's witnesses' enthusiasm for service-work presents as many problems for the Watch Tower Society as does their high turn-over rate, since they both have deleterious effects on the movement's evangelistic efficiency.

(c) In the manner of most sectarian organizations the Watch Tower Society takes care to insulate its members against, and to isolate them from, potential sources of ideological 'contamination', (see B. R. Wilson, 1967, pp. 37–8) but the very obligation to engage in evangelism necessi-tates frequent interaction with people of widely differing outlooks and increases the risk that Jehovah's witnesses will either compromise the purity of their outlook or replace it with an entirely different one.

To meet the threat of ideological contamination during service-work the Watch Tower Society has devised some measures to safeguard Publishers' ideological inviolability. No witness is encouraged to give door-step sermons unaccompanied by another Witness, so that they can keep a check on each other's doctrinal orthodoxy and intervene in situa-tions where the companion is in danger of losing an argument to the householder. This arrangement also ensures that, in cases of serious error or indiscretion, one partner can inform the Book Study Servant and set in motion the process of re-education and/or admonition. In fact, continual training in methods of evangelism at week-night meetings further reduces the likelihood of contamination: Jehovah's witnesses learn that every stage in the evangelistic interaction must be planned, and every con-tingency must be covered by a rule. Consequently, the Publisher learns so many strategies, tactics and gambits that the probability of engaging in an interaction that is either unstructured or unexpectedly structured is quite low.

Finally, pressure to satisfy service-work targets is so strong that the substance of each door-step interaction is not always of greater importance to the Publisher than the purely formal procedure of actually 'doing service-work'. The intended and unintended consequences of evangelistic education therefore help to minimize the risks of ideological contamina-tion from prospective converts, but the costs of such precautions entail utter routinization of evangelism and resignation to strictly limited suc-cess. This is a potential source of demoralization for some Witnesses.

(d) Since the formal declaration of the Theocracy there has been no safe opportunity for any Jehovah's witness to voice critical opinions of existing arrangements in the Society or to suggest even minor adjustments to them. Instead, the Watch Tower ideology holds that, as Jesus Christ is already in personal control of the movement, it must be pursuing the

correct policies in the best manner. The suppression of minor grievances
and idiosyncratic ideas probably serves to increase the movement's long-
term evangelistic efficiency by eliminating potential interruptions and
delays in implementing official policies, but it also precipitates occasional
outbursts of irrevocable dissent. The non-availability of channels for airing grievances and suggestions means that minor irritations can build up
into major sources of conflict with the Society's authorities and erupt in
total withdrawal from Watch Tower activities. Cases of individual withdrawal as a result of an accumulation of relatively small dissatisfactions
are not uncommon.

(e) Finally, a certain amount of strain is generated between the
expectations that Jehovah's witnesses have of their congregation Elders
and the actual patterns of Elders' behaviour. In their role as mediators
between the Watch Tower Society's directives and the mass of its
followers, the Elders sometimes experience a conflict of loyalties or a
sense of the incompatibility between the demands of these two parties.
Role-strain and role-conflict of this kind occur most commonly when local
officials are exposed to pressure from their superiors to reprimand or
punish members of their congregation. Not infrequently the Elders are
aware of extenuating circumstances and personal factors which convince
them that corrective action is not required, but the hierarchy tends to be
oblivious to such considerations. The admittedly scanty evidence available
to us from interviews indicated that Elders usually resolve the difficulty
in favour of obeying commands and overriding local pressures. This bears
out our earlier statement that Elders do not consider themselves to be
representatives of their congregations: their self-identity is as appointees
of the uniquely authoritative Watch Tower Society.

The rigorous suppression of any notion that *vox populi* could equal
vox dei is designed to rule out any suggestions of congregational autonomy
or of organizational democracy. Consequently, there is no ideological
incentive or justification for Elders to place considerations of their congregations before considerations of the wider Watch Tower Society. The
dominance of didactic and evangelical-administrative elements in the
ideology induces Elders to overrule the more affective aspects of their role
and thereby to weaken their potential bonds of identity with the congregation. These considerations do not mean that Elders are insensitive to
the strain inherent in their role but that there are strong reasons impelling
them to resolve it in the way that they normally do. The outcome is not
very different from what we know to happen among the *clergy* of other
religious groups.

In different ways, then these five areas of strain and conflict within the
movement illustrate some of the difficulties arising from the manipulation

of a value-oriented movement for utilitarian goals. Part of the cost of success for the Watch Tower movement in Britain has always been paid in the disaffection of people who might have remained loyal to a movement having a more flexible organization and imposing less demanding tasks on its members. The underlying problem, then, is no longer as T. W. Sprague understood it in 1943 to be the incompatibility between 'centrifugal' and 'centripetal' 'systems of sentiments among Jehovah's witnesses' (Sprague, 1943) but the competing demands of affectivity and instrumentality in a movement which has already been purged of centrifugal tendencies.

DEVELOPMENT AND GROWTH

In order to complement the synchronic viewpoint of the previous sections we must now turn to a diachronic analysis of the relationship between organizational factors and the Watch Tower movement's material growth. Chapters 1 and 2 accounted for some of the external constraints on its development, but internal dispositions were no less important in determining how the Society would develop.

The evidence from service-work returns, schemes for training and supervising evangelists and forward-planning of publishing developments indicates that the Watch Tower Society's present-day objectives are hardly different from its charter goals. One major reason for this high degree of continuity is the practice of top leaders of presenting and repeating the Society's goals as narrow and specific. By focusing followers' minds on clear and objective aims, they have prevented the incorporation of new or informal goals into the Society's programme and have tried to play down the importance to Jehovah's witnesses of the survival of the Society as an end in itself. Only in those Bible Student groups that seceded from Rutherford's movement in the 1920s were there signs that the social structure and the group's conventional arrangements were considered more important than the evangelical goals of the Watch Tower Society. Even the post-Second World War ideological reorientation towards ethical questions and the apparent thaw in relations with the 'outside' world do not, as we have emphasized, represent a shift in basic goals or values so much as tactical adaptations to changes in the social environment. The Watch Tower Society is not therefore likely to follow the example of the Townsend Movement[8] or the YMCA (Zald, 1970) in seeking radically new goals when its original primary goals no longer seemed important in the social context, nor is there any evidence that like the Church of England (see Thompson, 1970) it has historically shown outstanding concern with preserving for their own sake the set of characteristics that are said to constitute its essential identity.

One of the reasons for the Society's ability to keep its members' attention riveted to the question of ever-expanding evangelism has been the remarkably high degree of organizational *centralization*—not only in comparison with other religious groups but also with secular organizations. All 'critical' decision-making[9] is confined to the uppermost echelons of the Watch Tower Society's hierarchy, and the opportunities for autonomy at lower organizational levels are virtually non-existent. Without actually defying authority, no single Publisher or group of Publishers could hope to pursue goals that had not been officially prescribed without incurring the righteous indigation and wrath of all superiors. Similarly, *standardization* of all Watch Tower procedures and processes has aided the movement's continuity and rigid application to narrowly defined objectives. The code of behaviour for Jehovah's witnesses covers all routine events and is universal in application, mainly because official handbooks set out correct procedure in great detail and because the Service Meeting is partly devoted to inculcating standard attitudes. These considerations are vitally important for a movement aiming to expand its outreach to countries with widely varying cultures for it can be demonstrated that overseas groups conforming with Brooklyn standards have enjoyed a higher rate of membership growth than breakaway groups.

Given that the movement is almost 100 years old and that it has embraced millions of people, the slowness of change in its outlook and stance make it almost unique in comparison with other groups which also began as evangelical agencies. Unlike the Townsend Movement (Messinger, 1955), the YMCA (Zald, 1970), the Brethren (B. R. Wilson, 1967), the Faith Mission (Warburton, 1966) and some denominations (Winter, 1968), the Watch Tower Society has not acquired values and goals tangential to its earliest objectives nor has there been a noticeable shift in the focus of its members' commitments. The only significant changes that have occurred have been aimed at the rationalization and streamlining of organizational and evangelical arrangements.

In view of the premium placed on its organizational efficiency and effectiveness it is perhaps surprising that the Watch Tower Society has never regularly employed secular experts or professionals in any sphere of its work. It has certainly made good use of its own members who happened to have particular expertise, and the British Branch contains professional advisers and skilled labour in such things as accountancy, civil and criminal law, medicine, printing, public relations and engineering. But the lack of non-committed secular officials in the upper echelons of the organization has meant that a potential source of innovation in both means and ends has never been present. The presence of secular experts who would in many respects have fallen outside the hierarchical chain of authority relationships might have served as a lever for introducing radical changes which, in turn, would have required ideological legitimation.

Similarly, refusal to co-operate with other religious groups in evangelism, social service or ritual has obviated another potential source of ideological and doctrinal change for the Society, and significantly, the resultant isolation is now considered a commendable feature by many prospective members. By refusing to collaborate in ecumenical ventures and by steadfastly decrying such developments in other groups, the Watch Tower Society has succeeded in retaining a clear-cut identity for itself and in attracting the favourable opinion of some theological conservatives. Finally, a factor supporting the relatively unchanging character of Watch Tower teachings and outlooks is the strictly limited availability of economic resources and their immediate use in direct or indirect evangelism. Since the Society seems to have no interest in amassing either fixed or movable assets in themselves but only in so far as they facilitate evangelism, its steadily growing wealth does not constitute an obstacle to the pursuit of its traditional goals. Nor is it clear, on the other hand, that the accumulated assets have exercised any influence on the choice on high-level policies in the way that, for example, the Church of England's material situation influences its policies. Above all, and most remarkably, the Society has resisted the pressures towards a proliferation of leisure and welfare agencies which were felt by most British and American religious groups in the early twentieth century. In the process, of course, it has avoided the fragmentation of its followers into 'endless class-specific, age-specific and sex-specific "targets"'. (Yeo, 1973, p. 228) The Watch Tower Society's development has therefore been curiously unbalanced: the high rate of change and rationalization in organizational instrumentalities contrasts sharply with the continuity and unchangableness of its goals and doctrines.

COMPARATIVE PERSPECTIVES

An overall assessment of the Watch Tower movement's organizational structures and dynamics can be attempted by means of a comparison with similar groups. The most convenient way of tackling the task would seem to be to examine its relationship with a process that has been said to occur in most Christian sects, namely, denominationalization.[10] Yet, this apparently simple task turns out to be fraught with all kinds of difficulties:

H. R. Niebuhr's confident assertion that, 'By its very nature the sectarian type of organization is valid for only one generation (1957, p. 19) has been severely and justly criticized as being a partial judgement based on a highly selective sample of sects. Furthermore, David Martin has established the valuable point that some denominations did not develop out of sects but were *founded* on distinctively denominational lines. (Martin, 1962) We must therefore start from the stipulation that if the process is not universal, then it is extremely important to state the conditions under which it does occur and the characteristics by which it can be recognized. But sociologists have failed to reach agreement not only on these two critical points but also on an acceptable definition of the process. Perhaps a representative list of defining characteristics would include such things as growing tolerance of alternative religious outlooks, increasing reluctance to withdraw from the social order, increasing association with particular social status groups, developing differentiation between clergy and laity, and increasing centralization of bureaucratic functions, but the relative status of all these processes makes the concept problematic in the extreme.

When we turn to the question of the conditions under which this vaguely defined process is said to occur, the problems show no sign of abating, for most authors have simply argued that sects with denominationalizing tendencies are more likely to become denominations than are those without such tendencies. E. Isichei's study of organizational and ideological developments in the Quaker movement is an outstanding exception to the common practice; she stresses the historical alternation between sectarian and denominational orientations and identifies the cause of this curious evolution as 'fortuitous external circumstances (which) are unlikely to be subsumed in any widely and meaningful statement of sectarian sociology'. (Isichei, 1964, p. 221) Unfortunately, her conclusion is as pessimistic from the viewpoint of a comparative sociology of religious sects as it is realistic, but we hope to show in what follows that there is still scope for sociological analysis in this field.

In order to break out of this sterile debate, we propose to ignore the question of denominationalization and to focus the analysis instead on the typical patterns of organizational developments that have actually occurred in the course of the Watch Tower movement's history and to compare the patterns with that of other religious groups regardless of their current sociological classification. Only in this way can the baneful influence of sect/denomination speculation be countered. We might seem, on the other hand, to be merely heaping confusion upon confusion by contributing just one more typology to the plethora of such devices for analysing religious groups. But our project can be justified on two grounds: (a) specifically organizational characteristics have never been used before as the principal criteria for a typology of religious groups; and (b) only by spelling out in full a potentially controversial means of comparing such groups can fruitful discussion be stimulated.

Interestingly, A. Eister's frustration at the fruitlessness of available typologies of religious organization led him also to advocate that,

> One obvious line of procedure towards establishing some clarity and perhaps eventually some consensus as to the precise denotations of types (words) such as sect or church . . . would be to 'break down' the multidimensional conglomerates which presently pass for 'sect' or for 'church' entirely into their potentially component variables or attributes and then construct empirically-derived clusters of traits, with probabilities of combinations of various characteristics spelled out explicitly on the basis of observed instances of concurrent appearance, or other association, in various historical movements or organizations. (1967, p. 86)

We shall follow his suggestion, but narrowly in respect of the empirically-derived clusters of *organizational* attributes.

In the first place the number of Watch Tower followers has expanded enormously, and the organization has become correspondingly more complex and more highly differentiated in order to cope with the influx. Yet, numerical expansion has not seriously affected the Watch Tower Society's primary evangelistic goals nor has it lessened the effectiveness of Jehovah's witnesses as evangelists. One of the reasons for the movement's ability to absorb and to canalize such increases is that central directives have continued to be communicated to the mass of Jehovah's witnesses through their local congregations because they, in turn, have continued to increase in proportion to the aggregate of Witnesses. Thus, the mediated nature of the elite-mass relationship has not been forfeited nor has the relatively close-knit nature of the congregation, and these two constants have helped the Watch Tower movement to grow rapidly without compromising its single-minded pursuit of unchanging goals. The policy of splitting congregations whenever they approached a total of around 200 members has prevented local groups from assuming enough power and prestige to compete with the movement's central agencies, and the intrusive role of regional supervisors has checked the potential of congregation leaders to diverge from official policies. Finally, the Watch Tower Society's dogmatic refusal to sanction representative internal government or discussion has reinforced the power of its hierarchy to control the mass of Jehovah's witnesses and has therefore obstructed the normal process of transition from quantitative growth to qualitative change.

Secondly, it will be sufficient merely to recall briefly our findings that centralization and standardization have always been characteristic of the Watch Tower Society's method of operating and that, in combination, they have served to render the movement highly integrated. The autonomy of national Branches, regional groupings, local congregations and individual Jehovah's witnesses has been subjugated since the 1930s to the policy of allowing the greatest possible freedom of control to the Society's top leaders in the USA, and this policy has welded the witnesses into a more self-consciously unified and more determinedly united religious group than almost any other sect, denomination or church.

Thirdly, one of the Watch Tower Society's favourite self-images is that of an evangelical publishing organization, and this was indeed its principal function during Russell's younger days, but success soon obliged him to enlarge the scope of its functions to include the moral welfare and devotional needs of the consumers/distributors of Watch Tower literature. Thenceforward, the affective and ritual aspects of the Watch Tower movement assumed greater importance, but the primacy of publishing work has never been eclipsed by other considerations. This has entailed the almost unquestioned domination over Watch Tower affairs of a bureaucracy whose original functions in strict relation to publishing slowly expanded until they embraced all aspects of the Jehovah's witness's life as well as the collective affairs of the Watch Tower movement.[11] Whereas a bureaucracy is commonly believed to develop in a religious group only in proportion to the declining primacy of its pristine values and goals, the Watch Tower bureaucracy was from the very beginning the most forceful and important component of the entire movement. If anything, legitimation for the bureaucracy has traditionally been more plausible for Jehovah's witnesses than legitimation for those devotional and welfare arrangements which usually stand at the very core of most religious organizations' activities. We are therefore in complete agreement with J. A. Banks' view that innovative social movements require considerable management of practicalities before they can function properly and that what is normally thought of as 'routinization of charisma' or 'bureaucratization' should be more accurately termed 'sanctification of praxis'. (Banks, 1972, p. 39) An interesting contrast-class would include groups like New Thought, Unity School and Psychiana which, like the Watch Tower movement, began as religious publishing enterprises but failed to achieve the transition from a kind of mail order business into a fully fledged religious movement.

If a large membership, an integrated organization and a dominant

bureaucracy are the most distinctive features of the Watch Tower movement, it might seem perverse to deny that it has ceased to be usefully
understood as a sect. But we wish to argue that in fact it can be considered as a particular type of religious group which may or may not
display denominationalizing tendencies but whose organizational characteristics are clustered in a sufficiently distinctive fashion to constitute a
type *sui generis*. Needless to say, types in this context are merely heuristic
devices for rendering meaningful the confusing mass of empirical knowledge about religious organizations, and it is essential for their proper
functioning that they remain subject to revision or excision in the face of
new information. (See McKiney, 1966) Thus, in the present case we
suggest that the available schemes for typifying religious groups require
modification if they are to help explain the Watch Tower movement's
development and, more importantly, if they are to illuminate the interesting comparative aspects of religious organizations. But we must stress
that our concern is principally with the typification of this particular
group's *organizational* structure and not with the more inclusive typifications proposed by such sociologists as B. R. Wilson (1967, pp. 22–45) and
J. M. Yinger (1970, pp. 256–81). We have documented elsewhere (Beckford, 1972b, chapter 7) our strong reservations about the ability of their
respective divisions of religious sects into Adventist, Conversionist
Introversionist and Gnostic or Acceptance, Aggressive and Avoidance
types to accommodate unambiguously or instructively the case of Jehovah's
witnesses.

The chief criteria for the new typification are the degree of specificity
with which a religious group's official goals are stated and the degree of
intensiveness with which they are persued. If these two dimensions of
organizational character are arranged as crude continua ranging from
high to low in the form of the two axes of a graph, a four-fold property
space emerges. (See Figure 3, p. 98) Our reasons for selecting these particular criteria are that they help to throw into sharp relief some of the
organizational problems that partly determine a group's pattern of
development, but of course there are other, equally useful, ways of studying religious groups and they each focus on different features. Since we
have discovered the great independent importance of purely organizational
factors in the history of the Watch Tower movement, it is reasonable to
select this area as a fruitful ground for comparing it with other groups.
We are also mindful of suggestions from other authors that one or both
of our criteria are important sources of differentiation among religious
groups: Peter Worsley, (1957, p. 236) for example, regards the distinction
between activist and passivist types of millennial movements as more
crucial for their respective types of development than the distinction

between millennial and non-millennial types; Ernest Gellner (1973) attributes the astounding material success of the Moslem Mourides in Senegal to their intensive pursuit of narrow socio-economic goals; and Scalf, Miller and Thomas (1973; and Beckford, 1974) have demonstrated the usefulness of examining religious organizations in terms of goal-specificity.

Before sketching the major comparative insights deriving from the proposed typology, however, we must enter a note of caution about the necessary crudeness of this device for locating groups at the poles of continua which are in themselves ill-defined, and we must make a plea for provisional tolerance of its shortcomings in the anticipation of eventually useful results. Finally, the present context is unsuitable for attempting to develop all the possible implications of such a typology, so we have restricted the discussion to matters of immediate relevance.

FIGURE 3

A typology of religious organizations

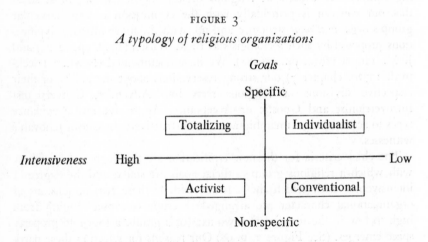

The *Totalizing* type includes, in addition to the Watch Tower movement, such groups as Scientology and the Holy Spirit for the Unification of World Christianity (Beckford, 1973; and Cozin, 1973) (the Unified Family), but the number of similar organizations is relatively small. They are characterized by a very assertive leadership above the level of local groupings, highly specific and narrow objectives, immense drive to achieve the goals, rigorous control over competing demands on members' time and energy, and stringent control over the quality of neophytes. Associated with this set of organizational features is a cluster of different characteristics, namely, a tendency for the group's ideology to have a totalizing grip on its members' lives, a strong likelihood that relations with secular authorities will be strained, a marked reluctance to co-operate with other religious organizations, a high rate of both recruitment and membership turn-over and a low rate of doctrinal change or adjustment.

The *Activist* type includes, *inter alia* and with varying degrees of appositeness, Pentecostalism, the Salvation Army, Seventh Day Adventism, Mormonism and Christadelphianism, and is characterized by a disparity between the single-minded activism with which the groups pursue their objectives and the lack of concerted agreement among their members on what their precise objectives are. In fact, their activities betray a plurality of not necessarily compatible goals, and the net effect is to diffuse the high degree of intensiveness over a wide area. Their organizational characteristics include a rudimentary division of labour between clergy and laity, a mildly democratic system of government whereby professional leaders are not entirely free from control by lay representatives, some means of selecting appropriate entrants to full fellowship but weak devices for controlling their members' use of time and energy. Among the other kinds of characteristic associated with this type are a strong interest in the ethical correctness of members' lives, a tendency for members to find gratification for their expressive needs in the company of fellow-religionists, harmonious, but distant, collective relations with secular authorities, mildly co-operative attitudes towards some other religious groups and low rates of both recruitment and membership turnover.

The *Individualist* type includes Spiritualism, the Bahai Faith, Spiritual Healing, Christian Science in recent years and some branches of Oriental philosophical/religious movements. It is characterized by a fairly high degree of consensus among members and leaders about the group's specific objectives, a weakly articulated leadership structure, a general lack of interest in organizational matters, minimal selectivity of neophytes and a low degree of collective activism or purposefulness. This cluster of organizational traits entails a weak ideological hold over the members, a very fluid concept of membership, conformity with prevailing societal values, peaceful relations with secular authorities, high rates of recruitment and membership turn-over and indifference to co-operation with other religious groups.

The *Conventional* type includes the majority of British denominations and churches. In terms of organizational characteristics, they share a weak sense of purposive leadership from the central agencies, a multiplicity of goals and functions, a corresponding multiplicity of factions and divisions, a sharp distinction between laity and clergy, low selectivity of members and a formally democratic or collegiate, but invariably cumbersome, system of government. Associated traits include minimal ideological influence over members, close identity with prevailing societal values, good relations with secular authorities, low rates of recruitment and membership turn-over and willingness to co-operate with other religious groups.

We must emphasize that the four type-cases are not intended to be water-tight or rigid: in fact, they are expressly designed to allow flexibility in scope and mobility between cases. It is immaterial for our purposes, for example, that Christian Science could be located between the Individualist and Activist types, because its very intermediacy gives an important clue to its organizational stance. Moreover, this particular group *in its formative years* might have been located on the borderlines between the Totalizing and Individualist types. The typology can therefore accommodate changes that occur in organizational characteristics even though the group's doctrines may remain unaltered. But the typology will serve its most useful purpose if it highlights previously unknown or unrecognized associations between types of religious organization and clusters of other characteristics. The following are proposed as a few of the relevant implications of the present exercise in typification:

(1) There is a close association between clusters of organizational characteristics and patterns of problems in the assertion, recognition and maintenance of stable authority relationships. Totalizing groups usually achieve the highest degree of short-term uniformity and stability but only at the risk of occasionally serious disruptions; by contrast, Conventional groups rarely suffer serious disruptions, but the concomitant degree of members' integration is correspondingly low. Activist and Individualist groups range between these two poles of the continuum and are characterized by moderate degrees of both stability and integration.

(2) The belief that the teachings of one's own group are exclusively true is not uncommon among members of all four types of religious group, but only Totalizing groups erect this belief into a dominant element of their whole ideology. Activist group members are also likely to feel that their views lay some exclusive hold over absolute truth, although it is uncommon for an Activist group to express this opinion in a collective statement. Members of Individualist groups judge the truth of the group's teachings primarily in terms of their pragmatic usefulness. The dictum 'If it works, it must be true' epitomizes this outlook, and the important implication for present purposes is that Individualist groups are unconcerned with collectively challenging the value of other religious views. Some Conventional groups are characterized by a discrepancy between the formal claims to the exclusiveness of their doctrines enshrined in constitutional statements and the actual tolerance displayed by nearly all members towards competing religious outlooks; other groups under the same heading do not even advance formal claims to exclusive truth, and

for most members the superiority of their group's teachings can only be justified on grounds of aesthetics or convention.

(3) In respect of recruitment, the Totalizing, Activist and Individualist groups are more successful than the Conventional groups in attracting new members, but the latter are better equipped to retain their members for a long time. They are also successful at retaining the loyalty of families for several generations and are therefore partly supplied with members who are born into the group.

(4) Major issues of political, economic, social or moral significance evoke three distinctive reactions from the four types: the Individualists pay little or no attention to such matters, whereas the Conventionalists and the Activists participate more fully in discussion and relevant action. The Totalizing groups show an interest in public affairs but only 'as a stick to beat them with' and as a useful device for publicizing their own views. But this should not be taken to mean that Totalizing groups do not share prevailing societal values, for we shall later demonstrate with reference to the Watch Tower movement that they do in fact uphold the majority of societal values—but in such a way that they *appear* to be deviant.

(5) The pattern of association between the four types of religious organization and the dominant social class of their members is not very clear and is certainly not sufficiently clear-cut to serve as an important distinguishing characteristic of any one type. One can be no more precise than to suggest that Conventional groups have a predominantly middle-class membership, Activists have predominantly lower-middle and working-class followings, but Totalizing and Individualist groups seem capable of attracting members from a wide range of social classes. This finding is consistent with our view that affiliation to religious groups is just as explicable in terms of their organizational characteristics as in terms of the modal social class characteristics of their recruits.

Factors which have been found to be crucial to the clustering of characteristics in other typologies but which show no consistent patterns of association in the present scheme include the overall size of the group's following, the principle of membership (voluntary or obligatory), the envisaged location of salvation (this world or another plane of existence), the availability of salvation, the subjective or objective nature of salvation and the total or partial scope of changes in the world order envisaged in the group's doctrines or ideology.

Our typology attributes critical importance to the general role of a religious group's elite in influencing the dynamics of development and in particular to its size in relation to the total membership, its internal cohesion, its remoteness from subordinates' pressure, its unanswerability, its methods and rates of recruitment, power to exercise centralized control over all the group's activities and its ability to pursue a policy of divide and rule. The present study of the Watch Tower movement's history and structure has confirmed the usefulness of this approach to the analysis of religious groups, and brief allusions to comparison with other types of group have indicated its potential usefulness in broader studies. But, in case it should be objected that our approach is undesirably one-sided in its emphasis on the independent causal efficacity of organizational factors, we shall now turn to an examination of the doctrinal teachings of Jehovah's witnesses in order to elucidate the role of ideational factors in the Watch Tower movement's development.

NOTES TO CHAPTER 4

1. For the sake of clarity we shall observe the following terminological conventions: 'field service' refers specifically to canvassing householders with religious propaganda, whereas 'service work' is a generic term for all the different types of evangelism practised by Jehovah's witnesses.

2. They are actually descendants of Russell's 'Pilgrims' and Rutherford's Regional Service Directors or Zone Servants.

3. The absence of ill-feeling towards them on the part of rank-and-file Witnesses indicates that they have been more successful than the executives of, for example, the North American Baptist Convention in avoiding the appearance of remoteness and unaccountability. See Harrison (1959).

4. An instructive contrast can be made with the arcane rationales and procedures for promotion in the Roman Catholic Church. See Fichter (1961), pp. 165–75.

5. Harrison (1959), p. 14 has aptly labelled this type of legitimation for authority as 'expediential'.

6. For elaboration of this concept see Kornhauser (1960).

7. See, *inter alios*, Dencher (1966); Stevenson (1967); and Tomsett (1971).

8. The Townsend Movement began as a purely political movement in the USA but adapted to declining membership and dwindling financial resources by marketing health foods and emphasizing the expressive rather than the instrumental aspects of its meetings. For a commentary on the theoretical significance of this evolution, see W. H. Starbuck (1971), p. 51.

9. For an explication of the distinction between 'critical' and 'routine' decision-making, see Selznick (1957).

10. The volume of literature dealing with this topic is immense, but among the most relevant contributions are B. R. Wilson (1967), pp. 22–45; Isichei (1964); and Chamberlayne (1964).

11. For fuller treatment of this theme, see Beckford (1972a).

CHAPTER 5

DOCTRINES

THE NINETEENTH-CENTURY CONTEXT

The Watch Tower movement is organized in such a way that it facilitates, indeed demands, uniformity of beliefs and teachings from its members. There are two principal reasons for its success in this respect. On the one hand it has always relied on the written word as the dominant medium for communication, and on the other its leaders have invariably insisted that Jehovah's witnesses *learn* its doctrines and learn how to present them methodically to other people. In the case of this sect, then, it is permissible to talk of its doctrines and of its members' beliefs in a way that implies a higher degree of uniformity than can usually be expected of a comparably large religious group. In this chapter, we are justified therefore, in using the terms 'teachings' and 'religious beliefs' interchangeably, since Jehovah's witnesses acquire even their initial beliefs on the understanding that they will later be required not only to make a public profession of them, but also to teach them methodically to prospective converts.

In our earlier sketch of the intellectual and religious context within which C. T. Russell founded the Watch Tower movement we underlined the formative influence of Calvinistic Protestantism, a democratic social ethos, a popularized scientific philosophy and a nascent rationalistic positivism. Russell made a selective synthesis of these influences and adapted it in a novel fashion to the popular traditions of American fundamentalism and Second Adventism. The resultant amalgam served as a rallying cry for many opponents of contemporary trends towards liberal or modernistic theology and the anticipatory signs of what was to become the Social Gospel movement.[1]

Yet, one of the most striking features of the original set of Watch Tower ideas is that, despite sharp changes in the intellectual and religious milieux, it has continued until the present day to function as the irreducible core of the movent's theology and ideology. Although the precise issues that had stimulated Russell to construct a conservative, antimodernist outlook had virtually receded into insignificance as early as 1919, his outlook maintained some relevance to much later periods.

In Britain, as we indicated in Chapter 1, Protestants did not share exactly the same concerns as their American brethren, but Russell's writings were found to have a relevance to British affairs that he had certainly not foreseen. His writing had a tangential bearing on the late nineteenth-century debate about the relation between science and religion, and his arguments were welcomed by some evangelicals who were reacting very strongly against the increasingly liberal *Zeitgeist*. Although the precise issues were different in the USA and Britain, a general weakening of faith in traditional religious outlooks and a corresponding increase in sceptical, yet optimistic, agnosticism were common to both countries.

Russell diverged sharply from the contemporary pattern of conservative evangelicalism in insisting that the criteria of absolute truth were twofold: correspondence with Scripture and conformity with human reason. In asserting that all Scripture was reasonable and that nothing unscriptural could conform with reason, Russell was under-scoring the debt that he owed to the rationalist current of the late nineteenth century. In fact, his early writings concentrated on the reasonableness of God's plan for the world, and considerations of emotion or mystery were largely lacking. He therefore had nothing in common with the emotional, revivalistic preachers of his day. Yet, not only was Russell's approach unique in this respect; it also embodied the view that the strategies of groups which might have been considered as his allies were totally misguided and that the points of difference between his group and its putative allies were somehow critical for the disclosure of religious truth.

The proclivity towards emphasizing points of difference from groups having a basically similar religious outlook has always been a feature of the Watch Tower movement, and Russell devoted a large part of his energies to increasing the marginal differentiation between Bible Students and other Millennialists–Fundamentalists. This had the effect of encouraging him to *systematize* Watch Tower doctrines in order to accentuate all the more clearly their uniqueness. Moreover, his successors in the Watch Tower movement have never abandoned the search for didactically efficient ways of arranging and of 'marketing' their beliefs. This makes our descriptive task much easier, but we have no intention of trying to 'understand' Watch Tower doctrines by subjecting them to any independent test of inherent value or truth. Our aim is, rather, to examine them within the *Gestalt* of the Watch Tower movement's history and unique symbolic universe in order to elucidate the interdependence between ideas and social structures.

Although present-day writers of Watch Tower literature usually ignore the spiritual heritage of C. T. Russell, there can be no doubt that variations on his ideas still constitute the core of Jehovah's witnesses' beliefs. We shall therefore begin the review of Watch Tower doctrines by outlining those elements of the whole system which have remained essentially unaltered since Russell's time.

STABLE TEACHINGS

The central tenet upon which all other Jehovah's witnesses' theological beliefs are dependent is the postulated existence of a deity called God or Jehovah. Jehovah's witnesses insist nowadays on referring to God as 'Jehovah' because that is allegedly His personal name: 'God' is merely a title like 'President'. (*The Truth...*, p. 17)

Rather than tackling the question of whether God exists, much effort has been expended in analysing God's character and intentions, and the overall theology of Jehovah's witnesses gives the appearance of being God-centred rather than Christ-centred. Nevertheless, their conception of God differs only marginally from that which is common to other theologically conservative Christian groups. They believe that there is only one true God who created all things and who has existed as a 'spirit being' since the beginning of time and who will continue to exist forever. His powers are believed to be limitless and His purposes are never frustrated: His existence may be invisible but His intervention in human affairs is undoubted. Moreover, since He is represented as the source of all life and of all meaning in life, it is assumed that (some) human beings can, albeit imperfectly, understand His purposes and His reasons. Similarly, God is believed to possess and express to the highest degree all the known virtues and laudable personal qualities.

The Witnesses' conception of God departs appreciably from more common conceptions in stressing His rational, purposive characteristics rather than the mysterious, affective side of His nature. This selection of emphasized characteristics is consistent with, and essential to, the Witnesses' view of history, for the Creation and all subsequent events are believed to be the programmatic outworkings of a divine intelligence. But more important is the belief that, since human intelligence is modelled on the divine format, *men* can grasp the ends towards which God strives and the means by which He attains them.

The purposes of God in history are readily and completely subsumed

under human categories of thought, emotion and action. Jehovah's witnesses believe that His purpose in creating His son, the Angels and the
earth was to give expression to His capacity for love and consideration. In
return, He endowed men and Angels with freedom of will so that they
might enjoy the opportunity to express their own love for the Creator.
When, according to the Bible story, a jealous Angel abused the love
shown towards him by enticing Adam and Eve into disobeying God's
commands, the Creator experienced sorrow, regret and the dual desires to
punish mankind and to restore it to its former position of trust in the
order of Creation. At the same time, God is believed to have banished
from heaven a number of 'wicked spirit creatures' who are understood
to be the main source of human frustration on earth. Consequently,
Jehovah's witnesses learn to cultivate a very noticeable fear of phenomena
connected with the occult; they 'believe in' ghosts, for example, to the
extent of shunning conversation about them and of refusing to listen to
ghost-stories.

The concept of sin, as employed by Jehovah's witnesses, is simple compared with its complexities in 'mainstream' Christian theologies. 'Sin' is
understood to refer to any act or thought of disobedience to the rules laid
down by God in the Bible for correct living. According to the Witnesses,
so long as Satan is allowed to corrupt men's minds, sin will continue to be
inevitable, but forgiveness for sins will be guaranteed to all at the general
resurrection of the dead following the Battle of Armageddon.

Jehovah's witnesses' conception of the nature of human beings is among
the most fundamental of their deviations from conventional Christian
doctrine, because it denies that the soul is analytically distinct from 'the
self'. Since it is assumed that Adam and Eve forfeited the gift of immortality and perfection through disobedience to God, man is believed to
be a mortal creature for whom death has always entailed a state of total
unconsciousness. In this context, 'soul' is often used to refer to the living
person: a dead person is said to have lost his 'spirit' (or his 'life force')
and to have become a 'dead soul'⟨ The loss of immortality and perfection
is also believed to have had the consequence of rendering mankind vulnerable to bodily and mental afflictions.⟩

Human history, for the Witnesses, is the progressive unfolding of God's
plan for the restoration of mortal mankind to its formerly immortal
condition. Not only is God thereby said to display love and consideration
for His suffering creatures, but He is also believed to be disciplining
mankind for its original sin of disobedience. The highly anthropomorphic
conception of God is to be seen in a recent explanation of His relations
with Adam and Eve:

God was not going to encourage wrongdoing by a failure to enforce his own law. By their disobedience Adam and Eve showed a great lack of love for the One who had provided so wonderfully for them . . . Jehovah owed it to himself and to all his universal family to uphold the law. This he did. (*The Truth*, p. 31)

The plan is considered to be perfectly just and equitable in the sense that the length of time for which man has been sentenced to mortal status supposedly corresponds to the impudence of Adam's disobedience, to the appropriate severity of the punishment and to the pain that it caused God to suffer. (In another sense, God has permitted man to suffer for a long time in order to underline the fact that earthly systems of government and human patterns of living are unsatisfactory and are not preferable to direct rule from God.)

Justice and rationality also loom large in a further feature of God's plan to administer appropriate discipline: Adam's lost state of perfection must be balanced by the corresponding sacrifice of another perfect human being. The perfection that was lost must be bought back at the same price. The role of Jesus Christ in God's plan was, therefore, that of a sacrificial ransom-price for man's lost immortality. Only a spirit creature which had never compromised its perfection through disobedience could serve this purpose, but even then, it was necessary for that creature to take on human form in order to approximate as closely as possible to the condition of Adam before the Fall.

The doctrine of Christ, as taught by Jehovah's witnesses, differs in important respects from the way in which it is taught by most other Christians. In the first place, the Witnesses' views on the nature of God are clearly antitrinitarian: God, Christ and the Holy Spirit are believed to be distinct entities. God is eternal; Christ was His first creation; the Holy Spirit is the force through which God intervenes in earthly affairs. Secondly, Christ's ontological status while on earth was not that of a God-Man, but that of a human son of God who had been anointed as Messiah when the Holy Spirit had inspired Him in the course of His baptism. Thirdly, the Witnesses teach that, on being restored to immortality after the crucifixion and the resurrection Christ was rewarded with the promise of organizing and ruling the Kingdom of God on earth at the termination of the time specified by God for disciplining mankind.

Jehovah's witnesses teach (allegedly in the further interest of rationality and justice) that God undertook to make His plans known to mankind in order to explain them and to allow people to exercise freedom of will in either respecting His arrangements or in rejecting them. For, just as Adam and Eve had the choice between obedience and disobedience, so all people who will have been ransomed by Christ's sacrifice will have to choose between sincere repentance for sins and indifference to God's offer of redemption. The Bible was allegedly designed by God to serve as a guide to His plans for mankind's restitution and as a guarantee of His good faith in implementing them. The Witnesses regard the Bible as the exclusive and inerrant source of all necessary knowledge about God and about world history: they focus nearly all their attention on the Bible in their meetings and in evangelistic situations, and it clearly plays a more important role in their religious life than in that of almost any other Christian group.

In so far as the Witnesses hold to a doctrine of their 'church', they distinguish between 'the true church' or 'congregation' and 'the sheep-like persons'. The former is composed of 144,000 predestined people who began to be 'called out from spiritual darkness for a special purpose' (*The Truth*, p. 115) during Christ's life on earth. The present-day members of the 'true church' are united in worship and gathered in one organization—'the faithful and discreet slave' or the Watch Tower Society. The 'sheeplike persons' constitute a complementary part of God's 'church' in the broadest sense by virtue of their 'doing good' to the remnants of the 'true church' on earth. In addition, they are expected to associate with the remnant and to share in proclaiming the message of God's Kingdom. In seeking legitimation for their claim to represent 'the true Church', Jehovah's witnesses argue that only the Watch Tower Society's arrangements satisfy all the scriptural criteria for 'true religion'.

It is believed that, in fulfilment of certain prophecies, Christ returned invisibly to earth in 1874 in preparation for extinguishing the root-cause of evil in the world and for establishing a righteous new system of human existence. The first objective will be allegedly achieved with the defeat of Satan, the original jealous Angel, in an impending Battle of Armageddon. But work towards achieving the second objective has already been in operation since 1874. The work has mainly consisted of completing the collection of a body of 144,000 pre-ordained people who have displayed unalloyed devotion to God and who will, by way of reward, serve as assistants to Christ in Heaven in ruling the earth after Armageddon. It is the firm belief of Jehovah's witnesses that, in addition to some people who had died before the Watch Tower Society began operating, only workers for the Society during roughly the first fifty years of its existence were anointed as members of this elect body; all other faithful members of the Watch Tower Society fall into the class of people who will survive the Battle of Armageddon and live on earth in a paradise for a thousand years. The distinction between these two classes of people, the 'little flock' and the 'great company', does not have this particular meaning in Russell's early writing but is a later doctrinal invention.

The self-appointed commission of Jehovah's witnesses consists in firstly 'gathering the saints' and secondly in witnessing to God's existence, loving nature and plans for the world. This is what the term 'vindication' means in the context of Watch Tower doctrines. The importance of the 'vindicating' task in the history of the Watch Tower movement has usually been reinforced by the conviction that God is on the very point of drawing to a close the period when people might still heed the Witnesses' message, repent of their disobedience and dedicate their lives to propagating the news of the imminent millennium.

The precise timing of the stages of God's plan for judgement and restitution has been of perennial interest to the followers of C. T. Russell and to their successors in turn. In fact, Russell's overriding concern was for obtaining an accurate understanding of God's historical intentions and of reliable indicators to their practical implementation. With the assistance of several published works on the same topic, Russell constructed an account of God's plan for restoring man to immortality in terms of prophetic types and their antitypical fulfilments.[2] He argued that God had inspired the authors of Scripture unwittingly to include in some of their writings a number of hidden prophecies about the subsequent course of human history. The prophecies, or types, would remain concealed or misunderstood until the general plan required that men should be allowed the opportunity to discover that prophetic fulfilments or antitypes had already occurred or were about to occur.

Successive generations of Watch Tower followers have gradually relegated intricate prophetic exegesis to a relatively insignificant position in the total body of their doctrines. Even the most knowledgeable Jehovah's witnesses today accept only some of the following as so-called prophetic fulfilments:

1874 – Christ returned invisibly to earth for the purpose of gathering His prospective 144,000 co-rulers of the Kingdom of God.

1878 – Beginning of the end of the Gentile Times.

1881 – Nominally Christian churches finally forfeited the prospect of serving Christ's interests on earth.

1914 – End of the Gentile Times, ejection of Satan from Heaven and the beginning of his last-ditch attempts to confound God's plan.

1918· Christ entered the symbolic Temple by adopting the Watch Tower Bible and Tract Society as His agent on earth.

circa 1957 – Battle of Armageddon resulting in the destruction of wicked people on earth and in Christ's subjugation of Satan for a thousand years. Beginning of a progressive resurrection of all the dead.

The Witnesses most general prophetic beliefs are that the closing stages of the 6,000 year period of punishment for Adam's disobedience is marked by increasing strife and hardship on earth, that the Battle of Armageddon will be a distressing and painful period of destruction of all social institutions and that those who can prove during the judgement of all resurrected souls that they wish to remain faithful to God's law in the millennial Kingdom will be allowed to survive until its conclusion.

Jehovah's witnesses depart from some other adventist beliefs in holding that Satan will be released again for a short period at the end of the millennium in order to present a final test of the loyalty of those who will have already enjoyed paradisial existence. A second judgement will follow Satan's final defeat by Christ, and only those who will have refused to compromise their love for God will survive into eternity. The 144,000 members of Christ's millennial government in Heaven will not be subjected to the second test nor to the second judgement, because in their earthly lives they would already have given sufficient evidence of their undivided devotion to God.

The fate of those who are either destroyed at Armageddon, or who are refused entry to the millennial paradise or who are judged to be unfaithful at the second judgement is everlasting death. Death is understood to be a state of total unconsciousness lacking in all sensation or intelligence. It is thus very far removed from the idea that death entails either a period of purgatory or an immediate judgement before God; equally, it contains no notion of either torment or bliss.

The concept of salvation, as it is used by Jehovah's witnesses, is also different in important respects from its meaning in other Christian theological contexts. It does not refer to a state of spiritual excellence which is sufficient to warrant a favourable judgement from God; rather, it refers in Watch Tower theology to Christ's mediation of God's scheme for granting man everlasting life. Salvation is, therefore, a gift from God in return for faith in Christ's ransom-sacrifice and for appropriate works in the context of God's plans for the restitution of the earth. It is available as a freely-given gift from God to all men who respect His laws and it involves potential deliverance from death and preservation during the Battle of Armageddon. It is therefore more tangible than other Christian conceptions of salvation and it places more emphasis on purely personal benefits.

Similarly, Jehovah's witnesses understand the Kingdom of God in a more concrete way than is common among other Christians. Instead of conceiving of it as a spiritual realm existing in parallel with the earth, it is restricted in meaning to the dominion which Christ has allegedly already begun to prepare over the 'great company's' imminent millennial paradise on earth. They interpret what they claim to be the accelerating deterioration of human institutions and conditions of life as proof that Christ assumed control of the Kingdom of God in 1914 and that Satan has, in turn, begun to struggle for continued hegemony over the earth. The seat of power for the Kingdom of God resides in Heaven, but its subjects will enjoy an earthly existence. They will benefit most of all from a righteous and just administration which will, according to the Witnesses, promote harmony and peace.

The phrase 'New World Society' refers mainly to the Witnesses' everyday, pre- and post-Armageddon existence on earth. This phrase is a shorthand summary of all the social arrangements and *minutiae* of life under the Kingdom of God at the present time and during the promised one thousand years of peace and prosperity. No publication of the Watch Tower Society has yet endeavoured to set out systematically all the envisaged millennial arrangements, but some projected features can be gleaned from incidental references to them. Thus, it seems that the witnesses look forward to a physical existence in an abundantly fertile and unpolluted earth in company with the resurrected and perfected members of all previous generations who could prove they were willing to obey God's laws. Social arrangements are likely to be fluid; the family institution would be out of place,[3] since everybody will share a common age, and reproduction of more people will be the privilege of only those who will have physically survived Armageddon on earth; their marriages will remain intact, but resurrected couples will not remarry. There would be no necessity for political, social or economic divisions in the population, and everybody will enjoy equal material, mental and physical conditions. Miraculously, it is also believed that each resurrected 'person will come forth with the same personality that he had at death . . . You will recognize those you knew before'. (*The Truth* . . . , p. 110) Equal opportunities to learn the appropriate ways to eternal life will be offered to every subject of the New World Society.

DOCTRINAL CHANGES

A full account of all the revisions and adjustments that have been made to Watch Tower doctrines is unnecessary in the present context,[4] so we have concentrated on only those changes that have some sociological relevance for the movement's historical development and present structure. Indeed, many of the changes that have occurred in Watch Tower doctrines amount to little more than a reorientation of basically stable beliefs; changes of emphasis have also occurred as part of the Watch Tower Society's response to its changing intellectual and social environment. In other cases, however, doctrines have passed through alternating phases of acceptance and denial, and it is not unlikely that this process will continue in the future.

The principal elements among Watch Tower doctrines which have remained more or less constant since C. T. Russell's day include: the belief in the literal truth of the Bible, the nature of God, His relationship to the Creation, to Jesus Christ and to man. Similarly, the general outline and purpose of His plan for restoring man to perfection has remained unaltered, although different features of Russell's original understanding of it have enjoyed distinct vogue at different times. The notions of a general resurrection and of two judgements by God at an interval of one thousand years have been retained in almost pristine form, and the envisaged features of Christ's millennial reign have remained constant.

On the other hand, Russell's ideas have sometimes been contradicted, refined or altered in ways which produced significant effects on the fortunes and structure of the Watch Tower movement. Disputes over the 'correct' interpretation of Scripture or of Russell's teachings have been at the centre of some far-reaching upheavals and schisms in the social group allying itself with Russell's doctrinal system, and the continued existence of such schismatic groups as the Pastoral Bible Institute or the Laymen's Home Missionary Movement is testimony to the enduring importance attaching to early doctrinal disagreements. (See Rogerson, 1972) This is most evident in the changes that have occurred in the Watch Tower Society's teachings about the role of C. T. Russell and about his own status in God's plan for mankind.

Those who denied that Russell was the personal fulfilment of Old Testament prophecy and argued that symbols such as 'the man with the writer's inkhorn' or 'the faithful and wise servant' were intended as references to the Watch Tower Society as a corporate whole tended to subscribe to the view that God had made Russell the 'watchman for all Christendom' until 1884 when the Zion's Watch Tower Tract Society took over his increasingly important work. The opponents of this view tended to argue that Russell's personal status in God's plans could not be legitimately inherited or usurped by anybody else or any other institution. In the event, Rutherford imposed the former view on the Watch Tower movement, and it has remained orthodox. The only slight modification is that nowadays, the 'faithful and wise servant' is identified as both the Remnant of the little flock *and*, by implication, the governing body of Jehovah's witnesses. Thus,

> The 'slave' remnant has faithfully and discreetly cared for the Lord's earthly belongings, extending his care over them to the four corners of the earth, into 197 or more lands and in 164 leading languages of the world. This worldwide care of the Kingdom interests is being carried on under the supervision of 95 branch offices of the Watch Tower Bible and Tract Society of Pennsylvania, with which the governing body of Jehovah's Christian witnesses is connected. (*Life Everlasting* ..., p. 186)

By legerdemain the Watch Tower Society has become inseparable from the Remnant and therefore claims legitimation from the same scriptural sources.

Doctrines about salvation have also undergone an interesting evolution. Russell's original teaching was that Christ's self-sacrifice had served as a ransom for the whole of mankind regardless of spiritual condition, attitude towards God or record of behaviour. Under Rutherford's influence, however, a progressive restriction on the applicability of the Ransom came to contradict Russell's views. An article in *The Watch Tower* in 1953 briefly reaffirmed Rutherford's view that,

> It is to obedient ones that the ransom does and will apply. Without ... works salvation is impossible. (*W.T.*, 15 May 1953)

Only when the prospects for greatly increasing the size of the Watch Tower following were unquestionably good was the scope of the Ransom extended again to embrace the whole of mankind.[5] Yet, in its latest form, the Ransom doctrine allows that some evildoers might be assigned to everlasting death before the termination of the millennium if they showed signs of unrepentance for sins and unwillingness to observe the millennial laws. Thus, the doctrine of salvation, as presently taught by Jehovah's witnesses, bears more similarity to the views of C. T. Russell than to some much more recent teachings of the Watch Tower Society.

This is also true of the evolution of the Watch Tower Society's views on the nature of the Battle of Armageddon at which it is believed that Christ will defeat the forces of evil and bring Satan under control as a preliminary stage in the process of a general resurrection of the dead. Russell's view was that all human societies would disintegrate 'from within' as a result of bitter conflicts between political and social factions. In particular, he had in mind a widening gulf between employers and employees, an insoluble division between socialistic or communistic and *laissez-faire* economic policies and a collision between anarchists, trade unionists and the forces of order. In the 1920s and 1930s, on the other hand, Rutherford envisaged that Armageddon would take the form of a Hobbesian war of all against all. He saw signs of the impending battle in European militarism and he imagined that formal warfare would be the means by which the forces of evil would finally destroy each other. This view remained current until the 1960s, when it was to some extent superseded by an up-dated version of Russell's views, namely, that Armageddon will consist of the break-down of known social structures and institutions. The role of warfare in Rutherford's views on Armageddon is replaced in present-day views by such devices as racial conflict, epidemic diseases, 'moral collapse', political fission, etc.

The fact that some Watch Tower doctrines have alternated between orthodoxy and heterodoxy suggests that the character of Watch Tower ideology and the sect's social structure are intimately linked to the total environment in which evangelism is practised. A full sociological understanding of the Jehovah's witness movement can only emerge from a consideration of the two-way relationship between it and social, political and economic factors. In this way, for example, it may be possible to understand the reasons for changes that have taken place in the interpretation that Jehovah's witnesses have placed upon the statement in *Romans* 13:1,2 'Let every soul be subject unto the higher powers. For there is no power but of God: the powers that be are ordained of God.' Russell had been in no doubt that 'higher powers' referred to secular or governmental authorities, but in 1929 Rutherford chose to interpret the same passage as an injunction to obey the Watch Tower Society's leading officials. Only since 1962 has the Society advocated a return to Russell's interpretation (without, incidentally, acknowledging the *volte-face*) which enjoins Jehovah's witnesses to show due respect for governments in so far as they do not impose conditions of life which contravene God's laws. (See, for example, *Life Everlasting . . .*, p. 199)

These doctrinal changes begin to make sense when it is remembered that in both Russell's day and in present times, the Watch Tower movement meets relatively little resistance to its work in the Western world, whereas during Rutherford's presidency Jehovah's witnesses were widely persecuted. Similarly the 1920s, 1930s and 1940s were years of great material hardship for most Witnesses and they were probably more aware of political instability than many people. In these circumstances, it seems plausible that an attitude of resistance or even defiance towards governmental powers should have been recommended to, and accepted by, Jehovah's witnesses.

Fascinating changes have occurred since the origin of the Watch Tower movement in the precise manner of classifying people according to their envisaged fate under the Kingdom of God on earth. Russell talked of the existence of four classes of men after Armageddon: the 144,000 *Saints* (or 'little flock') who would join Christ in ruling the Kingdom of God from Heaven; the *Ancient Worthies* who would assume leadership functions on earth during the millennium in return for faithfulness to God before Christ had sacrificed himself as a ransom-price; the *Great Company* of all people from past and present generations whose loyalty to God had not been sufficiently strong; and the *'rescued of the world'* who had positively rebelled against God's laws but who had responded eagerly to the offer of restitution. Of these four classes, only the saints were of the 'higher calling' which entailed access to heaven and membership of the true congregation of God, while the other classes were expected to be resurrected and to live on earth during the millennium.

The constitution of the class of 'saints', known successively as the 'little flock', the 'anointed', the 'remnant' and the 'slave class' has remained basically unaltered in Watch Tower theological formulations since Russell's day. The only slight changes in doctrine pushed further and further forwards the date by which the full complement of members was believed to have been collected, until it was announced that a few new members were still to be recruited in very exceptional circumstances, i.e. disloyalty to God by an existing member. The case of the Ancient Worthies, however, is different; in recent times they have lost their exclusive claim to fulfil princely functions during the earthly millennium. Symbolically, their collective title has recently suffered down-grading to 'Men of Old Times'.

In spite of their similarity in collective titles, Russell's 'great company' and the modern 'great crowd' include widely different groups of people. In response to the continually growing public interest in the Watch Tower Society after the First World War, its ideologists were clearly under pressure to achieve a doctrinal and scriptural adjustment to this unexpected situation. Accordingly, they made a formal announcement in 1935 that the 'great multitude' of *Revelation* 7:9 referred exclusively to people who were not anointed members of the 'little flock' but who were nevertheless assisting in its evangelistic work. (*W.T.*, 1 June 1935) Thenceforth, it was believed that nobody outside the ranks of Jehovah's witnesses (i.e. the 'little flock' and the 'great multitude') had been prefigured in scriptural descriptions of the millennial inhabitants of the earth. Adoption of the name 'Jehovah's witnesses' in 1931 had laid the foundation for this doctrinal adjustment by underlining the collective identity of Watch Tower followers as a group distinct from others whom Russell had expected to benefit equally from the ransom-sacrifice. In playing upon the importance of the wider group of Jehovah's witnesses, Watch Tower ideologists steadily eroded the distinction between the 'saints' and the 'great crowd' (or Jonadabs, as they had been called); similarly, the Ancient Worthies were virtually relegated to the status of 'honorary' Jehovah's witnesses. Consequently, those whom Russell had termed 'the rescued of the world' fell outside the boundaries of salvation and played no further part in God's Plan of the Ages.

Doctrinal changes since the Second World War have done little to alter the constitution of the classes of man outlined by Rutherford, but there does seem to have been a relaxation of the exclusion of non-Jehovah's witnesses from the opportunity to win eternal life. Nowadays, it is believed that all people will be resurrected and given the chance to prove their loyalty and devotion to God, but naturally Jehovah's witnesses estimate their own chances to be much better than those of non-Jehovah's witnesses. They also expect to survive the ordeal of Armageddon on earth without experiencing physical death.

One of the clearest examples of the process of reorienting Watch Tower doctrines rather than changing them concerns the interests which Russell had displayed in covenants. His study of Scripture had persuaded him that God's plan for mankind's restitution was divided into three principal stages, each of which had been sealed by a covenant between God and man. A covenant with Abraham had specified the material benefits to be derived from observing the rite of circumcision as a mark of continuing faithfulness to God. The Abrahamic covenant gave way to the Law covenant, for which Moses acted as intermediary between God and man in securing physical protection and assistance for Israel in return for observing God's law in detail. At the same time, the promise of atonement with God was reiterated and strengthened. The Law covenant was believed to have remained in operation until Christ ('the seed of Abraham') returned to earth. At that point, the New covenant was believed to supercede the Law covenant and to impose new terms on the relationship between God and man. Thenceforth, obedience to God's laws and faith in Christ's redemptive sacrifice were to be rewarded by eventual resurrection from death and the offer of everlasting life. In contrast to the earlier covenants, however, the beneficiaries of the New covenant were collectively described by Russell as 'members of the New Creation' or 'spiritual Israel' and 'fleshly Israel'.

Just as the scope of the ransom-sacrifice was narrowed during Rutherford's presidency to apply only to those who performed the requisite works for God (i.e. public evangelism), so the applicability of the New Covenant underwent a number of refinements until it was said to embrace only the elect members of the 'true congregation of God' after 1918. In this way, a sharp symbolic distinction was created between the spiritual elite among Russell's followers and those whose induction to the Watch Tower movement had occurred since the First World War. In attempts to reduce the confusion, the New Covenant became known as the Kingdom covenant and, later still, the covenant for the Heavenly Kingdom. Accordingly, only members of the 'little flock' or 'remnant' are nowadays called 'spiritual Israelites', and 'fleshly Israel' is specifically denied inclusion in the New Creation. Yet, what is perhaps more important than the precise changes in conceptions of God's covenants with mankind is that like prophetic chronologies, they have come to play a very minor role in the total body of Jehovah's witnesses' doctrines. No longer do the Society's ideologists scour the Bible in search of prophetic types and antitypes of covenants, and no longer do the Society's magazines carry whole series of articles in exposition of covenant details.

As the sharp outline of Russell's research into covenants and prophetic chronology[6] receded into the background, Rutherford tried to divert his followers' attention away from scriptural foreshadowing and on to contemporary events. Referring vaguely to the general chronological framework, he stressed the everyday 'signs of the times' which, it was argued, confirmed the view that an important juncture in God's Plan of the Ages was imminent and urged his followers to ever stronger devotion to evangelism. Thenceforth, collective identity was phrased in terms of shared tasks and divine mandates as well as in terms of prophetic foreshadowings.

When the magazine *The Golden Age* was launched in 1919, the editorial policy was to highlight 'the many wonderful events [which] are transpiring today, all of which have a scriptural meaning', but more attention was devoted to the events than to their scriptural meaning. This was because the prophetic/scriptural context was in process of becoming conventional and taken-for-granted among Bible Students; no sustained attempt was made to examine Scripture in the search for new light on covenants or on the timing of God's plan. This is not to say, however, that scriptural, non-prophetic exegesis was ignored; on the contrary, intricate textual exegesis was probably more common in the 1920s than in the pre-war period but it was directed towards clarifying organizational goals and structures rather than prophetic schemes. Even the ideas of the ransom-price and of the covenants between God and man were eclipsed by 'ecclesiological' considerations during Rutherford's presidency.

One might have expected that in recent years there had been a resurgence among Jehovah's witnesses in the 'time features' of God's plan, since it was announced in 1966 that:

> Six thousand years of man's existence on earth will soon be up . . .
> How appropriate it would be for Jehovah God to make of this coming
> seventh period of a thousand years a sabbath period of rest and
> release. (*Life Everlasting* . . . , pp. 29–30)

Yet, the similarity with Russell's statements about chronology is only
superficial, for the belief that 1975 will be a year of prophetic significance
is based on very little explicit scriptural evidence and is discussed in
heavily guarded terms. Interestingly, a subsequent publication of the
Watch Tower Bible and Tract Society does not specifically refer to 1975
but merely suggests that the 'present wicked system of things' will be
seen to disappear by people who will be old enough to remember events
from 1914. (*The Truth* . . . , p. 94) This means, in effect, that Armageddon
is believed to be very near, but there is no parallel in the Watch Tower
movement at the moment of the extreme state of expectancy that was
apparently widespread before 1914. The fact that two of the latest books
of doctrinal exegesis published by the Society are extended commentaries
on *Revelation* and *Ezekiel* is also an indication of at least a superficial
reversion to the interests of C. T. Russell. Significantly, however, the
modern approach to these biblical sources emphasizes their general
prophetic import rather than their specific predictions. This is another
reason for believing that very few Jehovah's witnesses will repeat in 1975
the kind of excited behaviour that some Bible Students displayed in
anticipation of a prophetic event in 1914.

We can best summarize the distinctiveness of Watch Tower doctrines
by briefly comparing them with Yonina Talmon's authoritative ideal-
typification of millenarian beliefs. (1966) First of all there can be no doubt
about the appropriateness of her definition of millenarism to Jehovah's
witnesses' beliefs: 'the quest for total, imminent, ultimate, this-worldly,
collective salvation'. (Talmon, 1966, p. 166) Each element of this definition
is clearly reflected (with minor qualifications) in Watch Tower teachings,
but it fails to indicate the significantly different ways in which millenarian
doctrines can find institutional embodiment. In fact, Talmon rather
surreptitiously adds further elements to the definition in the course of
tracing 'major characteristics of milleniarism'. Significantly, for our
purposes, the additions are mainly concerned with the social expression
of millenarian beliefs. But the link between doctrine and social expression
is precisely the key-issue, for in our opinion it displays considerable
variation. Talmon's answer to this problem takes the following, logically
dubious, form:

Organizationally, millenarian movements vary from the amorphous and ephemeral movement with a cohesive core of leaders and ardent believers and a large, ill-defined body of followers, to the fairly stable, segregated and exclusive sect-like group. The organizational form of the more or less ephemeral movement is, however, more typical. This is no doubt closely related to the nature of the millenarian message. (Talmon, 1966, p. 177) (emphasis added)

Our findings on the Watch Tower movement suggest, on the contrary, a very different conclusion: the nature of the millenarian message is so highly ambiguous that it is largely determined by the organizational form dictated by the founders or members of the groups that carry the message. Thus, Russell's organizational blueprint for the Watch Tower movement has ensured the maintenance of millenarian doctrines (as defined by Talmon) but it has also, and more importantly, ensured that some of what she terms the 'major characteristics of millenarism' are thereby excluded, e.g. ecstatic and antinomian tendencies. A comparative glance at Christadelphianism, (B. R. Wilson, 1961) Shakerism and the Oneida Community (Whitworth, 1971) confirms our general point that their goals and imposed organizational design were heavily determinant of their respective, and widely differing, ways of embodying millenarian doctrines.

SOCIOLOGICAL IMPLICATIONS

At the beginning of this chapter we drew attention to the uniqueness of Russell's original synthesis of theological and intellectual resources and to the didactic orientation of the Watch Tower doctrinal system, but in the course of the chapter two extra features have claimed our attention. In addition to being characterized by simplicity and methodicalness, the doctrines of Jehovah's witnesses could also be described as relatively unchanging and outstandingly coherent. The high degree of continuity may be unexpected in view of the fact that the Watch Tower Society does not issue any single, comprehensive 'statement of faith'[7] but prefers to express its doctrinal position in a multiplicity of ways in various publications. Yet, there is a number of structural, procedural and organizational factors which combine to produce a much higher degree of continuity in Watch Tower teachings than any other religious group's statement of faith could possibly achieve.

Since the very early days of Russell's Bible study meetings in Allegheny, the Watch Tower movement has lacked anything approximating to a high-level forum for doctrinal discussion, that is, a legitimate occasion or procedure for criticizing, or contributing to, the canon of official teachings.

Creativity has been carefully restricted to the inner councils of the Society's elite, with the result that Jehovah's witnesses are more accurately considered in this respect as consumers of a packaged product rather than participants in a productive process. This situation has been reinforced by the lack of doctrinal specialists among Jehovah's witnesses whose role could be likened to that of theologians *vis-à-vis* mainstream Christian churches. Only Gilead graduates and the school's teaching staff are in a strong position to develop critiques of current orthodoxy, but the rules governing their behaviour and the exhausting nature of their tasks virtually preclude the possibility of criticism from them. Renegades, by definition, must have withdrawn from the Society, and this very act disqualifies them according to Watch Tower teachings and in the eyes of most practising Jehovah's witnesses from being credible critics, so there is no realistic opportunity for rebels to bring about doctrinal changes 'from the outside'. Furthermore, the fact that the Brooklyn elite has always retained exclusive control over the Society's magazines and has systematically obstructed the communication among Jehovah's witnesses of ideas which were inconsistent with its views of orthodoxy has minimized the potential for doctrinal change 'from below'. Incessant pressure on members to learn doctrines formally and to rehearse them in public completes the set of factors contributing to the unusually high degree of historical continuity in this religious movement's doctrines.

'Coherence' in a doctrinal system is a measure of its overall truth as perceived by the believers, whereas 'consistency' is a measure of the logical fit between separate components of the system.[8] In practice, of course, the two terms usually coalesce to form a unitary, but vague, indication of a belief system's credibility, but the distinction between them is important for sociological purposes, because it brings out their differential significance for human behaviour. Thus, to argue, as do some opponents of the Watch Tower movement, that its system of doctrine is riddled with logical inconsistencies is to miss the point as far as sociology is concerned. What is sociologically interesting about Jehovah's witnesses is that they derive psychological satisfaction from perceiving a coherent pattern in their beliefs regardless of possible inner inconsistencies, and that, even if they do notice inconsistencies, they can then abrogate personal responsibility for their own beliefs in the safe conviction that *someone, somewhere* in the Watch Tower Society must be able to solve the problem. An implicit premise in the argument is usually that, if the perceived inconsistencies were real, then the beliefs would not have gained widespread popularity.

The import of the distinction between coherence and consistency in religious beliefs to the study of Jehovah's witnesses is that the Watch

Tower Society's emphasis on the alleged logicality, conformity with reason, methodicalness and widespread popular support of its doctrines is much more effective in attracting and retaining its members than would be a sincere attempt to tackle questions of doctrinal consistency. This is why we have devoted relatively little attention in our study of Jehovah's witnesses to their beliefs in detail: analysis of the way in which the Watch Tower Society *presents* its doctrines is more enlightening for our purposes than analysis of the doctrines themselves. This is also why a later chapter on Ideology is necessary to supplement the present description of teachings, for it is important to study the normative and emotive power of the symbols that compose the general *Weltanschauung* of Jehovah's witnesses. 'Mere intellectual or logical construction, however impressive, is insufficient' as a means for the individual to attain 'emotionally experienced meaning'. (Fawcett, 1970) Thus, our bare description of what the Watch Tower Society considers that its members should believe must be supplemented later with an account of both its underlying ideology and the more inclusive outlook of Jehovah's witnesses. The only justification for describing doctrines at all in a work of sociological analysis is that the very unusually high degree of doctrinal awareness among these particular believers is an important reflection of the Watch Tower movement's organization and has crucial consequences for the course of its development.

NOTES TO CHAPTER 5

1. For an account of 'modernism' in the USA, see Hudson (1961).

2. For an account of this procedure in the European literary tradition, see Patrides (1972).

3. Contrast this statement with the exalted status that the family nowadays enjoys in the Society's prescriptions for correct living in the 'theocratic' age. See pp. 53-4 above.

4. Extensive documentation on this point is available in T. White (1967). Many of the minor doctrinal adjustments that took place in the 1920s and 1930s were a source of great irritation to those Bible Students who joined schismatic Watch Tower movements in protest against Rutherford's regime. See Rogerson (1972), chapter XI.

5. 'We now see that more are to return than we expected.' *The Watchtower*, 1 October 1966.

6. For examples of his work, see Beckford (1972b), pp. 409-13; and Rogerson (1969), p. 192.

7. Perhaps the closest approximation to an authoritative statement of Watch Tower faith was the series of questions and model answers comprising the *Verbi Dei Minister* test in 1916. See p. 31 above.

8. The following discussion benefits from the perceptive contribution of Piker (1972).

CHAPTER 6

CONCEPTS AND THEORIES

TYPIFICATION AND EXPLANATION

A recurrent theme of the preceding chapters has been the suggestion that recruitment to, and continuing membership in, the Watch Tower movement must be understood primarily in terms of the organizational 'stance' of the Watch Tower Society. More particularly, the intrusive role of its elite in (a) determining and promoting the specific goals of its members (or, more accurately, workers), and (b) eliciting from Jehovah's witnesses an exceptionally high degree of intensiveness in pursuing their goals has emerged from the foregoing analysis as the principal factor accounting for the movement's pattern of development and present social structure. It was found that even its doctrinal system could not be properly understood as an independent factor influencing Jehovah's witnesses' thought and behaviour without also taking into account both the way in which the organization mediates the doctrines and the methods of the elite for manipulating doctrines to suit their long-term goals.

But we must also study the 'religious career' of individual Witnesses in order to present a balanced view of the conditions influencing the Watch Tower movement's development. For, if the present findings are to have any value in a comparative context, they need to be supplemented with information about Jehovah's witnesses deriving from examination of factors to which students of other religious movements have attributed causal significance. As most studies of sects have been focused on the personal and social characteristics of sectarians, we shall now have to abandon the collective level of analysis that we have so far maintained and concentrate more closely on the level of individual Jehovah's witnesses.

A brief allusion to the conceptual confusion that reigns in the realm of the sociology of religious sects is needed here to indicate the main source of difficulty in identifying and operationalizing the factors which have been said to influence the processes of recruitment to, and continuing membership in, religious groups.

In part, the typologies of sects devised by B. R. Wilson[1] and J. M. Yinger (1970, pp. 274–80) have helped to lessen the confusion by introducing general principles for ordering the mass of heterogeneous data into a small number of convenient type-cases. But the typification process, however imaginative and important, can only sensitize the sociologist to factors that might be crucial in the explanation of variation between sects. The task of *testing* the proposed explanation still remains to be done, and it is not unjustifiably harsh to say that neither Wilson nor Yinger has framed insights in such a way that they could give rise to conveniently testable hypotheses. This problem is not, however, serious, because it is theoretically possible to 'read into', or distil from, their work a small number of implicit explanatory principles. A more serious obstacle to the adaptation of insights from typological schemes is that they confuse the 'group' level of analysis with the 'individual' level, thereby raising awkward questions about the advisability or practicability of 'converting' insights from one level into propositions about the other. Wilson's work is free from this problem because it is designed explicitly to account for development at the group level of analysis, but one might still question whether a collectivity can be reasonably said to display a 'response to the world'. This question might arise purely from terminological difficulties, since it is clear from Wilson's typification that he does not impute individualist dispositions to whole collectivities, and his substantive account of sectarian evolution displays no signs of 'switching' between individual and group levels. In our opinion, then, a less ambiguously collectivist label for the criterion of the typification than 'response to the world' would meet our objections perfectly.

Yinger's typological procedure, on the other hand, is open to the criticism that 'response to undesired situations' can only be attributed to individuals and that it is therefore methodologically unjustified to proceed from this level to frame propositions about collectivities. Even if every single member of a sect reacted in the same way to an undesired situation individually, one could not legitimately infer that the sect, as a group, would necessarily behave in the same way. For the very fact that the sect is a collectivity introduces a factor over and above the aggregate of individual responses, and the possibility must always be kept open that the collectivity will react in a way that is only indirectly related to the individual dispositions of its members. The confusion in Yinger's work about whether the typology refers to individual or to collective behaviour prevents us from extracting from it any usable hypotheses for empirical testing in the case of Jehovah's witnesses.

Turning from the typologists to other students of sectarian religion we find, in addition to a morass of confusion in definitions and conceptual explications,[2] a surprisingly small number of underlying frameworks of explanation. That is to say, most usages of the term 'sect' in sociological literature embody, usually implicitly, a latent set of assumptions about the reasons why some people join sects and why sects develop in characteristic fashions. Their assumptions reflect a broader 'theoretical orientation' or set of deep-rooted, though not necessarily conscious, notions in the sociologist's mind of the basic principles governing social action and social processes. If the theoretical orientations can be uncovered and made explicit, we believe that the foundations can be laid for the methodical derivation and eventual testing of useful hypotheses. This aim is worthwhile not only because it will hopefully lead to continuity in comparative research, but also because it will help to cut a way through existing terminological and conceptual confusion in the sociological study of sects.

In particular, it could obviate the danger of explanation 'by definition'. At the moment, the widely varying definitions of 'sect' can embody unstated assumptions which determine that any hypothesis in which a particular use of the term is made can only be confirmed. A sociologist who believes, for example, that sectarian religion can fulfil a function in compensating people for deprivation and frustration is likely to define the term 'sect' in such a way that it can denote only groups composed of deprived people. Consequently, no hypothesis about the sect's functions as a compensating agency can be disconfirmed because of the *logical* connection between the theoretical assumptions and the definition employed. Conflicting or embarrassing evidence is merely overlooked, or it is stated that the group in question is not *really* a sect.

The proposal to devote more attention than has usually been the case to *explanation*, rather than to definition, of religious groups would have the added advantage of making explicit the constraints imposed by theoretical orientations on methods of research. To revert to our example of the 'explanation by definition', the sociologist who starts from assumptions about the compensating functions of sectarian religious outlooks will be largely prevented by a kind of 'methodological blinkers' from adopting research methods which could examine features of religious sects unrelated to their allegedly compensatory function. In general therefore, we sympathize with Ian Jarvie's creed:

> I do not believe there is such a thing as a theory-free statement of fact; on the contrary, I hold that all alleged statements of fact are theories or interpretations. (Jarvie, 1964, p. 31)

But in the face of the daunting prospect of an infinite regress of determining orientations, we can only suggest that a clear understanding of each orientation's logical and methodological implications is the most hopeful, albeit partial, solution to the problem.

A final bonus from the study of underlying theoretical orientations and encapsulated theories is that it cuts across conventional ways of conceptualizing religious groups. The concepts 'church', 'ecclesia', 'denomination', 'sect', and 'cult' were for the most part framed in such a way that a range of implicit explanations was built into them.[3] The implicit explanations related to a socio-cultural context in which it was still meaningful to distinguish between broad types of religious groups in terms of their position of relative strength and salience in Western societies and in which there was a clear association between particular social strata and particular types of religious groups. In some areas of the Western world this socio-cultural context still obtains, but we would argue that in Britain the situation has changed so drastically in the past two or three decades that the formerly taken-for-granted explanatory principles are now in need of serious revision. At a time when churches, for example, could exercise an influence over the lives of a large proportion of British people, when church leaders played important roles on the national and international political scene, when church wealth constituted an impressive part of the country's economic resources and when church doctrines enjoyed almost a monopoly of legitimate religious beliefs, it was obviously necessary to treat dissenting religious groups as a different and distinctive type of sociological entity. Yet, wholesale changes in the pattern of inter-relations between British institutions have eroded the power and authority that was once exclusive to churches. Relations between formerly distinctive types of religious groups now approximate to relations of equality, or at least, the sharp distinctions enshrined in the classic conceptualizations of church-and-sect-types have been blunted. To retain the conventional ways of thinking about religious groups is perhaps to overlook the gap that has opened between the concepts and the reality which they are expected to grasp.

In a different, but instructive, context R. Bendix (1967) has argued along similar lines for the necessity to treat sociological concepts as heuristic devices which naturally vary with the user's purposes and which must alter in response to changing circumstances. If the situation being studied changes, then those aspects which are considered significant for its conceptualization must be adapted accordingly. In Bendix's chosen example of changing conceptualizations of bureaucracy, 'the exclusion of every personal feeling' (Bendix, 1967, p. 73) was crucial to the nineteenth-century view of the concept but in mid-twentieth century this particular characteristic has become so engrained in so many aspects of social groups and processes that it no longer requires special emphasis.[4]

We conclude that, although the present study is narrowly focused on the personal and social characteristics of the members of one so-called sect, the theoretical frameworks and derivative hypotheses which we shall examine could be profitably consulted in the sociological study of *all* the conventionally conceptualized types of Christian group. In fact, our understanding of contemporary religious phenomena leads us to believe that the results of such a study would either suggest a thoroughgoing revision of the classic typologies or would suggest new reasons for upholding some of the old ones.[5] In the rest of the book, therefore, our use of the term 'sect' must be qualified as provisional or problematic, and it can be assumed that the hypotheses which will be tested in the following chapters are applicable to all religious groups.

THEORETICAL FRAMEWORKS

In the main, sociologists of religion have directed their research on sects towards answering two questions: Why do people join them? and Why do people remain in membership? Our present purpose is therefore to expose the theoretical orientations and assumptions underlying the principal types of answer. We shall artificially rearrange the disparate explanatory tendencies under three headings:

 1. Frustration-compensation
 2. World-view construction
 3. Social solidarity

But it should be made clear that these three frameworks are neither mutually exclusive nor collectively exhaustive: they admit of considerable overlapping. In practice, sociologists often combine them, but we shall attempt to keep them at least analytically distinct.

Three general remarks on explanation are in order before we begin to analyse the components of each framework and elaborate their corresponding hypotheses.

Firstly, a common feature of sectarian studies is the implicit understanding that the dynamics of sect-type groups and the conduct of individual sectarians are in some unspecified way more problematic than those of the church-type. Consequently, sociologists have tended to ask separate sets of questions about the two types of religious group which reflect deep-rooted cultural biases. Assumptions about the normality or abnormality of the respective types exercise a strong constraint over the sociologist's view of what needs explaining and therefore condition the kind of research that will be conducted. Nowhere is the effect of personal and cultural bias more glaringly evident than in the work of Werner Stark (1966; 1967a; 1967b; 1969; 1972). He clearly uses a double standard of judgement in studying churches and sects which are, after all, two forms of the same thing, i.e. religious sociation. To counter Stark's thesis, we would argue that one of the side-effects of secularizing tendencies in modern Western societies has been the erosion of historic differences in the perceived normality of *all* religious groups.

Secondly, explanations of sectarians' conduct have commonly been given in terms of their display of one or more characteristics which are crucial in distinguishing them from non-sectarians. What this procedure ignores is the possibility that at each stage in the *process* of an individual's affiliation to a so-called sect, different factors may be important in the explanation. In our testing of hypotheses, therefore, we shall try to avoid treating sectarian affiliation as a once-and-for-all event but shall specify what factors seem to be operative at successive stages in the whole process. If affiliation is conceived of as a 'career' in the way that Howard Becker has conceived of 'the process of becoming', (Becker, 1963) for example, a drug user or a jazz-band musician, we shall have to amend some of the available hypotheses to fit this extended view of becoming a Jehovah's witness. In addition to introducing control for the stage of the process, we shall also consider the career to extend from the individual's earliest awareness of the Watch Tower movement, through affiliation and continuing membership until, if necessary, withdrawal or disaffection.

Thirdly, in the present state of knowledge and resources all methods for testing explanations for sectarian conduct are necessarily, but regrettably, of the *ex post facto* kind. Judgement on the plausibility of competing explanations can only be made by reconstructing completed events and by studying people who have already passed through at least some stages of their Watch Tower 'career'. It is not therefore possible at present to evaluate the differential strength of various explanations by testing predictions deriving from their inner logic, but there is no insuperable obstacle to the possibility that this could be done in the future. Consequently, we cannot strictly claim that our research has *tested* the specified hypotheses: they have certainly guided the research-design by suggesting appropriate questions, and we have tried to answer the questions methodically. But far more intensive, detailed research is required on each hypothesis before the task of testing them properly can be said to have begun.

FRUSTRATION—COMPENSATION

'A strong contender for the major motivational theorem in sociology' (Zetterberg, 1957, p. 189) is how Hans Zetterberg has described the view that human beings experience frustration at meeting obstacles in the path of their attaining goals and that they search for alternative goals in compensation. John Lofland concurs with,

> It would seem that no model of human conduct entirely escapes some concept of tension, strain, frustration, deprivation, or the like, as a factor in accounting for action. (1966, p. 34)

Glock, Ringer and Babbie (1967) certainly found confirmation of this theoretical view in their study of the reasons for involvement in American Protestant churches, and R. K. Fenn (1972) has also noted with regret that this view amounts to almost a monopoly of theoretical insights in the sociology of religion. Yet it is rare for sociologists to make explicit the mechanics of this most common type of explanation; the usual practice is to conceal the underlying principles in bare statements to the effect that 'Anomic social conditions are associated with sect activity', (Young, 1960) or religious sects begin as 'religions of the disinherited' (Niebuhr, 1957, p. 26)

Even when the mechanics of this type of explanation *are* spelled out in detail, there remain outstanding problems in its use. Thus, those sociologists who have recognized the importance of studying the effects of deprivation only in so far as they can be shown to be (a) felt, (b) perceived as harmful and (c) related to the actor's reference groups have failed to devise adequate means of *ensuring* that the deprivation is actually felt; that the deprivation has not resulted from the actor's choice of negative reference-groups in an attempt to rationalize feelings of deprivation deriving from quite different sources; and that the deprivation has not resulted from the actor's comparison with unlikely reference groups. Explanations in terms of 'relative deprivation' are therefore subject to a number of practical difficulties, and at the end of Chapter 7 we shall scrutinize more closely the feasibility of applying this concept to the study of Jehovah's witnesses.

Hypotheses representative of the frustration-compensation theoretical framework include:

(a) The formation of, and affiliation to, so-called religious sects are functions of the desire of disprivileged people to protest against the unequal distribution of goods in their societies.

(b) There is a positive relation between the degree of economic and social unrest in a given society and the growth of membership of so-called religious sects.

(c) Interest in so-called religious sects varies directly with the degree of inconsistency between a person's perceived status rankings in different dimensions of his overall social status.

(d) 'The sect offers high social status to compensate those with low social status'. (Demerath and Hammond, 1969, p. 157)

(e) The more an individual perceives himself to be deprived relative to others of economic, social, psychic, organismic or ethical goods, the more likely he is to affiliate with a so-called religious sect.[6]

WORLD-VIEW CONSTRUCTION

Peter Berger and Thomas Luckmann[7] have helpfully systematized the heterogeneous collection of theoretical insights that cluster around the central notion that religious thought, behaviour and sociation are attempts to construct, and give expression to, an understanding of the world. Numerous theoreticians could have been cited in this tradition, but we shall restrict this exposition of its principal themes to Berger and Luckman because their work is representative of the general approach, highly systematic and quite comprehensive. Drawing from a wide spectrum of theoretical sources they have documented the argument that 'anthropological necessity' (Berger, 1967, p. 4) obliges men to construct a shared view of reality, to treat it as the only possible reality and to think in terms of that reality alone. The argument is sociological in so far as it insists that the process of world-view construction takes place in human groups and that the resultant world-views consequently derive a certain 'coercive facticity' (Berger, 1967, p. 11) from their group origins. With reservations about personality differences and the imperfect functioning of each stage in the socialization process Berger summarizes the argument as follows:

> To live in the social world is to live an ordered and meaningful life. Society is the guardian of order and meaning, not only objectively, in its institutional structures, but subjectively as well, in its structuring of individual consciousness. (Berger, 1967, pp. 21-2)

The relevance of these ideas to religion lies in the view that socially structured, taken-for-granted meanings enjoy a 'stability deriving from more powerful sources than the historical efforts of human beings' (Berger, 1967, pp. 25-6) and contribute therefore to the establishment of

ultimately powerful and meaningful notions of reality ('sacred cosmoi').
A complementary proposition is that the consequence for individuals of
failure to integrate into social groups where people are constantly engaged
in the process of world-construction and world-maintenance is a kind of
nightmare chaos.

In addition to providing a framework of ultimate meaning, religion is
also said by Berger to function as legitimation for social institutions by
giving them 'an ultimately valid ontological status, that is, by locating
them within a sacred and cosmic frame of reference'. (Berger, 1967, p. 33)
The potential of religion to legitimize social institutions is dependent on
support from social groups in the sense that unless the group-members
continue to take the sacred cosmos for granted, the plausibility of religious
symbolism is lost. Instability or discontinuity in such groups ('plausibility
structures') may result in the members' 'conversion' to another group-
supported view of reality, or they may produce social isolation and its
attendant moral problems. This theoretical scheme has clear relevance for
a study of dissent from mainstream religious groups.

But several difficulties arise in operationalizing and testing Berger's
concepts. In the first place it is very difficult to discover exactly how
people construct and maintain a view of reality without relying on formal,
doctrinal statements of belief which are notoriously misleading. The only
satisfactory solution is to look for broad patterns of attitudes, beliefs,
emotions and motivations which are evidently shared by large numbers
of people in specific social groups. Paradoxically, the second difficulty
follows from the solution to the first. If the sociologist is justified in
talking of a relationship between plausibility-structure and world-view
only when the relationship is manifestly clear, then he is by implication
unable to study those critical situations in which either plausibility-
structures are indeterminate or the world-view is ambiguous. The best
solution is to remain sensitive to the possibility of varying degrees of 'fit'
between social structures and ideational forms and to refuse to accept that
the relationship is always 'symmetrical'. Finally, to say that a change of
plausibility-structure is associated with a change in world-view is not to
offer an explanation of the reason why an individual chooses to leave one
group and join another. What is missing is a reference to the *motivation*
necessary to account for purposive behaviour such as joining a new
religious group. This factor is not forthcoming merely from a consideration of the background or 'facilitating' conditions. But, of course, consideration of the influence of changing plausibility-structures on a person's
world-view is an essential preliminary to the search for motivating factors.

Hypotheses stemming from the 'world-view construction' framework
include:

(a) The more severe the individual's sense of confusion about moral standards, the more likely he is to respond positively to the offers of help from evangelists.

(b) A change in the individual's plausibility structures precedes acceptance of a new *Weltanschauung*.

(c) The more a so-called sect member's social relations are restricted to other sectarians, the more likely he is to remain in membership.

(d) The lower a person's social class position, the more disposed he is to adopt extremist political and/or religious views.

SOCIAL SOLIDARITY

The most obviously sociological approach to the study of religion rests on Durkheim's view that the relation of men to important groups in their society is such that the men experience feelings of exaltation, awe and respect in contemplating the group's superiority and historical priority over their individual selves. Subsequent subscribers to this view have tried in various ways to specify precise modes of association between types of social group and types of religion. Despite their different interests they have agreed that religion can function as a celebration of, and a means of maintaining, a sense of the integrity and solidarity of dominant social groups. A recurrent theme of later sociological studies of religion has been the idea that sects, in particular, supply a social context within which individuals who failed to feel integrated into the wider society can find a point of attachment and a sense of meaningful solidarity with others. Confirmation of this mechanism has come from studies of, *inter alia*, Puerto Rican migrants to New York, (Poblete, 1960) pioneer settlers in Canada, (Mann, 1955) slum-dwellers in Guatemala City (Roberts, 1968) and the dispossessed middle class in the Weimar Republic. (Cohn, 1955) But one of the most faithful attempts to work out the full implications of this theoretical tradition has been Mary Douglas' (1973) study of the relationship between, on the one hand, two ways of conceiving of social solidarity and, on the other, corresponding modes of symbolism. In rejection of explanations of religious symbolism in terms of deprivation or strain, she propounds the thesis that the nature of the relationships linking people together in groups has a strong influence over the kind of symbols through which they can express their view of the world. Such a simple thesis confronts formidable problems in its application to religion in complex, modern societies, but it can nevertheless serve as a fruitful source of less ambitious, but testable, ideas.

Practically all the variations on the social solidarity theme share the drawbacks of any functionalist approach in sociology: statements about function are not causal statements; the focus on function emphasizes eufunctional and integrative aspects of religion at the expense of its divisive and harmful aspects; the functionalist approach does not readily lend itself to the study of change; and it is notoriously difficult to specify what kind of evidence is required to challenge successfully a functionalist explanation. No short solution to these problems is available, but an awareness of them will at least help us to avoid some of the more egregious methodological hazards in the testing of functionalist hypotheses.

The following are a small selection from the vast range of hypotheses deriving from the social solidarity theoretical framework:

(a) The less extensive an individual's associations with social groups, the more likely he is to join a so-called religious sect.

(b) The faster the rate at which large-scale social change takes place, the greater the likelihood that people will join so-called religious sects.

(c) The more a person rejects his social environment, the more likely he is to join a so-called religious sect.

(d) The stronger an individual's felt desire to achieve integration into warm, emotive primary groups, the more likely he is to join a so-called religious sect.

The frustration-compensation hypotheses will be tested in the following chapter, not, we must emphasize, with a view to validating or invalidating the whole theoretical framework, but with the intention of using the hypotheses as devices for throwing explanatory light on the conduct of people who become Jehovah's witnesses in Britain. The wider question of theoretical validation cannot possibly be tackled in the present context and may not be a practicable or wise undertaking for the future. Chapter 8 will attempt to examine critically hypotheses from the other two theoretical traditions.

NOTES TO CHAPTER 6

1. The most explicit accounts of Wilson's typological work are found in Wilson (1959) and (1969). References to his other attempts at typological formulation are contained in the Bibliography.

2. For a lengthy and detailed analysis of the majority of contributions to this field, see Beckford (1972b), pp. 429–68.

3. R. Bendix and P. Berger (1959), p. 94, in criticizing some of the founding fathers of sociology for claiming high-level generality for concepts that were actually rooted in extremely limited empirical evidence, made an observation that is appropriate here: 'Differences among various theories were often due to different purposes of cognition itself.'

4. Martin Albrow (1970), p. 123, has coined the useful phrase 'terminological conservation and conceptual change' to refer to this kind of phenomenon.

5. This point is argued more fully in Beckford (1975), chapter 8.

6. This is a condensed paraphrase of statements taken from Glock (1964).

7. Berger (1967); Luckmann (1957); and Berger & Luckmann (1967).

CHAPTER 7

SOCIAL STRATIFICATION AND JEHOVAH'S WITNESSES

SOCIAL STRATIFICATION AS A SOCIOLOGICAL VARIABLE

The findings of sociological research into the whole gamut of ways in which human beings associate with one another have confirmed the general point that material and symbolic indicators of social class and social status are useful predictors of all kinds of behaviour-patterns. Sociologists of religion have studied, amongst other things, the relation between certain kinds of religious beliefs and particular social status groups or classes; they have examined the relevance of social class as a variable constraining the 'style' of religious expressions; and they have emphasized the importance of social class as a determinant of whether people merely participate in religious groups or whether they assume leadership-roles. In many different ways, then, the relationship between social stratification and religion has been profitably used to explain social behaviour, processes and structures. But there has been a regrettable tendency merely to *posit* a relation between social class and Christian sectarianism as if it were a sufficient explanation of religious deviance. In fact, such a relation can only serve as the starting-point for explanation, for it needs to be fitted into the framework of an explanatory apparatus which can spell out the reasons why particular social class characteristics conduce towards particular forms of behaviour.

But the first task is to describe and analyse the social class composition of the Watch Tower movement in Britain. This will enable us to comment on two relevant features of the movement which have already raised doubts in our mind about the widespread belief that sectarians are lower class. On the one hand, the Witnesses' extremely high levels of participation in formal meetings seem out of keeping with research findings on the behaviour of lower-class people. On the other hand, one might have expected that an ideology which is apparently as revolutionary as that of the Watch Tower movement would attract people from largely disprivileged strata, but we have argued in several places that objectively middle-class people have also played an important role in it. The public stereotype of Jehovah's witnesses' social class therefore requires close examination.

The sources of information from which a satisfactory description of the social-class profile of British Jehovah's witnesses can be drawn fall sadly short of the ideal in several ways. The Jehovah's witnesses themselves were mildly antagonistic towards the idea of research which would include questions designed to elicit a profile of their social status,[1] and some answers to questionnaire items were deliberately obstructive. Similarly, Watch Tower literature was largely unhelpful because the movement's ideology pointedly devalues the importance of factors associated with social stratification. A further complication is that many authors of studies of Jehovah's witnesses have been motivated for a variety of personal reasons to present the worst possible image of the Watch Tower movement and have therefore deliberately understated the group's modal social status characteristics. For different reasons, but with similar consequences, the mass media in the West have chosen to promote a selective image of Jehovah's witnesses as uniformly low class, indigent people. The situation is aggravated from our point of view by the fact that the most widely quoted studies of Jehovah's witnesses were done in the USA where the group may well have had a different social composition from that of the British Branch, and at a time when the modal social class of members was probably as low as it has ever been. Finally, it is unfortunately necessary to treat with some reservation the findings from our own questionnaire survey, especially since there was no opportunity to secure a reliable sampling frame, a properly random sample and a chance to ask all the most probing questions. Nevertheless, some of the findings are so clear in their implications that they cannot be ignored, and in the absence of better resources, we feel justified in subjecting them to analysis.

In Chapter 1 we described briefly the historical changes that had occurred in the social class composition of the Watch Tower movement from Russell's day to the present. The most remarkable feature of the findings was that the post-Second World War situation more clearly parallels the pre-First World War situation than any intermediate stage. Many of Russell's earliest followers were middle class in terms of educational attainment, cultural style and occupation, but they were joined around 1900 by increasingly large number of recruits from the American working class. Evidence from Britain is even less satisfactory than for the USA but in general it suggests that the composition of the British Bible

Student movement changed from being overwhelmingly middle class before 1900 to having a more even balance between middle-class and working-class followers at the time of the 1914–18 war.

The period of Rutherford's presidency was marked in both countries by the numerical predominance of working-class Bible Students, although it is likely that the movement's leaders remained largely middle class. The latter point is extremely important, for as J. M. Yinger observed,

> if one sees religion as a cumulative product of many persons, making their religious interpretations in a specific social and cultural environment, then the shaping influence of the values and needs of the stratum in which it develops is highly important. Once the 'tone', the basic view of the nature of man and the problem of evil, is fixed in a religious system, under the selective emphases of one stratum, that tone will affect other strata who come within the religious tradition. (Yinger, 1970, p. 290)

But preliminary analysis of later developments has suggested that the recruitment of lower-middle-class Jehovah's witnesses has increased sharply since 1945. This alternating pattern in the Watch Tower movement's social class composition is not only interesting in itself but also has important consequences for many other organizational and ideological features. We shall eventually inquire whether the hypotheses deriving from the frustration-compensation theoretical tradition can help to explain this pattern in its present-day form.

SOCIAL CLASS COMPOSITION

Table 8 shows clearly that, on the basis of an occupational criterion of social class, the Jehovah's witnesses in our sample are predominantly drawn from the lower middle and upper working class.

The statistical predominance of the clerical and supervisory grade is increased when wives who have employment outside the home are included in their husband's occupational group. To have called the second largest occupational grouping 'Junior Managerial and Technical' may be misleading, because a close analysis of the respondents' job-descriptions reveals that the number employed in technical posts is much greater than that of Junior Managers. By contrast the Skilled Manual workers, who ranked third in order of statistical frequency, were appropriately classified as such, because three-quarters of them had received special training for their work. These three grades, in combination, contain 99 out of the 164 respondents who gave adequate information about their own, their husband's or their pre-retirement occupation.

TABLE 8

*The distribution of British Jehovah's Witnesses
by occupational status**

	N	%†
Senior Managerial and professional	23	13
Junior Managerial and technical	28	15
Clerical and supervisory	44	24
Skilled Manual	27	15
Semi-skilled Manual	22	12
Unskilled Manual	20	11
Housewives not describing husband's occupation	6	
Schoolchildren	7	10
Retired, disabled or unemployed	2	
No answer	1	
Total	180	100%

* Married women are included under husband's occupational grouping where given, and retired people under
their pre-retirement grouping as far as possible.
† Figures are corrected to the nearest whole number.

Yet, the *range* of occupational grades represented in the sample is just as significant as its central tendency. The grades of Senior Managers and Professionals, Semi-skilled Manual and Unskilled Manual are all of roughly the same size, and this feature is indicative of some of the group's important sociological characteristics. It implies, firstly, that the sect can draw on a sizeable group of people with managerial experience to occupy leadership positions and that the British Branch Headquarters has at its disposal a sufficiently varied pool of secular skills that it rarely needs to use 'outside' assistance or advice. It also helps to maintain sectarian exclusiveness by reducing the likelihood that the group would become closely associated with the interests of only one social class. Even evangelism benefits from the wide range of class backgrounds because it ensures that Witnesses of the appropriate social class can work among people of similar backgrounds. This factor is also important in helping newcomers to feel at home in congregations.

It should be pointed out, however, that the number of respondents representing the major liberal professions and the management of large enterprises was extremely low; respondents classified in this grade were mainly self-employed businessmen, traders and minor professionals. This must be borne in mind when comparing the social class profile of Jehovah's witnesses with the distribution of social classes in the British population at large. An exact comparison is impossible because (a) the sources of information on the general population are not always reliable, (b) the methods of classifying vary widely, (c) our own method of classifying occupations is different from those used in other surveys and (d) the surveys were conducted in different years. Yet, since in some respects the contrast between Jehovah's witnesses and the British population is quite striking, it seems worthwhile to proceed with the comparison in Table 9.

TABLE 9

Comparison between the social class profile of Jehovah's witnesses
and four samples of the British population

	(a) British Institute of Public Opinion 1952 %	(b) Hulton Readership Survey 1955 %		(c) Research Services Ltd. 1961 %		(d) Registrar General's Census of G.B. 1961 %		(e) Jehovah's Witnesses 1969 %	
Self-rated									
Upper	1	A	4	A	4	I	3.9	1	13
Upper middle	6	B	8	B	8	II	14.4	2	15
Middle	27	C	17	C₁ ⎰	20	III	49.8	3	24
Lower middle	16	D	64	C₂ ⎱	35	IV	19.9	4	15
Working	46	E	7	D	25	V	8.6	5	12
				E	8			6	11
Unclassified	4						3.4		10
Total	100		100		100		100		100

(a) The British Institute of Public Opinion conducted a Gallup Poll in 1952 of a sample of adults in Great Britain in which the question was asked: 'If you had to say what social class you belong to, which would it be?' The categories provided were: Upper, Upper Middle, Middle, Lower Middle, and Working. 4 per cent of the sample did not answer the question.

(b) The British Market Research Bureau conducted annual surveys of a sample of the British population for the Hulton Readership Survey between 1947 and 1955. The interviewers assessed the social class of the respondents on the basis of their appearance, manner of speech, occupation, type of house and district lived in. They were classified under five headings: Class A the well-to-do, Class B the middle class, Class C the lower middle class, Class D the working class, the Class E the poor.

(c) Research Services, in their survey of the adult population of Britain in 1961, classified the respondent's households into six socio-economic grades on the basis of the head of household's annual income. The six grades were:

A   the Upper Middle Class with incomes over £1,750 per annum.
B   the Middle Class with incomes between £950–£1,750 per annum.
C_1 the Lower Middle Class with incomes under £950 per annum.
C_2 the Skilled Working Class with incomes between £650–£1,000 per annum.
D   the Working Class with incomes between £350–£625 per annum.
E   the Poor with incomes under £340 per annum.

(d) In the Registrar-General's Census of Great Britain in 1961 the economically active and retired population was classified into the following five social classes by occupation: Professional etc., Intermediate, Skilled, Partly skilled and Unskilled.

(e) Respondents to the questionnaire on which the present research was based were asked to provide a 'full description of the kind of work you do for a living'. They were classified under six headings: Senior Managerial and Professional, Junior Managerial and Technical, Clerical and Supervisory, Skilled Manual, Semi-skilled Manual and Unskilled Manual.

Leaving aside for the moment the top two grades of the Jehovah's witnesses sample, the rest of it displays a much more even distribution than the various profiles of the population at large. Nevertheless, it is also apparent from Table 9 and from personal observations that the Watch Tower movement contains a disproportionately small number of people from social classes at society's extremes. It cannot emulate Moral Rearmament, Christian Science or Mormonism in deliberately attracting and retaining eminent people from the political, business or intellectual spheres, nor has it ever received patronage from anybody even loosely associated with the British 'ruling class'. Similarly, the poorest strata are under-represented in the sect, and it may be significant in this respect that the Watch Tower ethos would seem to frown upon anything but the most unavoidable instances of prolonged unemployment. Finally, it is most unlikely that very poor people in Great Britain could afford the necessary expense on books, magazines, travel and personal appearances for performing satisfactorily even the most basic duties of a Kingdom Publisher.

In order to achieve comparability of criteria with the other samples, it is necessary to count the vast majority of Senior Managerial, Professional and Junior Managerial and Technical Jehovah's witnesses among the middle class rather than the upper middle or upper classes. This brings our study into closer alignment with the others and facilitates more meaningful comparisons. The principal result of the adjustment is an accentuation of lower-middle-class predominance in the Watch Tower movement. This finding will be supported later by additional evidence on the group's dominant cultural style.

The occupational status profile of British Jehovah's witnesses is in the main congruent with the pattern of their *self-rated* occupational status, although it is again necessary to introduce strong reservations about the accuracy of the labels for the top two grades.

TABLE 10

The self-rated occupational status of Jehovah's Witnesses

	%
Senior managerial and professional	15.5
Junior managerial and technical	12.0
Clerical and supervisory	16.0
Skilled manual	24.0
Semi-skilled manual	10.5
Unskilled manual	6.0
Schoolchildren ⎫ Retired, disabled ⎪ Housewives ⎬	16.0
No answer ⎭	
Total	100.0

Precise comparison between Table 9 and Table 10 is not possible because of differences in the size of unclassifiable responses, but there is substantial similarity in the shape of the two distributions and in the broad division between manual and non-manual strata. But perhaps the only safe interpretation of the findings is that Jehovah's witnesses hold neither exalted nor humble views of their occupational status and that the discrepancy between notional and actual status (in so far as the latter can be discussed at all) is unlikely to have an important influence on their behaviour.

As might be expected from a religious movement drawing members from a wide range of social classes, the leaders tend to be drawn from the group with obviously middle-class occupations. In our experience only a very small number of Congregation Elders have manual occupations, and even the routine tasks in each congregation fall to the responsibility of white-collar or skilled manual workers. *A fortiori*, officers of the Watch Tower Society's regional organization are almost exclusively middle class in terms of their occupation prior to working full-time for the Society. Full-time officers from working-class backgrounds are more likely to remain in the Special Pioneer Branch than to become Circuit or District Servants, although we are given to understand that until the Second World War it was still possible for working-class men to occupy the highest positions in the British Branch organization.

Yet, despite the clear correlation between social status and opportunities for advancement in the Watch Tower movement, there is no evidence to show that middle-class Jehovah's witnesses have a different orientation towards the Society from that of their fellow-religionists. In this respect the Watch Tower movement may differ from N. J. Demerath III's prediction that:

> If a lower-class individual is committed to religion at all, his internal involvement is likely to be higher than that of his higher status church-fellows. (Demerath, 1965, p. 25)

One of the consequences of the wide range of social classes represented among British Witnesses may be to counteract the tendency for class-related 'styles' of religiosity to develop and, of course, the standardization of service-work and worship requirements militates against a patterning of religious practice by social class.

In terms of their formal educational qualifications British Jehovah's witnesses do not appear to have received disproportionately inferior education in comparison with the national population. As with their occupational status, there are relatively few who have reached the highest levels of attainment, but the modal qualifications are probably slightly better than the national mode. Again, the range of educational experience is comprehensive, but there are few representatives of the highest and lowest echelons.

Of the 173 respondents who had left school before the survey was carried out, 71 had done so before the age of 15; 81 between the ages of 15 and 16; and 21 over the age of 17. Unfortunately we have no evidence on their educational qualifications gained whilst at school, but it is possible to describe the kinds of training they received after leaving school. Of the 173 respondents who had left school, 35 underwent some form of further training in trade and technical matters; 23 in clerical matters; and 19 in professional studies. Ninety-six underwent no further training. But 34 of the people who had no further training after school were housewives and were less likely to have had career prospects in the first place.

It is extremely difficult to make a clear comparison between Jehovah's witnesses and the general population in respect of further educational experience, because the sample contains people from many different age cohorts whose educational expectations have differed widely. It is all the more surprising, consequently, to discover from the Central Statistical Office's Annual Abstract of Statistics for 1969 that of the age group 15–20 in England and Wales between 1967–8, only 59.27 per cent were engaged in further education (excluding courses in Colleges of Advanced Technology). It is surprising because the percentage of Jehovah's witnesses having been engaged in further education is also around 50 per cent. The difference is very slight when it is borne in mind that people in the age group 15–20 today are much more likely than the rest of the older population to be engaged in further education, and that the Jehovah's witness sample contains many people whose opportunities for further education were far inferior to those of the present generation of youth. Without wishing to make pretensions to unjustified precision, then, it seems reasonable to infer that Jehovah's witnesses display an unusually high degree of interest in further education of a variety of forms.

Our analysis of the social class composition of British Jehovah's witnesses has so far relied on the two more or less objective indicators of occupation and education. Together they have revealed that the sect contains a wide range of members in terms of their occupational status and their educational qualifications. But the sect lacks representatives of both the highest and lowest echelons of the occupational status scale and the ladder of educational achievement. The social composition of the Jehovah's witnesses could be likened to a slightly flattened microcosm of the general population: the extremes are under-represented, and the centre over-represented.

Broadly the same picture emerges from an analysis of the newspaper and magazine reading habits of British Witnesses. The advantage of this particular criterion of the sect's social composition is that it provides a guide to the dominant *cultural style* of the membership. Although interpretation of reading habits is sometimes fraught with problems of subjective bias, the pattern of the Witnesses' choice of magazines and newspapers is sufficiently distinctive to obviate most of the difficulty. The sample was fairly evenly divided between those who read no newspapers regularly and those who read a small number of mass-circulation dailies. In view of the oft-quoted maxim that sectarians are 'in' society rather than 'of' it, the fact that so many Jehovah's witnesses do read newspapers regularly may be unexpected. Yet, the witnesses are still clearly out of line with the adult British population in this respect. Whereas 22 per cent of the sample read no newspaper regularly, and 33 per cent read no daily newspaper regularly, estimates of the percentage of the general population who read daily newspapers regularly have been put as high as 88 per cent by Raymond Williams (1961, p. 209) and 82.9 per cent for the period 1963–8 by the Joint Industry Committee for National Readership Surveys (see Curran, 1970, p. 128).

The most popular dailies among respondents are the *Daily Express* and the *Daily Mirror*, and the most popular Sunday newspapers are the *Sunday Mirror* and the *Sunday Express*. In all, these four publications account for 107 out of the 220 options made for newspapers, and it is tempting to speculate about their cultural 'appropriateness' for Jehovah's witnesses. They all share a certain ambivalence towards the political divisions of Left and Right, and their self-proclaimed independence from rigid party allegiances might enhance their appeal to people who deliberately take very little interest in political affairs. A second ground for affinity between Jehovah's witnesses and the *Express* and *Mirror* groups' newspapers might be the fact that their readers, like Jehovah's witnesses are drawn almost uniformly from all social grades. (See Abrams, 1966) We must stress, however, that these interpretations of cultural appropriateness are highly speculative and clearly require more rigorous testing, although like all topics in the sociology of knowledge, it is difficult to see how the testing could be adequately carried out.

Jehovah's witnesses are no less unusual in their magazine reading habits than in their low level of newspaper reading. Less than 25 per cent of the 87 women in the sample read non-Watch Tower magazines regularly, and the range of choice was narrowly confined to such mass-circulation products as *Woman, Woman's Own* and *Woman's Realm*. The number of female magazine readers was so small that it is not worthwhile attempting to relate their reading habits to social-class characteristics, but it was most noticeable that they ignored completely all the so-called sophisticated magazines. A similarly narrow range of magazine choices was reported by the male Witnesses. Again, the habit was not widespread and was virtually confined to *Readers' Digest* and *Geographical*. Only a few men reported reading magazines about hobbies or practical pastimes, but nobody mentioned any sporting, sensationalist, prestige or sexually stimulating publications. Respondents from the managerial and clerical grades more frequently read professional and general interest magazines, while skilled manual Witnesses were the most assiduous readers of journals on hobbies and on practical pastimes. The fact that Jehovah's witnesses from the lower occupational grades did not, in sharp contrast to other members of the working class, report reading sports magazines indicates the great strength of the cultural influence exerted by the sect's middle-class leaders over the thought and behaviour of its acolytes. The level of magazine reading for both sexes is much lower than for the British population at large (see Fletcher, 1970) and can be accounted for in terms of the extremely limited spare-time available to conscientious Witnesses and of their lack of ideological sympathy with the content of much secular journalism.

Only 3 out of 180 respondents did not have a radio in their home and 80 per cent of the sample had a television set. These figures are not widely out of line with the national averages, but they do not of course provide the crucial information about Jehovah's witnesses' choice of programmes. Regular attendance at all congregation meetings would naturally restrict the extent of their listening and viewing, and many Witnesses revealed in the course of conversation that they were highly selective in their choice of programme. They were uniformly reluctant, moreover, to visit the cinema and to attend dance-halls. A tentative explanation for this pattern may be that the latter activities would expose Jehovah's witnesses to potentially corrupting influences over which they would have little control in a public setting, whereas in their own home they would be in a stronger position to insulate themselves against unwanted influence. For present purposes, the important implication of these findings is that British Jehovah's witnesses display a distinctive pattern of cultural affinities and characteristics, but it cannot be unambiguously associated with any specific social class.

The question of the social class 'style' of Jehovah's witnesses' behaviour is further complicated by the influence of American culture on members of the Watch Tower movement in all parts of the world. Missionary movements usually induce (deliberately or accidentally) converts to adopt some of the outlooks, manners and mannerisms of the missionaries' culture. Perhaps modelling themselves, for example, on the extremely stylized illustrations in Watch Tower literature, male Jehovah's witnesses in Britain tend to wear rather sober suits of traditional design, white shirts and dark ties for congregational meetings. The habit of carrying Bibles and other religious literature in leather briefcases is also widespread, and it is undoubtedly considered appropriate to adopt an air of business-like purposiveness in meetings and during service-work. Female Jehovah's witnesses, on the other hand, enjoy greater freedom in their style of dress and personal appearance, but strict limits on the range of acceptable styles exclude extravagant fashions and encourage utilitarian moderation. Thus the extremes of sartorial elegance, informality and shabbiness are all clearly discouraged; respectability and purposiveness are positively valued. These characteristics undoubtedly show an affinity with British lower-middle-class styles of self-presentation in public but they are also qualified by a few 'Americanisms' which become even more apparent in language habits.

In the process of socialization into the culture of the Watch Tower movement neophytes learn to articulate a number of expressions and conversational gambits which, when mastered, lend them an air of self-confident 'outward-goingness'. In ways certainly more characteristic of American than British culture, Jehovah's witnesses learn to greet both fellow-religionists and outsiders with positive expressions of personal interest and benevolence. Conversations are studded with such positive reinforcements as 'right', 'good' and 'good thought', while the customary vocabulary includes such borrowings from the USA as 'to tie in with' or 'to point up'. Conversations are commonly closed with the formula 'I've enjoyed talking to you' or 'I hope we shall have an opportunity to talk again', and the other party is left with the feeling that the interaction has been methodically managed. These formalities enable working-class Jehovah's witnesses with 'restricted' speech codes to give the appearance, at least, of a superficially 'elaborated' code (see Bernstein, 1971) and thereby to transcend the limitations imposed by their social class background on their ability to argue persuasively in public.

About half of the Jehovah's witnesses whom we interviewed in their homes owned, or were in process of buying, their house. A few lived in large, expensive houses but the majority lived in small, semi-detached or terraced houses. The style of interior decoration was conventionally lower middle class with patterned wall-coverings, carpeted floors and moderately well-equipped kitchens. Expensive, fashionable furnishings were rare, and it was apparent that comfort and utility were considered more important than novelty or prestige. Similarly, most families owned a motor-car, but the preference was almost exclusively for modest saloons. In contrast to the conversation of their peers outside the sect, male Witnesses very rarely talk about motoring, and the car has only utilitarian value for them. In part, these findings are a function of the area in which interviewing was conducted, but visits to congregations in other parts of the country provided the opportunity to observe variations in Jehovah's witnesses' standards of living. Contrasts between, for example, Newport in Monmouthshire, Llandudno in Caernarvonshire or Hoylake in Cheshire in terms of the local economic and occupational structures are reflected in widely different age-structures and patterns of the social class composition of the respective congregations.

The principal sociological relevance of these contrasts lies in the correspondingly different 'tones' of congregational meetings and social activities despite the apparent uniformity in procedures and programmes. But it is certain that unless standardization of procedures remained at least an ideal for congregation leaders, the movement's coherence and purposiveness would be seriously threatened.

SOCIAL MOBILITY

The assumption underlying the insertion in the questionnaire schedule of the question 'What kind of a job do you do for a living?' is that respondents' occupational status is an elliptical guide to the class of people with whom they share most of their material, social and cultural interests. We have indeed seen that a pattern characteristic of the British lower middle class does pervade many aspects of Jehovah's witnesses' lives and can be meaningfully associated with some sociological features of the Watch Tower movement. But it is just as important to discover what the social status of Jehovah's witnesses is relative to that of their parents,[2] because intergenerational social mobility has been said to cause a wide variety of socially and psychologically significant effects.

Some preliminary explication is required of the methodological problems involved in using the concept 'social mobility'. Neither inter- nor intragenerational changes in occupational status can be unreservedly taken as indicators of 'social' mobility in all its diversity. But in the absence of reliable measures of all the possible indicators of the concept we can invest some faith in the predictive usefulness of changes in occupational status because it is probably the most comprehensive guide to the whole complex of social class characteristics. Secondly, it is not entirely valid to make comparisons of occupational status between generations, because the structure of the occupational hierarchy has changed considerably in recent decades. This problem can be met to some extent by restricting the analysis of mobility to those cases alone of *marked* intergenerational differences. It is less easy to deal with the third problem, namely, the questionable procedure of comparing sons and daughters who have only

TABLE II

Intergenerational occupational mobility of British Jehovah's Witnesses

Respondents' Occupation	Father's Occupation							
	Senior Managerial	Junior Managerial	Clerical and Supervisory	Skilled Manual	Semi-Skilled	Unskilled Manual	N/A	Total
Senior Managerial	4	5	2	4	1	6	1	23
Junior Managerial	1	7	8	9	0	3	0	28
Clerical and Supervisory	3	6	6	11	11	7	0	44
Skilled Manual	2	4	6	7	1	3	4	27
Semi-skilled	0	3	3	6	7	2	1	22
Unskilled Manual	0	2	0	6	7	3	2	20
Housewives	0	1	1	0	1	1	2	6
Retired etc.	0	0	0	0	0	1	1	2
Schoolchildren	1	0	1	1	4	0	1	7
N/A	0	0	1	0	0	0	0	1
Total	11	28	28	44	32	26	11	180

just embarked on a career with their fathers who are much more likely to have already attained their optimum occupational status. The only reasonable solution is to keep the difficulty in mind when interpreting results and to remember that, for the reason given, they will tend to exaggerate both differences and similarities between the generations. Finally, it is essential to supplement analysis of the rates and magnitude of social mobility with controls for the points in the occupational hierarchy at which respondents began and completed their movement (i.e. 'origin' and 'destination' status). This factor has an effect on the consequences of mobility that may be independent of its other measures. (See, for example, Vorwaller, 1970)

Table 11 contains the basic data on which estimates of intergenerational social mobility can be constructed.

It is immediately apparent that the social class profile of our respondents is not remarkably different from that of their fathers. The modal occupational status of Jehovah's witnesses is only one grade higher than that of the parental generation, and this small difference could be plausibly understood to be a function of historical changes in the British occupational structure. Indeed, the extent of similarity between the generations is considerable: 21.6 per cent of the sample shared their father's occupational status, and 35 per cent had moved no further than one grade away from their fathers' position. Given our reservations about the crudeness of the available data, we can do no more than simply infer that about half of the respondents have experienced very little upward or downwards social mobility.

TABLE 12

Magnitude and frequency of social mobility among Jehovah's witnesses

	Up	Down
Two moves	25	16
Three moves	11	5
Four moves	4	2
Five moves	6	0
Total	46 (68%)	23 (32%)

Of the 43 per cent who have been identified as socially mobile, 68 per cent are upwardly mobile and 32 per cent downwardly mobile. But the figures conceal some noteworthy indications of the magnitude and frequency of movement in both directions.

On balance, then, more Jehovah's witnesses are upwardly mobile than downwardly mobile, and the magnitude of upward mobility is greater than that of downward mobility.

The same general conclusions emerge from consideration of the amount of mobility between manual and non-manual occupations. Exactly one-third of the sample had fathers with manual occupations but had acquired non-manual jobs for themselves. Only 28 per cent of the sample shared a manual occupational status with their fathers. One reason for the high frequency of upward social mobility among British Jehovah's witnesses is that they are considerably over-represented in urban areas and therefore in a better position than people in rural areas to benefit from the provision of white-collar jobs in industry and the tertiary sector of employment.

In comparing our findings on the rates of intergenerational social mobility with those of British society in general, it is convenient, but not entirely satisfactory, to refer to Glass's study of Britain in 1949. (Glass, 1954) Fortunately, Glass used categories which are as broad and inclusive as our own and which clearly facilitate comparisons between very general types of mobility experience.

Expressed as a percentage of the total group of respondents, the number of sons in Glass's sample whose occupational status was higher than their fathers' was 39 per cent. The percentage of Jehovah's witnesses in the same position *vis-à-vis* their fathers' occupational status was as high as 56 per cent. The sample of Jehovah's witnesses appears to be more up-wardly mobile than one would expect, but the difference between the two samples may result partly from factors which will receive consideration later. As a percentage of the total group of sons in Glass's sample, those whose occupational status was lower than their fathers' constituted 61 per cent whereas the comparable group among Jehovah's witnesses was only 44 per cent. The rate of downward mobility among Jehovah's witnesses would appear to be considerably lower than among the general population in Britain, and a final confirmation of the differences between the two groups emerges from a comparison of the differential measure of congruence between sons' and fathers' occupational status. As a percentage of Glass's sample, those whose occupational status was the same as their fathers' amounted to 35.1 per cent, whereas the comparable figure for Jehovah's witnesses was 21.6 per cent.

If Lipset and Bendix (1959) considered that rates of social mobility were high when between one-quarter and one-third of a population were mobile in either direction, then we may seem justified in inferring that the Jehovah's witnesses in our sample are unusually mobile. The difference between the rates is not, of course, inordinately great, and we should bear in mind the likelihood that national rates have risen since the year when

Glass was conducting his survey (1949). Moreover, the fact that our scheme of classification is not exactly the same as the one used by Lipset and Bendix should also deter us from reading too much into the comparative figures. Yet, a recent study of middle-class families in Banbury (Bell, 1969) also showed that no more than 25 per cent of heads of families in the sample were upwardly mobile across the manual/non-manual dividing line. Thus, we are strengthened in our view that contemporary Jehovah's witnesses are more socially mobile than their peers. But perhaps the only 'safe' interpretation to be placed on the findings is that the witnesses are possibly more socially mobile than the rest of the British population and are clearly not predominantly downwardly mobile.

At present we have no means of knowing whether the magnitude of mobility (i.e. the distance travelled between occupations measured in terms of differential status) among Jehovah's witnesses is abnormally high or low. We can only reiterate in passing that the magnitude of the sample's upward mobility is greater than the magnitude of downward mobility, but it is impossible to compare these figures with the findings for any kind of control group.

If the conclusion to be drawn from our data is that Jehovah's witnesses differ to only a small extent from the population as a whole, then it is not possible to isolate this factor as an important condition of becoming a member of the Watch Tower movement. It may still be the case, however, that individuals have been predisposed by intergenerational changes in their social-class position to treat the message of Watch Tower evangelists more seriously than do most people in Britain, but there is no suggestion that this biographical factor has produced a marked effect on anything like the majority of Jehovah's witnesses. Nor was it found that they had experienced frustration through failing to achieve the magnitude of upward social mobility to which they had aspired. The fact that Watch Tower doctrines and ideology may induce Jehovah's witnesses to curb their aspirations towards higher social status must be acknowledged, but this is irrelevant to the present consideration of factors which might have predisposed them to show an interest in Watch Tower affairs in the first place.

The above findings on the relatively 'normal' pattern of social mobility among Jehovah's witnesses (coupled with reservations about the methodological reliability and usefulness of the concept itself) make it inadvisable to attach clear explanatory significance to this factor. Until 'social mobility' can be operationalized in a more sophisticated way and until its implications for social behaviour can be more fully clarified, it seems wise to suspend judgement on the hypotheses which embody the concept.

THEORETICAL INTERPRETATIONS

As we stated at the beginning of this chapter, one of our principal aims in discussing at length the evidence of the social class base of the British Jehovah's witness movement was to stimulate reflection on the kind of general propositions about the relation between religion and social stratification which have achieved widespread currency in sociological literature. The most questionable proposition has taken many forms but can be reduced to the statement that:

> Premillenarianism is essentially a defence mechanism of the disinherited; despairing of obtaining substantial blessings through social processes, they turn on the world which has withheld its benefits and look to its destruction in a cosmic cataclysm which will exhalt them and cast down the rich and powerful. (E. T. Clark, 1949, pp. 218–19)

A wealth of empirical evidence could be cited in support of Clark's statement, and it is not our intention to cast serious doubt on the view that lower social strata in many societies are the most fruitful sources of recruits to millennial movements. Our immediate interest lies, however, in considering the complementary, but largely neglected, view that millenarianism may also be an appropriate mode of religious thought for some sections of the middle class in Britain. Admittedly, the phenomenon of middle-class millennialism may be much less commonly found than lower-class millennialism, but our findings suggest that lower-middle-class support for the Watch Tower movement is a crucial element in the sect's past and present composition.

There have, in fact, been few sociological studies of Jehovah's witnesses, and only two sources are commonly referred to by sociologists of religion: H. H. Stroup's *Jehovah's Witnesses* of 1945 and Werner Cohn's article 'Jehovah's witnesses as a proletarian movement' (1955), but as Cohn cites Stroup as the main source of evidence for his interpretation, it seems that sociological generalizations have been largely based on the evidence of one piece of work carried out in the USA in the early 1940s. If Stroup's work is closely examined, it becomes clear that he was unable to obtain hard-and-fast data on the social class composition of the sect at that time. In this particular matter he relied on the impressionistic accounts of journalists to supplement his own unsystematic observations. There are grounds, what is more, for arguing that his observations in the 1940s could not be valid for any other period of history. Stroup's analysis of the movement's social class base in the USA should therefore be treated with some caution, although it must in all fairness be added that the same reservations need not extend to other parts of his valuable pioneering study.

The slightly earlier studies by T. Sprague (1942 and 1943) and M. Czatt (1933) are of strictly limited relevance in this context because they did not focus upon the social class characteristics of American Jehovah's witnesses. It is, however, significant that Sprague stressed the fact the lower-class Witnesses did not predominate in the congregations and that only the extremely wealthy and the extremely indigent were not represented in the proportions in which they occurred in the wider American society. Roughly the same picture emerges from D. Manwarings' (1962) study of Jehovah's witnesses in relation to American flag-saluting laws and from Sibley and Jacob's (1952) survey of American Witnesses who registered as conscientious objectors in the Second World War.

Outside the USA empirical study of Jehovah's witnesses has been equally rare and equally deficient in reliable evidence in the matter of the sect's social class base. W. J. Schnell's (1957) work provides some tantalizingly cryptic insights into the social class profile of German Bible Students at the time of the First World War, but it is otherwise silent on this important sociological topic. Similarly, Jean Séguy's (1966) analysis of the transcripts of some radio interviews with French Jehovah's witnesses at an assembly in Paris in 1964 was potentially valuable but ultimately disappointing from our point of view because he gave no information about the way in which the quoted interviews were selected from those available. But a valuable exception to the pattern of unsystematic or unfounded pronouncements on the social class base of Jehovah's witnesses is Norman Long's (1968) careful study of Zambian Witnesses, and it is interesting to note that he had little hesitation in claiming that they tended to be more prosperous than their kinsmen. An equally careful study of Dutch Jehovah's witnesses by Q. J. Munters (1971) showed that they are more likely than are members of the Dutch Reformed Church to suffer from various forms of deprivation. We shall postpone critical comment on the methods that he used to achieve these results until the point where we can review all similar methods together.

As far as the social class characteristics of British Jehovah's witnesses are concerned, the picture that emerges from post-Second World War studies is both vague and confusing. Since Royston Pike (1954) made no systematic attempt to discover precisely what kind of people belonged to the sect in the 1950s, we must be highly suspicious of his bland characterization of them as 'the frustrated, the hard-pressed, the underprivileged' or as 'men and women who are intensively dissatisfied with their lives but who do not know what to do about it'. (Pike, 1954, p. 135) Equally impressionistic accounts of the social class profile of the Jehovah's witness movement in Britain have appeared in the works of two more recent writers about the sect, but it is significant that neither Stevenson (1967) nor Rogerson (1969) appears to attach much importance to this aspect of the group to which they once belonged. There is a clear implication in their books that the attributes of British Witnesses which are associated with their social class position are not sufficiently striking or unusual to deserve close attention.

Not only are our findings on the social class composition of the British branch of the Watch Tower movement incompatible with some of these descriptions and with popular stereotypes but they are also difficult to reconcile with the hypotheses deriving from what we termed the frustration-compensation theoretical framework. Firstly, there appears to be only qualified confirmation of the hypothesis proposed by Bryan Wilson that:

> religious movements, as essentially social movements, can be expected to stand in specific relations to social classes, to the prevailing economic and social conditions, and to the cultural and social ethos obtaining within such social groups. (1955, p. 10)

The Watch Tower movement does not stand in one specific relation to a social class: it recruits from a wide range of social classes, although the range does not effectively include the extremes of privilege and disprivilege. Nor is it the case that the sect stands in a specific relation to the cultural and social ethos obtaining within one particular social group. Rather, the cultural and social ethos of the middle-class Witnesses predominates and sets the 'tone' for the whole group which has a broadly based social composition.

Secondly, the hypothesis relating membership of religious sects to rebellion against social class oppression does not receive even qualified confirmation from the present findings. The wide range of social classes represented in the sect makes it unlikely that the oppressed members of one class would make common cause in their rebellion with members of supposedly oppressing or more oppressed classes. The crude Marxist explanatory model is of minimal assistance in accounting for the representation of varied social classes within one allegedly 'revolutionary' body. Chapter 10 will explore more fully the implications of this finding for the Watch Tower movement's ideology.

Thirdly, the hypothesized relation between periods of economic or social unrest and increased interest in millenarian religious sects does not find confirmation in the historical development of the Watch Tower movement in Britain. The period immediately following the First

World War, which is often said to have been a time of severe material hardship and of social disruption, was not conducive to a numerical expansion of the Jehovah's witnesses. In fact, the inter-war years were marked by stagnation in membership and magazine-subscription statistics. Only with the succession of new leaders at the time of the Second World War did the number of British Witnesses show signs of increasing, and the rate of growth remained more or less steady during the 1950s and 1960s despite evident fluctuations in the general standards of living and temper of life.

A fourth hypothesis demanding consideration concerns the relation which is said to hold between status inconsistency and support for 'liberal or radical movements designed to alter the political *status quo*'. (Lenski, 1966, p. 88) Gerhard Lenski, for example, postulated a relation between status inconsistency and sympathy with liberal or radical political ideologies, but there is no reason why the concept should not be thought to apply to religious outlooks as well.

What evidence is forthcoming from our findings about the sources of status inconsistency among British Jehovah's witnesses? Even if one shelves methodological problems in the use of this concept for the moment, it is immediately clear that no *prima facie* case for the influence of status inconsistency on the motivation of people who have become Jehovah's witnesses can be made. Thus, male Witnesses with senior managerial posts tend also to have undergone long periods of formal education and to read 'quality' newspapers. Patterns of consistency between ranks on several dimensions were also characteristic of workers in other socioeconomic groupings. But judgement on the final reliability of our assessment must depend on the solution of major methodological problems and the availability of more conclusive evidence.[3]

The final hypothesis on questions of social stratification concerns the relation between relative deprivation and the predisposition to join a religious sect. We have already discounted the possibility that *absolute* deprivation could be instrumental in precipitating affiliation to the Watch Tower movement and we have voiced some preliminary reservations in Chapter 6 about the feasibility of successfully operationalizing the concept of *relative* deprivation. But the latter concept has come to play such an important role in recent sociological studies of religion that it requires especially careful consideration.

We may define a relatively deprived person, following W. G. Runciman's usage, (Runciman, 1966) as someone who does not have X, who sees some other person or persons, which may include himself at some previous or imagined time as having X (whether or not they have X) and also wants X (whether or not it is feasible that he should have it). But before any such hypothesis can be tested, the following three conditions must be satisfied:

(1) Steps must be taken to ensure that the posited deprivation is actually *felt* (though not necessarily perceived) by the subject and is not simply a figment of the researcher's imagination.

(2) Since the standards against which the subject can compare himself may assume a variety of real or fictive forms, the researcher must be attentive to forms of felt relative deprivation which do not seem to stand in any expected relation to the subject's personal circumstances.

(3) Like all comparative concepts in sociology, the concept of relative deprivation must satisfy two basic conditions: (a) it must be possible to state whether a relatively deprived person feels *more* deprived than others, *less* deprived than others or *equally* deprived; and (b) if subjects are placed on a ranking scale of relative deprivation, then the logical law of transitivity must apply. These conditions can be satisfied only when objective measures of the *magnitude* (i.e. the distance separating the subject from his standard of comparison), the *intensity* (i.e. the strength of discomfort) and the *frequency* with which relative deprivation occurs in determinate groups are available.

Since the present study was unable to fulfil these basic conditions, we can only make rough assessments of the evidence for and against the argument that perceived relative deprivation disposes people favourably towards the idea of joining the Watch Tower movement.

C. Y. Glock (1964) may appear to have conveniently prepared the ground for our study by breaking down the concept into five broad areas in which different types of deprivation were said to be operative: economic, social, organismic, ethical and psychic. We are particularly interested, then, in his delineation of the economic and social kinds of deprivation in so far as they seem to be directly relevant to the general hypothesis under discussion:

> Economic deprivation has its source in the differential distribution of income in societies and in the limited access of some individuals to the necessities and luxuries of life.
> Social deprivation is a derivative of the social propensity to value some attributes of individuals and groups more highly than others and to distribute societal rewards such as prestige, power, status and opportunity for social participation. (Glock, 1964, p. 27)

It is not, of course, necessary that people suffering from relative deprivation should give any outward expression of their feelings, but unless some indicator of perceived deprivation is available, the sociologist is not justified in imputing motives to behaviour for which there is no evidence. Our interviewees gave no indication, however, that they felt economically or socially deprived relative to others, nor were any objective indicators of such deprivation prominent in their reported backgrounds. In the absence, then, of clear indicators of relative deprivation among British Jehovah's witnesses we cannot test the hypothesis adequately.

A more optimistic evaluation of the explanatory potential of relative deprivation is embodied in Q. J. Munter's study of Jehovah's witnesses in Holland. (Munters, 1971) He used a 'chance of deprivation' scale ranging from 0 to 2 in order to calculate the comparative deprivation scores of a sample of Dutch Witnesses and a sample of Dutch Reformed Church members in Utrecht. Scores were assigned *on the basis of his assessment* of the deprivation that each individual suffered in 57 different situations. By grouping the situations into five categories (socio-economic, 'organic', church-religious, primary relations and diverse) he was able to demonstrate (a) that the Witnesses had an average 'D-score' of 0.65 compared with only 0.46 for the Reformed Church members, and (b) that the former had higher scores in all the separate categories than the latter. His conclusion was that the Witnesses displayed,

> ... a higher incidence of unemployment, less favourable prospects of social advancement, a parental background of church-religious heterogeneity, and so on. (Munters, 1971, p. 97)

But, in our opinion, this method does not study relative deprivation: only deprivation defined as such by an observer. The weakness of Munters' interesting approach is that it cannot articulate the link between deprivation and membership of the sect in any way other than by the dubious logic of affinity or conguence. Nor can it answer the question why all people with a 'D-score' of 0.65 or above do not become Jehovah's witnesses.

In addition to these methodological objections there is a further reason for doubting the relevance of relative deprivation to a reliable explanation of Jehovah's witnesses' behaviour. During neither the socialization process nor in the routine meetings of the sect is there an opportunity for expressing explicit resentment against the prevailing distribution of material and social goods. In fact, Jehovah's witnesses accord less importance to scriptural references to this-wordly or other-wordly privilege than do the clergy of mainstream Christian churches and denominations. They certainly do not rejoice in the prospect of 'virtue rewarded' or 'positions reversed' in the New Kingdom on Earth, and it is difficult to allot the Watch Tower ideology to either of Max Weber's theodicies—good fortune or suffering. Consequently, the person suffering from economic or social relative deprivation would find little to attract him to the Jehovah's witnesses, unless he was prepared to abandon all hope of obtaining redress for his disprivilege. In this case, joining the sect might be interpreted as a purely expressive act of withdrawal from the struggle to achieve tangible improvement in his material or social position. It is unlikely, however, that such a negative action could provide motivation for the exacting tasks of learning and evangelizing which are demanded of mature Witnesses.

In view of this ideological feature of the Watch Tower movement in Britain we do not feel that relative deprivation plays the same kind of role in stimulating membership as it seems to have done, for example, in the British Israelite movement. John Wilson (1966) saw fit to describe the members of that movement as being 'drawn' or 'attracted' by an ideology which presented a view of the world in accordance with the material and social position of civil servants, clerks, teachers, and minor officers in the armed forces. The principal attraction of the movement was the possibility that it offered for restructuring the definition of their collective position and promoting identifiable common interests. A movement which *attracts* members by an ideology and a programme of action standing in commonsensical relations to the material and social position of identifiable social groups lends itself more readily to an analysis in terms of relative deprivation than does the Watch Tower movement.[4] The latter does not so much 'attract' members as it actively *seeks them out* and creates the grounds for its own attractiveness. Since the movement does not necessarily stand in a commonsensical relation to the collective material and social position of its followers, it does not lend itself easily to explanation in terms of collective relative deprivation.

A more general, but closely related, criticism of explaining recruitment to a religious sect in terms of relative deprivation is that it invokes only the conditions which may or may not result in the individual's motivation to join. At best, it can amount to no more than positing a number of initial or facilitating conditions within which the motivation to act in a particular way may be stimulated, but there is no automatic or straightforward link between conditions and action. It is during this intervening stage that the decision to accept or reject the evangelist's view of the world is made, but very few explanations have accorded it the importance that it deserves.

Finally, a general methodological problem confirms us in the opinion that relative deprivation cannot easily function as an explanatory device in present-day sociological research. The concept is too gross and indiscriminating; it clearly applies to so many people that it cannot possibly succeed in distinguishing between those who are motivated by it and those who are not. It at once 'explains' everything and, *ipso facto*, nothing. Blanket explanations of this kind are an interesting exercise in metaphysics but hardly a convincing demonstration of scientific precision. Perhaps the concept would be more useful and reliable if the necessary and sufficient conditions for a contrast-class could be clearly stated. The question is never asked, How could it be shown that relative deprivation was *not* a cause of something? But until such questions are asked and receive satisfactory answers, there can be no point in continuing merely to seek confirmation of the concept's plausibility.

In fact, none of the hypotheses from the most celebrated theoretical tradition in the sociology of religion is able to shed much light on the reasons why people became Jehovah's witnesses in Britain. Nor does the evidence concerning historical changes in the Watch Tower movement's social class composition admit of either simple or straightforward interpretation. Our findings, then, support the need to revise the stereotypical notion that Jehovah's witnesses display low or inconsistent social class profiles. In a wider perspective we have shown the desirability of questioning the relation that is believed to hold between these characteristics and affiliation to *any* sectarian religious group. For it seems that through a process of methodological 'synecdoche' a relation that was actually found to obtain in one or more particular cases has come to be applied unquestioningly to all cases.[5] We have tried to argue that the association is far more subtle and flexible than previous studies have suggested. In particular, our argument stresses that it is essential to transcend the limits of an approach which starts from a statement of the material or honorific position of social strata and works backwards through a logic of affinity and congruence to infer their 'appropriate' religious outlooks.[6]

We prefer to examine religion and social class in relation to the other factors which influence the process of conversion to the Watch Tower movement, the personal 'career' of Jehovah's witnesses and the development of a sectarian organization. In particular, we have in mind the crucial process whereby the sect articulates and promotes its arguments in favour of becoming and remaining a Jehovah's witness. The response of both prospective and actual members will clearly reflect in some ways their social class characteristics, but we have found little reason to believe that the motivation to affiliate is a direct, automatic or necessary outworking of the needs and interests associated with various social class positions. We suggest, therefore, that account should be taken of social stratification only in so far as it constitutes one, albeit important, condition in a whole set of conditions affecting the behaviour of individuals and groups.

NOTES TO CHAPTER 7

1. For full details of the questionnaire's design and application, see Beckford (1972b), Appendix A.

2. On the assumption that the nuclear family's social status is very largely determined by the father's occupational status, we have not taken our respondents' mothers' occupation into account.

3. For an equally plausible, but very different, interpretation of data on status inconsistency, see Kessin, 1971.

4. Aberle's (1966) account of revitalization movements among American Indians also makes plausible and sophisticated use of relative deprivation.

5. For a similar judgement on developments in criminology, see Box and Ford (1971).

6. In Chapter 10 we shall take up the parallel criticism that Portes (1971) has brilliantly levelled against the tendency for sociologists to try to explain left-wing political radicalism solely in terms of lower-class frustrations.

CHAPTER 8

MORAL AND RELIGIOUS FACTORS

Broadening the scope of this inquiry into the sociological reasons why some people join the Watch Tower movement in Britain, we shall now switch the principal focus of interest to hypotheses deriving from the 'world-view construction' and 'social solidarity' theoretical traditions. We have shown that analysis of Jehovah's witnesses' social-class characteristics provides no obvious clue to their motivation in joining the sect. Perhaps there would be justification for understanding their behaviour in terms of a search for compensation for frustration if it could be demonstrated that they had typically *sought* religious solutions to their problems, but our findings indicate that Jehovah's witnesses are not people who could be termed 'religious seekers'. They did not shop around for suitable religious outlooks before joining the Watch Tower movement, but, as Table 13 illustrates, their initial contact with the sect was most commonly mediated by an active Publisher.

TABLE 13

Ways in which Jehovah's witnesses made their first contact with the Watch Tower movement

	%
Through the door-to-door ministry	46.0
Through a member of the family	44.0
Through friends or workmates	7.0
Personal initiative	3.0
No answer*	—
	100.0

* Less than 1%.

160

These findings are in line with Q. J. Munters' discovery that in Holland '. . . more than 80 per cent of the Jehovah's Witness respondents had joined together with relatives or after relatives had done so'. He concluded that '. . . the significance of door-to-door recruiting methods followed with such zeal should not be overestimated'. (Munters, 1971, p. 98)

It is significant that of the few Jehovah's witnesses in our sample who *did* deliberately seek to establish personal contact with a Watch Tower group at least a half had done so in the 1920s before mass-evangelism had achieved its present degree of sophistication and methodicalness. But the vast majority of Witnesses appear to have been either passive recipients of the Watch Tower message or instigators of contact with the group in only a minimal sense. These results should alert us, then, to the danger of examining such factors as social class or relative deprivation without also taking into account the individual's disposition to be spurred by them into particular courses of action.

DIFFERENTIAL ASSOCIATION

An hypothesis bearing a close resemblance to one of the most influential insights of criminological theory can be derived in the following form from the world-view construction theoretical tradition:

The probability that a person will become a member of the Watch Tower movement will vary directly with the intensity and frequency of interaction with members of the sect.

Just as it has proved helpful in some respects to consider crime as normal, learned behaviour, so we are hypothesizing that affiliation to a religious sect like the Watch Tower movement can also be understood as a consequence of learning through association with sectarians.

The findings from the questionnaire show that many Jehovah's witnesses have relatives who are also members of the Watch Tower movement. Nearly 64 per cent of our respondents reported having at least one relative in the sect, and 11 per cent claimed as many as six. Forty-six per cent were introduced to the Watch Tower movement as a result of a door-step meeting with a Kingdom Publisher. Again, the *personal* nature of the message's systematic presentation to the householder in his home is undoubtedly important in influencing its outcome. Typically, the Publisher raised questions in the householder's mind which were consonant with the kind of question already occupying his own attention. The householder probably accepted the offer of free literature with a promise to read it and discuss it with the Witness when he called next time. As a result of the second meeting, a regular date for discussing further aspects of the Witnesses' interpretation of the Bible would have been arranged, and the long process of indoctrination and induction into the group would have begun.

The most significant aspects of the whole process for our immediate purposes are (1) the so-called sect's forceful policy of staging a personal presentation of its world-view to all people regardless of whether they have displayed an interest in religious affairs, and (2) the individual evangelist's concern to focus a discussion around matters of topical interest to the householder. These two factors, in combination, go a long way towards ensuring that, if the householder can be reminded or persuaded that his own reflections on important issues are compatible with the Jehovah's witnesses' outlook, there is a small probability of his subsequent induction to the group. In other words, the Witnesses' door-to-door evangelism serves to tap sources of sympathy and support which are commonly either unknown or over-looked by the prozelytizing agents of other religious or secular organizations.

Significantly, the Church of Jesus Christ and the Latter Day Saints, which is the only other religious organization to arrange systematic house-to-house evangelism in Britain, also enjoys a high growth-rate in membership. On the basis of admittedly slight evidence, we were willing to hypothesize that, as a consequence of their similar recruitment policies and tactics, the Church of Jesus Christ and the Latter Day Saints attracts people from social backgrounds very similar to those characterizing British Jehovah's witnesses. The findings of a survey of the 108 members of the Mormon church in Hereford bear out our prediction in general. (Buckle, 1971) One-third of the Mormon sample was described as middle class and two-thirds as lower middle class and working class. But more striking is the high percentage (74 per cent) of the Mormons whose first contact with the Church of Jesus Christ and the Latter Day Saints was with missionaries who called at their homes with the intention of converting them. These findings underline the importance of not ignoring evangelism and recruitment strategies in explaining the patterns of recruitment to religious movements.

Our experience in observing Jehovah's witnesses engaging in door-to-door evangelism and the evidence from interviews with active Publishers both confirm the point that the probability of conducting a successful 'doorstep sermon' varies directly with the ability to discover quickly a topic of importance and concern to the householder. The most successful Publishers seem to possess considerable skill in using an appropriate opening gambit in meeting the householder and thereby improving the chances that the encounter will last for longer than a conversation on strictly religious matters might be expected to last.

If the initial gambit meets with an unpromising response (as most commonly occurs), it is highly unlikely that the Publishers will be able to present the relevance of his religious outlook in a convincing manner. Even if he does manage to engage the householder's attention, the transition to a stage in the conversation where it can be realistically presented in the context of his religious beliefs is still fraught with difficulties. They are overcome to a small extent in an evangelistic tactic which has become increasingly favoured by Publishers in recent years, that is for the Publisher to present himself or herself in the role of literature-salesman only. It is common nowadays for the Publisher to omit all reference to religion in offering magazines and books which 'may be of interest' to the householder in the hope that the printed word may be a more familiar and acceptable means of conveying their message.

If either a doorstep sermon or a sale of literature elicits a display of interest by a householder, the Publisher must seize the opportunity to keep the communication going for a sufficiently long time to reveal as many sides of the Watch Tower Society's world-view as possible. But in the event of an individual Publisher feeling inadequate to realize the full potential of the relationship with a householder, he may enrol the assistance of more experienced Witnesses. Thus, constant evangelism serves not just as a means of maintaining and reinforcing the individual Publisher's personal commitment to the movement's aims, but it also serves to promote and preserve among the Witnesses a strong sense of the whole group's *corporate* involvement in pursuing the same ends.

An important implication of these evangelistic tactics is that, by means of the mid-week door-to-door canvass, Jehovah's witnesses establish contact with far more women than men. What is more, the kind of women whom they meet are likely to have young children at home or to be advanced in years. As will be shown in a later section, there are strong reasons for believing that women in both categories are disproportionately more receptive to the Witnesses' message than other women.

A further implication of the Witnesses' evangelistic strategy is that some people may have their curiosity aroused by a doorstep sermon and they may agree to read some of the group's literature without being very serious about it. If this is the case, and if their initial curiosity then develops into more serious interest, then it is clear that a different kind of explanation is needed from that which is required for the behaviour of people whose initial interest exceeds mere curiosity. In this respect, it is essential to treat conversion to the Jehovah's witnesses' world-view as a varied and gradual process and to examine separately the effects of the whole range of factors that may operate at different stages in that process.

Recruitment to the Jehovah's witness movement in Britain has been shown to be positively related to the intensity and frequency of interaction between Watch Tower evangelists and members of either the public or their own family. The most general hypothesis from the differential association theory finds some confirmation, therefore, in the present findings.

ANXIETY AND CREATIVE RESPONSE

An additional hypothesis from the world-view construction tradition may help to supplement the differential association hypothesis by suggesting that a positive relationship holds between a person's favourable responses to evangelists and the degree of perceived confusion that underlies his or her own outlook. A more specific formulation would be:

> If an individual experiences difficulty and confusion in trying to make satisfactory sense of what are considered to be important existential matters, then there is a high probability that he will respond favourably to the purveyors of a comprehensive religious ideology.

Provided that the individual considers the matters which give rise to his sense of confusion to be important, there is no need to stipulate that they be important to other people or in themselves. Nor is it necessary to hypothesize that the expression of confusion will somehow 'lead to' an interest in religious ideologies, since we have already established that very few 'religious seekers' have actually been recruited to the Watch Tower movement in Britain. We have preferred, therefore, to focus the hypothesis on the relation between perceived confusion and the response to social interaction with evangelists.

Interviews with Jehovah's witnesses who had not been 'born into' the sect yielded remarkable uniformity in their claims that conversion had taken place in a context of mental, and occasionally physical, anguish. They alleged that they had experienced so much doubt and confusion about the apparently aimless and chaotic condition of either their own lives or the world in general that the question of overall purposes in life was coming to occupy ever greater prominence in their thinking. Even in the statements of the less articulate there was an underlying implication that they had felt, consciously or otherwise, a painful discrepancy between what they thought should be the pattern of human existence and what was actually happening in the world. This comes close to what Glock called 'ethical relative deprivation' and represents perhaps one of the few instances when such a concept can be fruitfully and reliably used in analysis. For the sake of convenience we have summarized the wide range of anguished feelings under five headings, but the classification makes no pretensions to logical rigour.

(1) *General moral indigation* was frequently said to result from the estimation that certain moral values did not have the currency in contemporary society that they should have. The range of specific moral 'areas' includes declining standards of sexual morality, increasing incidence of dishonesty, growing prevalence of violent behaviour and the declining role of 'trust' in personal relations.

(2) *Anxiety about the future* and particularly about the quality of life which their children would have to live was a common theme in the Witnesses' statements about their feelings of insecurity and dissatisfaction prior to conversion. This particular set of feelings was said to emerge most commonly when the respondents' children were of school age, because it was then that the parents were likely to be confronted with questions about conflicting standards of historical and contemporary behaviour.

(3) Concern for the state of *world peace* frequently underlay the general anxiety expressed by Jehovah's witnesses. Their knowledge of the details of international affairs varied widely, but the strength of their conviction and fear that the world was in imminent danger of widespread warfare remained constant. This type of anxiety was often combined with a concern for the future of their children's lives, but was also common to childless people.

(4) It is possible to distinguish a class of statements about anxiety in which concern for the *stability of important social institutions* was uppermost. This class of statement was rarely unaccompanied by one or more additional themes of distress, but deserves separate treatment because it appeared as a common complement to more general moral indignation. It may be significant that the family often figured as an example of a social institution which allegedly showed signs of regrettable instability.

(5) A fifth class has been reserved for including more *personal and adventitious* attributions of anxiety. The range of these statements is very broad and includes such diverse themes as unhappy love affairs, stillbirth, death of a loved person and disenchantment with a religious group. We have included in this class statements of anxiety which might be taken as basic to any interest in religion: concern about life after death was a common example of this type of anxiety.

All these diverse types of anxiety-feelings could be characterized through their formal reflections of a discrepancy between expectations of how people should behave and perceptions of how they actually do behave, or between expectations of the values that social institutions should embody and realizations of what they actually represent. By the term 'value' we understand a criterion for selectivity; at a high level of abstraction it refers to the complex of cognitions and emotions which are said to inform the act of decision-making. Values are usually shared by groups of people and they are important in underpinning collective behaviour of individuals or groups, and they are commonly found in coherent sets. They are most fruitfully considered as abstract constructions of the sociologist who wishes to highlight the important patterns of preference and selectivity which seem to underlie empirical behaviour.

Feelings of anxiety would be less likely to result from a discrepancy between facts or ideas to which a person was not in any way committed, but what made prospective Jehovah's witnesses particularly anxious was the fact that they were *committed* to their values. This means that the values related closely to what they would have called the 'commonsense view of the world', that is, their values constituted an irreducibly basic part of the world as they had constructed it. For them, the world would have ceased to exist as a meaningful place if their values had not been seen to be current in it. Peter Berger has expressed these ideas as follows:

> Every society is engaged in the never completed enterprise of building a humanly meaningful world. Cosmization implies the identification of this humanly meaningful world with the world as such, the former now being grounded in the latter, reflecting it or being derived from it in its fundamental structures. (Berger, 1967, p. 28)

Values and meanings are thus intimately bound up in the process of constructing a view of reality and must, therefore, be called in question when they no longer seem to be accurately reflected in reality.

Prospective Jehovah's witnesses treated their values, then, not merely as the best available but more pretentiously as the most basic principles on which man's world is founded. If these principles were believed to be no longer embodied in social institutions, then they felt that the world was not only deviating from its ideal and necessary guidelines (which might be considered as merely regrettable), but that it was also in danger of total collapse, since its ideal and necessary foundation was being undermined. According to Allan Eister's apt characterization of such people, Jehovah's witness converts are drawn from those people 'who are more dependent upon a stable cultural base and more accustomed to thinking of logic if not of language, of rules of discourse, of criteria of "meaningfulness" as more fixed than they are'. (Eister, 1972, p. 327)

We must emphasize, however, that the individual rarely experienced the confusion consciously; but the evangelist was invariably successful in *stimulating* the belief that confusion was being, or had been, experienced. What is important at this stage of the conversion process is (a) the conviction that a confusing discrepancy exists between the ideal and the actual, and (b) the fear that the discrepancy contravenes some basic principle of order in human affairs.

These findings call in question the usefulness of trying to account for the pre-disposition to respond favourably to Watch Tower evangelists in the largely negative terms of rebellion, rejection, protest and frustration. In any event, statements to the effect that 'Sects are movements of religious protest' are notoriously misleading because they fail to make the crucial analytical distinction between the level of the individual believer and the collective level of the group's ideology. The two levels of analysis have very different implications for an explanation of affiliation to the sect, and it is essential to stress that collective ideological protest is not dependent upon the willingness of all sect members to protest.

Our respondents and interviewees reported that, prior to becoming involved with Jehovah's witnesses, they had taken very little interest in matters of political, economic or social concern and they had never seriously contemplated joining any kind of pressure-group. Indeed, they frequently indicated a mood of apathetic resignation and muted resentment. They also made it clear that alongside their general feelings of unease and anxiety they continued to entertain a number of fixed ideas or assumptions which constituted a kind of vestigial faith in such things as the existence of a Creator-God, the attainability of ultimate truth and the underlying meaningfulness of human existence. In this respect they were not suffering from extreme normlessness, nor could their lives be characterized as meaningless. Furthermore, very few took steps to look for an explicit ideology that could allay their anxiety and answer their questions. Anyway, their outlook was typically lacking in sufficient clarity and animus to motivate them to protest against their life-situation, and for the most part their character was antithetic to the very notion of protest.

The offer of support from Watch Tower teachings and social organization was interpreted by prospective Jehovah's witnesses not so much as an opportunity to give positive expression to feelings of resentment or to a desire to register a protest but more as a chance to introduce consistency into their beliefs. In some cases their previous outlook had been coherent in the sense of providing a satisfactory degree of meaningfulness in life but not consistent in the sense of displaying an inner logic or methodicalness.

This is why a large number of converts reported feeling that 'things suddenly fell into place', 'all my questions were answered' or 'I could see it was the Truth straightaway'. This is also why it is necessary to consider the process of conversion in its cognitive aspects as a creative act on the convert's part and not simply a mechanical reaction against material conditions.

Moreover, the interpretation of their behaviour as a 'creative' reconciliation of felt anxieties and proferred satisfactions has the advantage that it also accounts for the willingness of Jehovah's witnesses to take part in public evangelism. It is consistent with our interpretation that they should feel a strong desire to tell other people about their own sense of satisfaction at finding answers to questions that had been causing them anxiety. Many Congregation Elders reported that fresh converts usually experienced such strong feelings of elation that they undertook more door-to-door work than was considered suitable for them at that stage. It is also the case that congregations containing a large proportion of recent converts are more likely to fulfil the collective quotas for hours spent in service-work than relatively mature congregations.

Another corroboration of our view that it is profitable to interpret most cases of affiliation to the sect in terms of a positive, creative response to the possible satisfactions offered by the Watch Tower ideology is that strong feelings towards other ideologies and groups are fostered in, and acquired by, the individual Witness only as a result of intensive indoctrination. We met no recently converted Witnesses who were as eager to criticize and malign other forms of religious behaviour as were members of longer standing. On investigating the socialization of new members, we discovered that systematic analysis of other religious systems was not encouraged until the basic principles of Watch Tower ideology had been mastered. This would suggest that it is unusual for hostile feelings towards other religionists to constitute a *predisposing* factor to an interest in the activities of Jehovah's witnesses. Consequently, the view that people who become Jehovah's witnesses are motivated by a desire to register their protest against the inadequacies or corruptions of existing religious organizations is at best mistaken, and at worst an expression of a prejudiced stereotype. This is a further illustration of the necessity to examine the behaviour of sectarians with careful regard for the precise stage of their 'career', for it is a mistake to treat sectarians of varying degrees of maturity as alike.

Whilst we have some sympathy for I. C. Jarvie's suggestion (1964) that the adoption of millenarian beliefs should be treated as analogous to the scientific procedures of inventing and testing hypotheses, there is a danger that such an explanatory approach would unduly exaggerate the purely rational, objective and cognitive aspects of a phenomenon which is actually compounded of strongly emotional and sociological elements. Nevertheless, Jarvie's 'logic of the situation' approach has the distinct advantage for present purposes of shifting the emphasis away from the currently popular vogue for explanation in terms of psychological motives of resentment and protest. But it requires supplementation by consideration of the appeal to prospective converts of such non-rational factors as the intrinsically creative 'pleasure' to be derived from (a) learning the broad pattern and the intricate details of Christian sacred symbolism, (b) applying acquired knowledge in the interpretation of myriad stories and situations, (c) airing knowledge in public, (d) discussing the symbols with like-minded people, (e) feeling involved in the active pursuit of 'fresh light' on the symbols and (f) organizing or reorganizing life in accordance with the symbolic prescriptions.

In other words, we are suggesting that interest in esoteric religious systems can also entail a wide variety of different gratifications. We have in mind the sort of pleasure to be derived from listening to music, appreciating fine arts or even participating in sports. Admittedly, the strength of a sectarian's devotion to his chosen interest is much greater and more pervasive than, say, that of the music-lover, but the interests are analogous in so far as they may be indulged in *for their own sake*. That is to say, both kinds of interest embody a certain, gratuitous, non-instrumental value which may contribute heavily towards their respective appeals. Our reason for considering this matter important is that so many of the Witnesses to whom we talked gave unmistakable indications that being a member of the Watch Tower movement had given them a rewarding sense of creative satisfaction, and partly so because the activity was expressive as well as instrumental. In fact, the importance of these expressive factors was repeatedly underlined by people who had left the movement after being members for a long time and whose most intense regrets were often felt for the rituals and the non-instrumental aspects of membership.

In sum, although the desire to join a protest movement may have been a factor motivating *some* people to associate with Jehovah's witnesses, it was certainly not dominant among our respondents and interviewees. Indeed, many features of the Watch Tower movement would discourage potential protestors from considering it an appropriate channel for the expression of their feelings. Our findings indicated, rather, that the background experiences of converts and the evangelistic strategy of the sect combined to make prospective Witnesses feel that affiliation would offer a positive solution to some of their problems. The perceived chance to create for themselves a new sense of personal integrity and a meaningful view of the world was the converts' typical response to Watch Tower evangelism.

The world-view construction and the social solidarity theoretical traditions can be linked by a study of the sociological conditions within which people may be predisposed to respond favourably to the message of Watch Tower evangelists. This can be conveniently achieved by testing whether, as Peter Berger suggested, a relation holds between the disturbance of an actor's 'plausibility structures' and his readiness to reconstruct a view of the world in a new and more personally satisfying manner. The theoretical underpinning for the range of hypotheses within this tradition runs as follows:

> The world is built up in the consciousness of the individual by conversation with significant others (such as parents, teachers, 'peers'). The world is maintained as subjective reality by the same sort of conversation, be it with the same or with new significant others (such as spouses, friends, associates). If such conversation is disrupted (the spouse dies, the friends disappear, or one comes to leave one's original social millieu), the world begins to totter, to lose its subjective plausibility. In other words, the subjective reality of the world hangs on the thin thread of conversation. (Berger, 1967, p. 17)

The areas of discontinuity in plausibility structures which were common to many Jehovah's witness converts will be discussed under two broad headings: family and religion.

(A) *The family*

A large proportion of interviewees and respondents voluntarily characterized their upbringing as 'Christian' in the sense that their parents had been involved in church affairs for at least part of their lifetime. The norms of family life reflected the popular theology of major Christian groups, and the socialization of children into widespread Christian ethical and religious values proceeded unthinkingly. Moreover, the evidence of Table 14 indicates that, contrary to the downward trend in rates of participation in organized religious activities in Britain, our respondents displayed a more frequent and a more active interest in religion than their parents had done. This finding is all the more remarkable in view of the fact that since decline has been sharpest in Sunday School attendances, one might have expected the rate of adult involvement in religion to have dropped appreciably between generations.

TABLE 14

Comparison of the intensity of Jehovah's witnesses' previous religious involvement with that of their parents

	Active %	Occasional %	Nominal %	None %
Fathers	19.4	16.1	34.5	30.0
Mothers	28.3	16.7	36.7	18.3
Respondents	24.0	27.2	27.7	21.1*

* This figure is inflated by the inclusion of 23 respondents who were brought up as Jehovah's Witnesses.

A crude indication of the strength of the respondents' involvement in religion can be constructed by combining the figures for active and occasional participation. According to this measure, our respondents' percentage of 51.2 per cent is hardly different from that of their mothers. But in the context of a general decline in the level of participation in formal religious activities over recent decades[1] it is clear that people who subsequently became Jehovah's witnesses had earlier shown extraordinarily strong commitment to conventional religious groups.

It is to be expected that people who, in their childhood and early adult life, had acquired strong respect for Christian values, should have been all the more dismayed and alarmed at the realization that the majority of their fellow-citizens did not share those same values. In fact, the intensity of their resulting feelings of anxiety might be directly proportional to the strength of their commitment to 'old fashioned' Christian values. There is reason to believe that many of our sample, by virtue of an intensive and enduring integration in their family of orientation, had been artificially protected against the secular erosion of Christian values in the wider British society. Their families represented, as it were, islands of commitment and certainty in a sea of indifference and relativity. Only when the ties of the family were loosened did these people typically come to realize the extent of their 'moral isolation'. The situation became even more serious if the individual who had already formed a family of procreation had consequently felt responsible for the socialization of his or her offspring.

From an analysis of interviews with, and completed questionnaires from, Jehovah's witnesses, it is apparent that the family institution occupies a crucial position in their religious development. It is important both as a source of thought-categories by which the world can be ordered and understood, and as the source of social support ('conversation' in Berger's sense) for them. If the individual begins to suspect that the 'symmetry between the objective world of society and the subjective world of the individual' (Berger, 1967, p. 15) is no longer satisfactory, then we will expect him to endeavour to restore the symmetry either by seeking support for his own ideas or by adapting his ideas to suit his new perception of the situation. Until he manages to complete one of these courses of action, and so long as he continues to be worried by the dissonances between ideas and reality, we will assume that the individual is in a state of potential confusion.

(B) *Religion*

The discrepancy between our respondents' own values and the values current in the wider society at the time of their conversion is paralleled by a perceived discrepancy between their own ideas about the functions of religious groups and their understanding of what those groups were actually accomplishing. For a variety of reasons they lost their attachment to religious groups and failed to replace the former centrality of Christian teachings in their outlook with an alternative ideological position; their commitment to Christianity became latent. They did not, however, lose all interest in religious affairs but merely ceased to support any particular religious group. In fact, they retained sufficient personal interest to feel disappointed and sometimes angry at the church's alleged loss of influences and leadership. For they had learned to expect guidance from religious professionals, and their lack of active involvement in religion did not lessen their sense of indignation that religious leaders were not apparently meeting the standards expected of them.

Allowing for the intervening influence of Watch Tower propaganda in colouring their accounts of pre-conversion events, it is possible to extract some credible pieces of information from our interviewees' reports of their reasons for dissociating themselves from Christian groups. Of the highest importance for nearly all respondents who had not been 'born into' the sect was the charge that the clergy had abdicated from their traditional role as suppliers of firm advice and guidance about proper conduct in an age of moral, political and social confusion. These feelings were usually provoked by actual events which had caused the individual concerned to turn to religious agencies for guidance: they did not occur in isolation from specific events and were not simply the result of independent, critical reflection on religious and moral teachings.

In some cases, particularly for those people who had already lost personal contact with a church, the converts formulated their queries without voicing them and without explicitly testing the reactions of ministers of religion, but their feelings of disappointment were no less disturbing for all that. They seemed to feel that the churches should make their opinions and beliefs known, and that if there were people of good-will who were frustrated in their search for 'truth' and certainty, then this was the churches' fault.

It was also common for Jehovah's witnesses to complain that they had lost faith in traditional churches when these bodies had begun to show signs of losing their institutional identity. There seemed to be a strong feeling of resentment at the alleged reluctance of church leaders to propagate doctrinal and moral teachings which might have reasserted the distinctiveness of their churches' theological orientation.[2] Indeed, Jehovah's witnesses are prone to interpret the loss of traditional church identities as an indication that the Protestant clergy have either 'sold out to Rome' or become 'materialistic', but both interpretations smack so obviously of the mediating influence of Watch Tower propaganda that one cannot use this kind of remark as evidence of characteristic predispositions *before* conversion to the movement. It is much more likely that a generalized, vague sense of alienation from the churches has been rationalized *post factum* into specific grievances against the clergy. In a small number of cases, informants were sufficiently candid to admit that they had ceased worshipping in church for the simple reason that they had disliked the clergyman personally.

The fact that prospective Jehovah's witnesses had entertained such a variegated set of reasons for withdrawing from mainstream Christian groups and that some reasons were incompatible with others indicates that the precise reasons are of less importance in themselves than the indisputable fact that dissatisfaction was widespread among them. This cannot alone account for the predisposition to join the Watch Tower movement but it does at least point to the common experience among converts of having participated in religious groups and of them withdrawing. In no sense, therefore, can Jehovah's witness converts be classified as 'Godless' or 'unchurched', and it would be wrong to suggest that their lives had always lacked meaning in religious terms. What they have in common is the experience of an *erosion* of certain truths and axioms which formerly held the status of common-sense knowledge. It is during the period of time between the loss of faith in what had seemed to be a commonsense view of the world and the establishment of another that these people were vulnerable to the propagandists of alternative coherent ideologies.

We must emphasize, however, that our account of the transition from confusion to commitment or from scepticism to conviction is not founded on the view that 'nature abhors a sociological vacuum'. Whereas, for example, we agree in outline with Nigel Harris that 'Confusion prompts men to seek new guides', (Harris, 1968, p. 15) it is absolutely essential to draw attention to a critical, intervening stage in the conversion-process, namely, the deliberate attempts by Watch Tower evangelists to *precipitate* in the prospective convert's mind an awareness that (a) he has been suffering from anxiety, (b) the anxiety is an instantiation of a universal malaise, (c) the universal malaise is part of the outworkings of God's plan for mankind, and (d) his anxiety is shared by a large number of other serious-minded people. It is essential to underline this phenomenon if we are to avoid the mistake of treating converted Jehovah's witnesses as a class of people displaying one characteristic which suffices to distinguish between them and people who resist the sect's efforts to convert them. In our opinion the distinction is not so much a matter of whether they display feelings of anxiety or not, but rather a matter of whether they are susceptible to the arguments of the sect's evangelists. For in many cases there is no justification for believing that the potential convert was necessarily suffering from anxiety before encountering the evangelist's arguments; we should remain open to the possibility that the evangelist can create *ex nihilo*, or stimulate, feelings of anxiety in people who would not otherwise have been aware of them.

MARGINALITY AND MASS MOVEMENTS

The argument of the preceding section has sought to establish a connection between disturbance of two major plausibility structures and predisposition to respond favourably to the message of Watch Tower evangelists. Our findings in this respect have confirmed the usefulness of examining insights deriving from the 'world-view construction' theoretical tradition, but now they can be profitably supplemented with hypotheses relating more specifically to the social conditions which influence the cognitive aspects of the conversion process. The 'social solidarity' theoretical tradition embodies in part an argument which states that integration in social groups is a prerequisite for sharing religious views in common. For our purposes it is helpful to begin by considering the following insights from what has come to be known as the theory of mass-society. It holds that people who lack adequate integration into social groups are considered to be vulnerable to the propagandists of social movements which aim to mobilize them. One would expect, therefore, that people who had been accustomed to understanding the world in religious terms, but who had experienced confusion following the disruption of the supportive plausibility structures, would be especially open to suggestion from the propagandists of mass religious movements.

If this theoretical argument is valid, then it could be hypothesized that, prior to their conversion, Jehovah's witnesses had typically lacked sufficiently satisfying integration into social groups to generate resistance to the offers made by Watch Tower evangelists. The first step to be taken in preparing to test the hypothesis is to question whether it is justifiable to call the Watch Tower movement a mass-movement in the sense in which mass-society theorists use the term. This would seem justified in so far as the sect presents alternative channels for action to the mainstream, orthodox religious groupings, and in so far as it denies having a membership, only a mass of followers: its official self-image is of a centrally guided mass of individuals who have dedicated their lives to the vindication of Jehovah's name. Spokesmen for the Watch Tower Society give the people who undertake proselytism in its name the rather formal title of 'Publishers'. There is good reason, therefore, for examining the group as if it were analogous to the mass political movements which normally occupy the attention of students of mass society. We are further encouraged to adopt this perspective by Kornhauser's statement that:

> Classes subsist along with masses but they become less effective determinants of political behaviour insofar as society is a mass society . . . The primary utility of mass analysis centers in its power to explain *crisis politics* and the extremist response, whereas class analysis would appear to be more useful in the area of routine politics. (*Kornhauser*, 1960, p. 15)

We have already shown that analysis of the social class basis of the British Jehovah's witnesses does not produce any easy or straightforward explanations of their behaviour, and it is clear that their kind of religious activity is far from 'routine'. Since the sect qualifies, then, on both counts for analysis as a mass-movement, we shall now review the evidence for and against the hypothesis.

One of the central propositions of this theoretical tradition is that, in the absence of 'intermediate relationships and authorities', people lacking integration into secondary groups become vulnerable to the pressures put upon them by agencies which promote certain ideas without having firm foundations in social groups. The 'atomized individual' may be manipulated by these agencies because he lacks protection and support from secondary associations: and the mass agencies themselves are un-restrained in their activities by the social control exercised in cohesive social groups. If the Watch Tower movement is considered to display the defining characteristics of a mass agency, then we would expect that the people who subject themselves to its authority would typically lack inte-gration in voluntary associations and other secondary groups which might otherwise protect the individual from its influence.

Indeed, our findings are generally consistent with the theory's pre-dictions, for a large number of respondents reported that, prior to joining the movement, they had belonged to no voluntary associations, had participated in no organized sets of intermediary relations outside the family sphere (except by necessity in the place of work) and were no more than polite in relations with their neighbours. Their kin relationships, by contrast, were highly satisfactory, and there were no suggestions that prospective Jehovah's witnesses had lacked primary, affectual relations with immediate kin. They lacked, rather, relationships which might have given them a sense of participating in the wider society. The very close-ness of their family ties may have prevented this.

Even the most obviously middle-class Witnesses had not participated in voluntary activities organized by any formal associations except religious bodies. But their relative isolation becomes a little more understandable when it is learned that the occupations of middle-class Witnesses tend to be 'marginal' in the sense that their work does not entail interaction with the centres of political power and may not be conducive to the assimilation of values shared by most members of the community. The class of marginal occupations includes, among others, small businessmen, small shopkeepers and self-employed craftsmen, and these very occupations have been shown to be common among male Jehovah's witnesses in Britain. The reasons for this occupational pattern may be of two, not unrelated, kinds.

On the one hand a process of pre-selection operates to exclude people whose values are at variance with those that predominate in commercial and productive occupational spheres, and we have shown that even before their conversion Jehovah's witnesses tended to hold deviant values. On the assumption of a strain towards congruence between personal values and the values current in the place of work, one would expect prospective Jehovah's witnesses to opt for either self-employment or for employment in small-scale productive or service units where personal values might be allowed some freedom of expression and respect. In accordance with these expectations both white-collar and manual workers who became Witnesses seemed to have avoided employment in large-scale commercial or industrial enterprises. Those prospective Jehovah's witnesses who had held minor professional occupations rarely worked in the creative, socializing (see Campbell, 1967) or welfare professions. This negative preference may reflect distaste for the arts, distrust of government-controlled agencies and lack of sympathy with the ideals of social welfare; indeed, in this respect, prospective Jehovah's witnesses could hardly present a more vivid contrast to the occupational profile of the membership of such contemporary social movements as the Campaign for Nuclear Disarmament (see Parkin, 1966), the Communist Party of Great Britain (see Newton, 1966) or the British Humanist Federation (see Campbell, 1967). The range of professions common to Jehovah's witness converts was therefore virtually restricted to dentistry, accountancy, work-study engineering and shop management.

On the other hand it is plausible that prospective Jehovah's witnesses' occupational choice was constrained by the fact that some kinds of commercial and productive environments are intolerant of employees lacking commitment to the basic value of high secular aspirations. It would be entirely compatible with our findings on the pattern of anxieties felt by Converts that they would not be eager to work hard merely for the goal of maximizing earnings nor would they be willing to suspend judgement in the course of their secular job on matters of ethical concern. It is also likely that fellow-workers in certain occupations would refuse to tolerate such deliberate restraint in work-rates or reserved attitudes towards productive goals.

It would be quite wrong, however, to imply that Jehovah's witness converts typically lacked integration into *any* social groups or that their moral ties with the wider society were non-existent. Indeed, their respect for certain norms was in some cases strong enough to support the argument that they were upholders of some of British society's most basic institutions. Yet, for this very reason they felt set apart from large segments of that society because they respected values which had ceased to be widely respected. They evaluated highly such virtues as honesty, chastity, discipline and family-mindedness at a time when these virtues no longer seemed to find concrete expression to the same extent in the everyday behaviour of their fellow-citizens or in influential mass-media. Conversely, they did not typically place a high value on ambition, self-determination, scepticism and material comfort. It would be no exaggeration, therefore, to assert that, even before they had developed an interest in the activities of the Watch Tower Bible and Tract Society, the converts to whom we spoke had held enough values at odds with those of their fellow-citizens to justify the appellation 'marginal people'.

The plausibility for them of a comprehensive ideology derived in part from the fact that no secondary association was available to them to present an alternative view of the world. They lacked the means of comparing one view of the world with another, because they were not subject to the pressures towards conformity with the ideas and values current in intermediary groups. *A fortiori*, and in contrast to the majority of the adult British population, prospective Jehovah's witnesses had not acquired the kind of resistance to comprehensive ideologies which stems from participation in a variety of cross-cutting secondary associations. They were not inured to the relativizing perspective which can be cultivated only by means of involvement, or at least, interest in the views and activities of a plurality of different, and not necessarily mutually reconcilable, intermediary groups.

In view of all that has been said so far about the typical convert's lack of integration into a plurality of supportive social groups, lowered resistance to the ideology offered by Watch Tower evangelists and marginality in terms of leisure pursuits, cultural activities, political interests, occupational choice and personal values, it may seem strange (or even perverse) that we have avoided using the terms 'anomie' and 'alienation'. We certainly could have used them at various points in the developing argument, but there were overriding reasons for deliberately avoiding them. In the first place, 'anomie' and 'alienation' are potentially subject to so many different interpretations that it becomes counter-productive to use them, since each usage demands a lengthy explication. Secondly, the terms enjoy too many ideological connotations to be easily adapted for objective analytical purposes. Thirdly, they have become embodied in a highly conventionalized type of explanation for so-called deviant behaviour in which the critical aspects of the relation between perceptions of dissatisfaction and modes of adaptation are assumed to be too automatic. Our findings, for example, have repeatedly stressed the need to examine this relation closely and to take account of the strategy of evangelists in mediating it. To conform with the conventional usage of 'anomie' and 'alienation' would be to underplay the importance of this critical factor. For these, and other reasons, then, we have deliberately chosen to refrain from using the terms themselves and, instead, to analyse in detail only those aspects of their total range of meanings that were relevant to our purposes. The quick advantages of a 'blanket explanation', have been exchanged for the greater rewards of detailed analysis.[3]

THE SEARCH FOR COMMUNITY

Examination of hypotheses deriving from the world-view-construction and from the mass-movement theoretical traditions has confirmed the usefulness of understanding conversion to the Watch Tower movement against a background of cognitive, moral and social factors which influence a prospective convert's response to the evangelism of Jehovah's witnesses. We must now consider the role of a factor which has figured prominently in some of the best known sociological accounts of religious affiliation, namely, the gratification said to result from participation in primary social groups. (See, *inter alia*, Poblete, 1960; Roberts, 1968; and Klapp, 1969) A representative hypothesis from this tradition would read as follows:

> The less extensive an individual's memberships in supportive social groups, the more likely he is to join a religious sect in the search for integration into warm, affectual primary groups.

The fact that practising Jehovah's witnesses invariably describe their initial reception at a Kingdom Hall as 'warm', 'friendly' or 'sincere' should not be allowed to override certain other considerations about the early socialization of converts which are at variance with this stereotypical description. The only permissible evidence on this topic should therefore be statements indicating that *prior to conversion* individuals had seen participation in a Watch Tower congregation as a means of satisfying a desire for primary, affectual relations with others. But our findings suggest, on the contrary, that very few people who subsequently became Jehovah's witnesses had been primarily motivated in this way; rather, their initial concern had been typically to indulge their curiosity, to please a friend or to accept a challenge issued by an evangelist. This is not to deny that the friendly reception offered to newcomers does not eventually dispose them more favourably towards the sect, but it is to underline the necessity to retain an analytical distinction between separate stages in the process of interest-arousal and conversion. Our evidence indicates that perception of a friendly welcome is a more important factor in affecting *subsequent* behaviour than a belief that membership of a congregation will offer gratification for the felt need of primary relationships.

This argument is reinforced by several objective features of the conversion-process. The Watch Tower style of worship and the content of meetings are extremely arid and difficult to understand on first acquaintance. There is none of the emotionality or piety of other nonconformist groups to provide at least a modicum of resemblance with contemporary patterns of religious behaviour, and the trappings of more orthodox liturgies are entirely missing. It is difficult, therefore, for newcomers to feel 'at home', and there are few opportunities for neophytes to participate actively in the proceedings. Even if an individual did believe that participation in congregation meetings would satisfy an important and unfulfilled need in his life, gratification would be delayed for a long time after initial contact with an evangelist. Normally, a whole series of back-calls and Bible Studies precedes attendance at meetings, and outsiders are at first encouraged to attend only the Sunday Public Meeting at which a formal sermon is the major item. Finally, it is the express policy of the Watch Tower Society to discourage the development of any practice which might give the impression that participation in meetings was an acceptable end in itself. The policy has the immediate consequences of deterring Jehovah's witnesses from gathering together for purely social purposes at the close of meetings and from making the conduct of meetings less formal. *Newcomers* find very little reason therefore to consider affiliation to the group for its own sake as an attraction in the first place.

This finding is compatible with the view expressed in Chapter 4 that all aspects of the Jehovah's witness's career must be understood in the context of the sect's organizational, ideological and social characteristics. Thus, the Watch Tower policies for evangelism, recruitment, socialization and induction are important determinants of the rate, scope and quality of conversions. We have also tried to demonstrate the necessity to understand the behaviour of prospective and actual converts in terms of a creative response to the situation precipitated for, or suggested to, them by Watch Tower evangelists. Only in this way can the conversion process be seen as an end-in-itself in addition to being for some people an instrumental means of achieving certain desired states. This approach also enjoys the benefit of transcending the bounds of sociologistic and materialistic determinism. That is to say, it seeks to avoid the common practice of explaining sectarian religion by reducing it to a need for sociation or to a reaction against material disprivilege. Finally, it suggests the necessity to examine more closely the separate stages in the gradual and complex process of conversion to the Watch Tower faith and movement.

NOTES TO CHAPTER 8

1. Bryan Wilson (1966, p. 5) has estimated that no more than 25 per cent of adults in England and Wales are in membership of any religious denomination.

2. Their view is shared by more objective observers as well. See, for example, Lippman (1970).

3. Our argument parallels Worsley's (1957) reasons for being suspicious of the common use of 'charisma' in the study of Cargo Cults.

CHAPTER 9

CONVERSION, INDUCTION AND INTEGRATION

No hypothesis about reasons for becoming a Jehovah's witness from any of the major theoretical traditions has so far been unconditionally confirmed by our findings, but some hypotheses have undoubtedly received much stronger empirical support than others. But even the sum of confirmed hypotheses amounts to no more than evidence of 'predispositions' or facilitating conditions to affiliate with the sect: they cannot 'explain' the patterns of affiliation without also taking account of each individual's motivation. Since the psychological study of motivation lies outside the scope of the present work, we are unable to investigate it satisfactorily. (But see Zygmunt, 1972) Nevertheless, the underlying sociological factors are still an essential component of an ideally rounded explanation and deserve our further attention. For this reason we shall devote the first half of this chapter to a methodical review of the sociological context within which the process of conversion, induction and integration takes place. Most of the factors have already been introduced in earlier chapters, but for the sake of clarity, Figure 4 sets them all out in a convenient schema. It treats affiliation to the Watch Tower movement as a complex process having multiple points of departure and being subject to the influence of multiple contingent factors. It is seen as a career, and the convert's response to the forces operating at any stage will vary according to the whole complex of psychological and sociological factors.

The logical relation of transitivity does not hold between all stages of the schema because, while the predisposing conditions must historically and logically antedate the stages of suggestibility, it is feasible that critical events could precede and stimulate the latter.

FIGURE 4

A schema of the process of conversion to the Watch Tower movement
(excluding children and adults 'born into' the movement)

Stage 1 Predisposing social conditions	Stage 2 States of suggestibility	Stage 3 Critical Events	Stage 4 Affiliation	Stage 5 Retention
a) Christian upbringing; church participation	a) Perceived discrepancy between values and actuality	a) Door-step sermon	a) Attendance at meetings and assemblies	a) Acquisition of Watch Tower *Weltanschauung*
b) Marginal occupation	b) Vestigial dogmatism	b) Incidental witnessing	b) Friendship ties in congregation	b) Continuing service work
c) Lack of intermediary associations and communal ties		c) Active seeking	c) Participation in field-service	c) Extensive network of family and friendship ties in congregation
d) Young family of procreation			d) Severance of 'outside' social contacts	d) Posts of responsibility in congregation
e) Other family member in the Watch Tower movement				

(1) *Predispositions*

If we wished to rank the predisposing sociological conditions in order of importance, then a conventionally Christian upbringing would come first on the list. Not a single interviewee or respondent reported entertaining any atheistic or agnostic ideas, and for the most part they had earlier expressed their God-centred religious views in regular attendance at Sunday School or church. This conventionally Christian background has the effect of facilitating initial rapport between evangelist and audience through the common bond of basic religio-moral assumptions. The Publisher conducting a Bible Study has the task of elaborating on, rather than trying to instill, the prospective convert's basic set of views and is therefore spared the more arduous task of defending the very idea of God or belief in the Bible's divine inspiration. From the convert's point of view the early stages of contact with Watch Tower doctrines involve the reaffirmation of some basic Christian beliefs, the countering of persistent objections and the setting of new beliefs in a *systematized* framework. The amount of really new material to be digested is initially quite small, because Publishers consciously adopt the tactic of emphasizing continuity with previous outlooks.

Second on the list of predisposing conditions is a secular occupation which does not entail extensive personal interaction with fellow-workers or members of the public. Marginality to the main structure of occupations means that prospective converts are unlikely to be dependent on colleagues for off-duty friendship and are not imbued with driving ambition. The result is that they are correspondingly more suggestible to the arguments of Watch Tower ideologists and possibly more responsive to the offer of fellowship in a local congregation.

Lack of enduring ties with social groups outside the family and work-place implies that prospective converts have very little social support for their own ideas or for any resistance that they may wish to present to the arguments and blandishments of evangelists. Social isolation may also have the direct consequence of heightening the pleasure to be derived from the opportunity of having regular home visits from Publishers who appear to be genuinely concerned for one's personal welfare.

A further condition predisposing people to respond favourably to the evangelistic message of Publishers is the necessity facing parents to answer their children's ethical and religious questions. Those whose own child-hood was spent in a conventional Christian home environment are particularly prone to feelings of despair at being unable to give unambiguous answers to their children's ethical questions. They feel that their own unquestioned, nominally Christian values and standards have been stranded by rapid changes in public values and that they are no longer confident of the superiority of their own views.

The finding that couples with young children were especially responsive to evangelism accords with the fact that, excluding Jehovah's witnesses 'born into' the sect, the majority of our adult respondents had experienced conversion when they were in their thirties or forties. There is therefore no parallel of the pattern of adolescent conversions which characterizes entry to many mainstream Christian groups.[1] These findings support our contention that the nature of the group and of its ideology influence the mode of conversion to it, and that the Watch Tower movement, in particular, elicits a very unusual type of conversion.

People who have Jehovah's witnesses amongst their close kin are also more likely to respond favourably towards Watch Tower evangelists than are those who have no personal contacts with the sect. Unexpectedly, only a handful of respondents had been recruited by *friends* who were already in the sect, whereas Lofland, in contrast, reports that conversion to the Divine Precepts cult in California 'frequently moved through pre-existing friendship pairs or nets'. (Lofland, 1966, p. 53) This may be a reflection of the typical Jehovah's witness convert's lack of integration into social groups that might have afforded friendships. An additional consideration would be that Watch Tower converts cannot be described as 'religious seekers', whereas Divine Precepts members fit this description admirably.

Doubtless the list of facilitating conditions could be greatly extended, but we have covered the most prevalent factors found amongst our sample of Jehovah's witnesses. It remains to be said that it should not be assumed that any particular combination of factors is considered necessary or sufficient for the predisposition to crystallize into a positive desire to discover more about the Watch Tower movement. In fact, we wish to stress that the predisposing process is both complex and variable and, although there may be an additive relation between *some* factors, it is impossible in the present state of knowledge to specify more precisely the way in which they are interrelated.

(2) *States of suggestibility*

The suggestible states of mind that seemed to be facilitated by the foregoing list of predisposing factors can be briefly summarized under two headings: general anxiety and monistic view of truth. In the first case, anxiety typically arose for a variety of reasons from the perception that there was a serious discrepancy between deeply entrenched personal values and the values that seemed to inform the thoughts and actions of the majority of the British people. The discrepancy was only rarely painful enough to entail demoralization, but more commonly it led to a state of latent suggestibility to any ideology that might have offered to explain, and thereby to explain away, the anxiety. Given the strength of their Christian background, it is not surprising that our respondents should have eventually responded to a *religious* ideology. But no generalizations can be offered on the relation between type of anxiety and type of ideological relief until adequate control groups can be examined.

Under the second heading we would include all the variegated evidence indicating that factors in the respondents' social background and life experience had inculcated the basic notion that absolute, unitary truth was in principle accessible to mankind. Another facet of this outlook was the view that everything in the world had once been perfect and could theoretically be restored to its pristine perfection. The readiness to accept a comprehensive and unambiguous ideology claiming to represent all truth and perfection is in part at least fostered by the above set of predispositions and their associated states of suggestibility.

(3) *Critical events*

To reiterate a constant theme of this study, the transition from states of latent suggestibility to a favourable response to Watch Tower evangelism is by no means automatic: the mediation of critical factors is crucial for the transition. For unless the critical events are taken into account, there can be no way of explaining the distinction, within the population subject to the same facilitating conditions and experiencing the same stages of suggestibility, between those who accept and those who reject the Watch Tower ideology. In no sense, of course, do the critical events constitute sufficient cause for favourable attitudes towards the message of Jehovah's witnesses—at most, they amount to a set of necessary conditions for activating the long process of conversion and induction.

The 'door step sermon' is by far the most frequent critical event in precipitating conversion. Its importance is reflected in the fact that (a) 'religious seekers' do not predominate among Jehovah's witnesses, and (b) women outnumber men among initial contacts. There can be no doubt that the number of conversions would be substantially lower if methodical house-to-house evangelism were not employed by the Witnesses.

'Incidental witnessing' is the term used by the Witnesses to describe the type of critical event in which proselytism is not necessarily the Publisher's primary concern but which unexpectedly provides an opportunity for it. Chance encounters on public transport, in restaurants and transient social groupings or disembodied communication through the medium of literature left in public places constitute the commonest forms of incidental witnessing. In all cases the event can be considered as critical if it focuses the potential convert's ideas around the central notions of Watch Tower ideology and suggests modes of thought and action that would not otherwise have been adopted.

(4) *Affiliation and induction*

In faithfulness to the methodical ethos of the Watch Tower movement at all times in its history, the process whereby newcomers begin to learn of Watch Tower doctrines, values and practices usually follows a standard pattern and is subject to the supervision of several sect members. In fact, the Society publishes detailed instructions on the precise time-tabling of events in the overall process of inducting people into the Watch Tower faith and fellowship. It is important to stress in this regard that the analytically separable processes of learning and integration into a community of believers are in practice closely intertwined: at all stages of the conversion process learning takes place largely in social groups or in interaction with at least one other Witness. Thus, although neophytes undoubtedly spend a lot of time reading the Society's literature in private, their reading is always oriented towards subsequent group discussion and testing.

While there are no formal rules preventing neophytes from attending all congregation meetings, it is the practice of Publishers to invite them to meetings only when it has become clear that their attitude towards the Society is serious and that they have acquired sufficient knowledge of Watch Tower doctrines to benefit from group discussions. The situation changes markedly, however, when the neophyte decides to join the Theocratic Ministry School, for this is interpreted as a sign of intent to express personal commitment to Watch Tower doctrines in public argument. Accepting the first assignment to prepare a demonstration talk or an evangelistic episode functions as a disguised testimony of faith and usually represents the conclusion of the initial stage of integration into a local congregation. Indeed, one of the sociological peculiarities about this particular religious movement is that faith in doctrines and ideological positions cannot constitute 'being a Jehovah's witness' if it is not expressed in participation and involvement in the practical activities of the social group of believers.

Service-work usually begins in the form of accompanying an experienced Publisher in door-to-door canvassing and occasionally reading aloud passages of Scripture to support the argument of his sermon. But it may be a long time before the neophyte undertakes to deliver short sermons personally. At this stage of the conversion process outsiders might notice that the neophyte has already severed connections with people and activities that threaten the singlemindedness of devotion to the Watch Tower cause, but no formal ceremony necessarily marks assimilation to the group of co-religionists. In fact, baptism by total immersion, although obligatory at some stage for all Witnesses, takes place at a time determined largely by temporal and geographical proximity to a major assembly at which multiple baptisms are planned.

Just as it is impossible to talk of the 'act' of conversion to the Watch Tower movement, so the formal procedure for gaining fellowship lacks clarity and finality. In theory the Presiding Minister of each congregation examines the suitability of all aspirants to full membership by administering a short oral test of their doctrinal knowledge and personal qualities. In practice, however, the test is rarely administered until the Presiding Minister is confident that the candidate will pass, and it is certainly easy for candidates to discover in advance what sort of questions will be asked. Thus, the purely formal admission-test is of less importance than the informal discretion exercised by congregation leaders about the timing of the event, for it is they who decide when the test shall be taken. Similarly, applications for baptism are carefully vetted by local leaders and may be subject to lengthy delay if it is felt that a longer test of commitment is required before 'dedication to Jehovah God' should be publicly signified. In particular, of course, evidence is required of submissiveness to organizational imperatives and of exclusive canalization of social life along the congregation's approved channels.

It is for these reasons that affiliation to the Watch Tower movement must be considered as a process determined by, and controlled according to, the deliberate policies of Jehovah's witness personnel. The only freedom of manoeuvre allowed to the convert is the choice of whether or not to conform with the conventions: there is very little possibility of conducting the process according to personal preferences. This represents a variation on one of the most widely accepted defining characteristics of the so-called sect: to say that a *sign* of special merit is required of all aspiring members is only half of the matter. More important in the case of the Watch Tower movement (and probably of other sects as well) is the group's power to determine, almost arbitrarily, the form that the *test* of merit will assume. In this way the group retains very close control over its new members and ensures that they are admitted on its terms—not on theirs.

(5) *Retention*

The 'directed' nature of conversion and affiliation to the Watch Tower movement has extremely far-reaching implications for the subsequent 'career' of Jehovah's witnesses, for conversion produces cognitive, conative and normative consequences. What is more, interrelations between the various consequences help to produce an overall coherence in the converts' mode of thought and behaviour so that a complete transformation of outlook and action patterns becomes the hall-mark of the converted Jehovah's witness. Stability in the convert's relations with the Watch Tower movement is correspondingly conditional upon continuing subscription to expected beliefs and uninterrupted participation in service-work. This was repeatedly borne out in the statements of congregation officials that an individual's service-work record is the best indicator of his intellectual satisfaction with Watch Tower doctrines and practices.

The chances of long-term membership are also improved if the individual obtains 'promotion' to posts of responsibility in the local congregation, since there are relations of mutual reinforcement between commitment to Watch Tower ideas and integration into the sect's network of social relations. Our findings showed that responsibility was commonly awarded to men who had given proof of about two years' unalloyed dedication to the Society's programmes. The rate of defection by men in responsible positions is extremely low and may be at least partly attributable to the increased personal involvement in the mesh of congregational relationships that follows from the performance of a Servant's tasks.

Even if defection does occur, however, the Jehovah's witness's career does not necessarily come to an abrupt conclusion. Rather, as we pointed out in Chapter 4, many defectors pass initially into a stage of peripheral membership in which their links with a congregation are activated only at times of special religious significance. At all other times they may remain loosely connected with the sect through the intermediary of a practising Witness among their relatives or friends. In fact, given the extensive network of familial and friendship relations among British Witnesses it would be surprising if inactive members were able to make a completely clean break from the group. For unless the individual has been officially sentenced to disfellowshipment, former associates are under an obligation to try to secure a return to active fellowship. In our experience the period of peripheral attachment to a congregation can last for many years, and it is far from unusual for some Jehovah's witnesses to move in and out of full fellowship with some frequency. But in nearly all cases of both temporary and permanent disaffection, ex-Witnesses do not abandon their basic assent to the movement's values and general ideological outlook.

In this respect, we are justified in extending our consideration of a career in the sect beyond the point when active participation in congregational life comes to an end. Although it is impossible even to estimate the size of the peripheral membership and although our own data on defectors are slight, the available evidence does clearly show that Watch Tower leaders are worried about two main implications: the effect on the morale of practising Witnesses and the possible dangers that might arise from bad publicity created by 'ex-insiders'. The dilemma is basically between tolerating partial defectors in the hope of eventually restoring them to full fellowship and running the risk of alienating practising Witnesses by appearing to condone rebellious or lax behaviour. The length of a Jehovah's witness's career must therefore be judged in the context of the sect's prevailing attitude towards this dilemma.

The conditions that allegedly facilitate conversion, induction and integration are the primary focus of interest for the sociological student of Watch Tower recruitment. But an equally important, although usually neglected, subject is the set of conditions that *repel* potential converts and dissuade them from joining. The enormous size of the population that has resisted Watch Tower recruitment implies that the range of reasons for non-participation is vast and therefore sociologically intractable. It would be foolish to attempt to construct a schema of 'repelling factors' in parallel with the schema of facilitating conditions, but we do have some interesting evidence about the problems that nearly prevented a number of interviewees from remaining in fellowship. Briefly, the main 'repelling' factors included the obligation to undertake regular public evangelism, the expectation that Witnesses should always submit to the authority of local or regional officers of the Watch Tower Society and the prohibition on cultivating deep friendship ties with others. Difficulties over differences of doctrinal opinion or over the sect's ritual activities seemed to occur very rarely. We conclude, then, that doctrine gives rise to few insuperable problems but that the structural network of social relations among the Witnesses is a pregnant source of dissension and potential defection. These tentative interpretations are at least consonant with our view that the intellectual assent of converts can be relatively easily acquired: but their continuing commitment to an activist religious movement requires undisturbed social support. The 'translation' of doctrines into social forms and practices is the Achilles' heel of the Watch Tower movement.

CONVERSION IN COMPARATIVE PERSPECTIVE

It may be helpful at this juncture to examine the salient features of the process of conversion to the Watch Tower movement in the light of what has been written about religious conversion in general. First and foremost we must report the virtual absence of anything which closely resembles the phenomenon of religious conversion as it is customarily understood. Jehovah's witness converts certainly experience no sudden conviction that they have miraculously received God's grace nor that they have attained an immediate assurance of salvation. In fact, very few Witnesses can isolate a particular moment in time as a decisive turning point in their religious or spiritual development: certainly none could remember having an overwhelming religious experience. In so far as one can talk of 'conversion' to the Watch Tower movement at all, then, it is very different from the experience which is common to converts to a number of Christian fundamentalist groups and which H. Carrier (1965), borrowing from E. T. Clark (1929), has characterized as the *abrupt awakening*.

Carrier described a second type of conversion experience as an *awakening by emotional stimulation*, and, once more, it is virtually restricted to religious groups whose theological outlook posits the need for the convert to make a sudden identification with a role characterized by certitude and complete confidence in his faith. In this case, the transformation is not so much from 'sinful' to 'sinless' but rather from knowing what God expects of His faithful followers to identification with, and internalization of, the norms of that role. This type of conversion is undoubtedly closer to the pattern of Watch Tower conversions but it still differs in the apparent necessity for a decisive emotional experience.

Carrier called his final type of conversion experience the *gradual awakening*,[2] and it accommodates those people who do not have a decisive experience in spiritual terms but who assimilate themselves gradually to a religious role. For the most part these are people who were brought up in religious families and who have probably never questioned their religious views deeply. In one obvious respect the conversion of Witnesses is of this type: the transition from a state of doctrinal ignorance and indifference to a state of relative enlightenment and positive commitment to the Watch Tower Society's goals is mainly smooth and unemotional. (There are, of course, some Witnesses who allege that they resisted bitterly and vehemently all attempts to convert them to the sect's outlook, and this experience seemed common among husbands of women who had already been converted.) Very few Witnesses experience any kind of decisive moment in their conversion process, and the majority are con-

scious only of a steady increase in knowledge and of a deepening awareness of belonging, and of being obligated to the Watch Tower Society.
The progress of doctrinal knowledge is paralleled in its smoothness by a
gradual strengthening of the convert's affective ties with other members
of a local congregation and, ultimately, with all participants in the Watch
Tower movement.

On the other hand, however, Carrier's typification is suitable only for
the religious development of people who do not radically change their
denominational allegiance. It describes the 'spiritual career' characteristic
of people who are brought up in a particular religious tradition and who
simply conform throughout their lives with the expectations that are held
of them within that tradition. The contrast with Jehovah's witnesses is
therefore quite sharp: retaining only the most basic elements of their
original Christian viewpoint, they reorganize their whole cognitive structure and internalize the prescriptions of a role which rarely has any
connection with the type of role played in their previous religious tradition. Thus, although the conversion process in the Watch Tower movement is gradual and progressive, albeit far-reaching in its consequences,
Carrier's typification of conversion processes must be amended or
expanded if it is to include the case of Jehovah's witnesses.

A further sign of the distinctiveness of conversion to the Watch Tower
movement is the lack of heightened feelings of joy and love compared
with the experience reported in Starbuck's (1899) findings on adolescent
conversions in the late nineteenth century. His adolescent informants
reported feelings of unbounded joy of a non-specific kind and of altruistic
urges, but very few Witnesses mentioned experiencing comparable
emotions. For them, conversion was principally marked by the realization
that they had 'found the truth' and by the relief of their anxieties about
moral problems. Many Witnesses also reported what might be called self-
righteous feelings of gratification on learning that their long-held
suspicions had been confirmed and that their latent faith in unitary truth
and goodness had been rewarded.

The relative insignificance of the baptism ceremony among Witnesses
is further evidence that the precise experience of conversion is not
accorded great importance by them. It is a purely symbolic and outward
expression of the individual's self-dedication to Jehovah's service and does
not mark any radical change in spiritual status. It frequently takes place
long after the convert has formally begun to engage in active service-work
and certainly a long time after informal integration into the web of social
relations in a local congregation. There is in fact wide variation in the
norms: of the 180 questionnaire respondents only eight reported that their
baptism had taken place less than six months after they had begun to

follow a course of Bible studies organized by local Publishers. While forty took between seven and twelve months to decide on baptism, a further ninety-nine delayed making the decision for longer than one year. The remainder had been born into the sect. Furthermore, the actual ceremony, involving total immersion in any suitably sized pool of water, is almost devoid of emotive elements and often concerns hundreds of people in one session. Conventional bathing costumes are worn by candidates and baptizers alike, and the occasion takes place in a highly instrumental, matter-of-fact atmosphere.

One might speculate that the whole process of conversion could be accelerated if Witnesses were allowed to live in communities, but this would undoubtedly have deleterious effects on their evangelistic productivity.[3] It might reduce the tension between millennial expectations and everyday realities which contributes towards their high degree of commitment to unremitting evangelism. Given, then, the Watch Tower Society's overriding goal of maximizing recruitment and awareness of its teachings, the present arrangements are rationally efficient. It is unlikely that people experiencing any kind of 'abrupt awakening' would be as reliable and as persistent as Jehovah's witnesses in carrying out difficult evangelical tasks over long periods of time.

Finally, we have unearthed no evidence of the process that R. H. Thouless (1971, p. 106) has termed 'moral conversion' whereby a supposedly unregenerate person suddenly becomes aware of a burden of sin and guilt. Since Watch Tower converts usually adhered to a fairly conventional scale of Christian values before conversion, it is rare to hear Witnesses rejoicing in the contrast between their pre-conversion immorality and their post-conversion righteousness. The only contrasts that occur regularly in their autobiographical statements are between error and truth or light and darkness. But these are basically cognitive, as opposed to emotional-evaluative contrasts, and the difference is a further reflection of the unusually sober and matter-of-fact character of so many aspects of the Watch Tower movement.

Rather than accept the view that the similarities are only coincidentally interrelated, we wish to argue that the aims, structure and values of this religious movement exert a strong influence on the type of conversion process experienced by its recruits. It follows that conversion to the Watch Tower faith entails first and foremost an acceptance of the Watch Tower Society's claims to represent Jehovah's earthly organization and a readiness to submit to its authoritative commands. Until or unless potential converts agree to acknowledge the Society's right to exercise authority in Jehovah's name, their Bible studies and devotions are of no significance. Only when converts willingly obey orders emanating from the Society's leaders, can one say that the conversion process has been successful. This frequently occurs long before individual converts have fully familiarized themselves with the movement's ideology and is, in this respect, a more important element of conversion than changes in religious ideas and feelings. Thus, in so far as there is a critical point in the conversion process, it centres around the acceptance or the rejection of the claims to authority made by the Society's officers at all levels of the hierarchy.

Until about 1945 one might have described the feeling of some Jehovah's witnesses that they were chosen members of the flock of '144,000 faithful witnesses of Jehovah' who would enjoy an existence in heaven during the millennium as a kind of Entire Sanctification experience. In all probability the experience occurred after the initial conversion and was felt to be an additional deepening of spirituality and commitment. Yet there are signs that the parallels with Entire Sanctification go no further: the experience lacked emotional intensity and was not regarded as a normal spiritual development to which all Jehovah's witnesses should aspire. Furthermore, the incidence of such experiences has clearly been a function of both the internal and external situations of the Watch Tower movement at different periods in its history and cannot therefore be considered as a regular stage in the conversion process.

INTERNAL RECRUITMENT

This chapter has so far considered exclusively the recruitment process of people whose parents had not introduced them into the Watch Tower movement during childhood. But, as we showed in Chapter 8, 44 per cent of our sample of British Jehovah's witnesses had made their first contact with the sect through a member of the family. What is more, we were able to demonstrate that a pervasive and extensive network of kinship relations among Jehovah's witnesses reinforces the ideological pressures to conform and thereby binds the majority of them to the Watch Tower movement more closely. We would expect, therefore, that Jehovah's witness parents were more than usually successful in ensuring that their children were indoctrinated with Watch Tower teachings and were drawn into a lasting commitment to the movement's aims and values. Our findings on the number of respondents' children over sixteen years of age who were still in fellowship at the time of our inquiries are summarized in Table 15.

Since most of the interviewees who fell into this category had never known any alternative religious outlook in childhood, one can hardly talk of their 'conversion'. Rather, they reported that they 'had always been Jehovah's witnesses' or had 'become Jehovah's witnesses automatically', although a very small number did admit passing through a stage of doubt about the value of the Watch Tower Society as their exclusive religious mentor. These doubts commonly occurred in adolescence and concerned questions of self-identity and purpose rather than positive disbelief in Watch Tower teachings.

TABLE 15

The number of Jehovah's witnesses' children remaining in the Watch Tower movement

	Male	Female	Both sexes combined
Retained in membership	54	50	104
Not retained in membership	37	25	62
Under sixteen			127
		Total number of children	293

Unremitting isolation and insulation of Jehovah's witnesses' children against the allegedly undermining influence of the wider British culture are responsible for the Watch Tower Society's relative success in retaining successive generations of its members' families. The supportive structure of a tight-knit nuclear family and a cohesive extended family (frequently intertwined with a local congregation) help to reduce still further the probability that children of Witnesses would permanently withdraw from fellowship. Finally, the congregation Elders deliberately and methodically try to prevent the children in their congregation from severing contact with the movement and urge them strenuously to restrict their friendship relations to fellow-members of the faith. These findings are not, of course at odds with H. R. Niebuhr's assertions about the problematic consequences for a religious sect of retaining its members' children, since in the case of the Watch Tower movement, its beliefs and practices have never been marked by spontaneity or by effervescence. It is not therefore vulnerable to the allegedly common problem of declining religious vitality among succeeding generations of internal recruits.

In conclusion, we must repeat that it is essential to understand conversion as a process or career and to acknowledge the important role of extra-personal factors in the individual's experience of conversion. In other words, conversion has at least as much to do with the social and ideological structure of the 'host' religious group as it does with the individuals who undergo it. This is true of conversion to all such groups, but it is probably more noticeable in the case of Jehovah's witnesses because their conversion experiences reflect very faithfully the group's primary orientation towards the intellectual and consequential dimensions of religiosity at the expense of the experiential and ritual aspects. To appreciate the full implications of this characteristic, it is now necessary to examine the movement's ideology. This will further our understanding of the way in which its goals and values are articulated for the purpose of attracting new members and retaining practising ones.

NOTES TO CHAPTER 9

1. Research has shown (a) that the modal age of conversion is about fifteen years and (b) that conversion in the late twenties and early thirties is rare. See Argyle (1958).

2. This pattern was also found to characterize conversion of adolescents in a mature Swedish sect. See Zetterberg (1952).

3. This is borne out by the findings of a recent sociological study of three utopian religious communities: the Shakers, the Oneida Community and the Brüderhof. (Whitworth, 1971) Although the founders and leaders of each community intended evangelism to be a primary goal, in fact it merely alternated for primacy with periods of introversionism. Intense community life and evangelism seemed to be almost mutually exclusive.

CHAPTER 10

IDEOLOGY

We have deliberately chosen to supplement the earlier description of Watch Tower teachings with a separate account of ideology because the latter term refers in the broadest possible sense to the whole set of ideas promoted in the movement's propaganda. The Society's ideologists disseminate information not only about such theological notions as the nature of God and of His purpose but also about the allegedly appropriate ideas, attitudes, values and behaviour of those who believe in its theological teachings. Our use of 'ideology' therefore implies that the Society's leaders strive to defend its most general interests as a religious collectivity and to create the grounds for the legitimacy of its claims to authority.

Although, as was argued in Chapter 5, the vast majority of British Jehovah's witnesses accept and internalize the Watch Tower Society's ideology, it is at least analytically desirable to maintain a distinction between the group's ideology and the individual's *Weltanschauung*. That is to say, the patterns of meaning that Jehovah's witnesses read into their lives and their most fundamental perspectives on the world do not *necessarily* coincide with what the Watch Tower Society would like to inculcate in its members' minds. Clearly, their *Weltanschauungen* are grounded in the movement's ideology which is unquestionably geared towards altering their states of consciousness in determinate ways, but our findings have shown that there is not always a one-to-one relation between ideology and *Weltanschauung*.

IDEOLOGICAL STRUCTURE AND IMPLICATIONS

Without repeating many of the Watch Tower Society's doctrinal teachings that were described in Chapter 5, our intention is now to describe the principal features of its ideology and to analyse the formal structure of interrelations between its constituent elements. We shall arrange the features under the following headings: historicism, absolutism, activism, rationalism, authoritarianism and extremism. The reflection of the ideology in the typical Jehovah's witness's *Weltanschauung* and its implications for attitudinal and behaviour patterns will also be traced in some detail.

(a) *Historicism*[1]

First and foremost the Watch Tower ideology can be characterized as an *historicist* belief-system. By that, we mean that it purports to lay bare the 'rythms', 'patterns', and 'laws' of history as if they constituted an autonomous dynamic, or at least, an outworking of God's design for the world's development. This is reflected in the Society's consuming interest in both the remote past and the distant future. It is a common feature of groups having dogmatic ideologies, and Milton Rokeach (1960) has tried to account for it in terms of the unwillingness of people with relatively 'closed' minds to treat their everyday experiences on their own merits or at face value. Rather, he argued, in the interest of preserving the integrity of their dogmatic beliefs, such people focus their attention on remote events in order to avoid stretching the explanatory potential of their beliefs beyond their capacity. The more remote the event, the greater are the chances of finding confirmation of one's expectations and, thereby, validation of one's entire outlook.

An allied feature of the ideology's historicism is its in-built resistance to the possibility that its understanding of God's plan could be proved wrong in any respects. In fact, the ramifications of the plan are so all-embracing that 'apparent' disconfirmations are catered for by the provision that Satan will (necessarily, one must assume) attempt to deceive people into believing that the plan is fallible. Consequently, evidence that the plan is not being implemented paradoxically constitutes evidence in support of its operation. The literature and public discourses of the Watch Tower Society do not observe the normal canons of scientific method insofar as confirmatory evidence is the only permissible evidence. No search for disconfirming evidence is undertaken, and no limitations are placed on the scope of the plan's applicability.

One might almost suggest that every mature Witness has an *obligation* to analyse the functional significance of all kinds of events because their proselytizing depends so largely on techniques for making credible their own interpretations of human history. Indeed, if a believer finds it impossible to understand a particular event or phenomenon in terms of God's plan, it is counted as an indication of spiritual immaturity. In this way, the historicist character of Watch Tower ideology not only offers the believer a conveniently packaged, inclusive and allegedly incontrovertible key to history but it also imposes obligations and constraints on his thinking and behaviour which can only be obeyed by conformity with the Watch Tower Society's injunctions.

The division of human history into a specific number of discrete periods or dispensations is a common feature of fundamentalist religious ideologies and of some dogmatic political philosophies. We need only add to our discussion of biblical chronologies in Chapter 5 (pp. 117–18 below) that the ideologists have used such periodizations in order to support the Society's claims to represent the essence of a long tradition of witnessing for God. This helps to render human history manageable and *ipso facto* more real to the proselyte because it can be readily accommodated within the terms of reference of an apparently objective explanation of historical trends.

Evangelism is further facilitated by the fact that Watch Tower ideology incorporates a conspiracy theory of history according to which the forces of good and the forces of Satan have, since time immemorial, been locked in a bitter struggle for hegemony over the earth. The Witnesses teach that God has been steadily gaining the upper-hand since 1914 and that His final victory at the impending Battle of Armageddon will signify Satan's containment for a thousand years. Conspiracy theories of this kind have proven valuable in persuading many people to support a wide variety of extremist social movements,[2] and the Watch Tower version has undoubtedly helped to swell the ranks of Watch Tower recruits. But in this particular case, it has the further consequence of legitimating the Watch Tower movement's extreme exclusivism and disdain for other human organizations. For at the individual believers' level this historicist characteristic encourages them to focus on a readily identifiable cause of suffering in the world. The conspiracy theory functions as a convenient theodicy through its simplicity and its comprehensiveness, thereby instilling in its 'practitioners' considerable confidence in their ability to diagnose the world's problems, anticipate the future and act accordingly.

A further boost for Jehovah's witnesses' confidence stems from the fact that the historicism of Watch Tower ideology encourages them to take a holistic view of the past, present and future. They analyse the world in terms of extremely large, ill-defined groups and categories at the highest levels of abstraction and in such a sweeping fashion that adequate testing of their analyses is quite impracticable. For them, the 'really' crucial forces in human affairs are such entities as societies, lineages, ethnic groups or even mankind itself; the niggling details of events or arguments which might threaten the neatness and persuasive thrust of their analyses are merely brushed aside in the conviction that it is only the broad patterns and the widest view that are important.[3]

Ideological holism commonly attributes blame for social problems to highly abstract elements of the social structure. (See Portes, 1971) In the case of groups like the Watch Tower movement it can imply that responsibility for widespread frustrations in a society is imputed to agencies and forces which, by definition, are unable or unwilling to remedy them. This results in a form of fatalism which may or may not be pessimistic. What is sociologically important is that it is not enough to understand the proclivity towards either political or religious radicalism as simply an emotional reaction against material or symbolic frustrations. The holistic character of the Watch Tower ideology is a major determinant of the Witnesses' fatalism.

(b) *Absolutism*

'Absolutism' is the term that we have chosen to refer to the constellation of ideological characteristics whose combined effect is to strengthen the Witnesses' conviction that the Watch Tower Society dispenses absolute truth and to harden their resistance to the competing counter-claims of other ideological positions. On the strength of the belief that Adam forfeited man's ability to know anything with absolute certainty and was thereby consigned to the frustrations of relative truth, Watch Tower ideology argues consistently that there can be no logical mediation between these two orders of truth. Absolutism slides over into exclusivism with the argument that God works through one exclusive agency on earth in progressively revealing glimpses of absolute truth and that this agency provides the only channel to truth and salvation. The sharp opposition between allegedly absolute and relative truth which pervades all aspects of Watch Tower ideology induces Jehovah's witnesses on the one hand to adopt an uncompromising refusal to have any dealings with non-Watch Tower ideas and, on the other, to minimize social contact with non-Watch Tower groups.

One of the major implications of ideological absolutism is that the Society, to which the Witnesses are taught to owe exclusive loyalty, is able to prescribe detailed moral regulations for them. Authors of the Society's 'improving' literature reason that, since they alone have the privileged benefit of God's direct guidance and since truth or goodness is an absolute property, there can be only one true and good course of action in any situation, and they alone can know what it is. In return the belief that absolute truth does exist and can be made available to mankind (via the Watch Tower Society's interpretation of the Bible) heightens the obligation that the Witnesses feel towards the Society and renders them more obedient than are the followers of most other religious groups. In this sense, one can talk of the 'coherence' that is felt by Witnesses to pervade their *Weltanschauung* because it seems to them to be not only internally consistent as a set of beliefs but also generally valid as a way of understanding the world.

(c) *Activism*

A further characteristic of Watch Tower ideology is its activism, i.e. its capacity to stir people into action along predetermined channels and to keep certain practical tasks always in its followers' minds. This is partly achieved, as was emphasized in Chapter 4, through the rigid orientation of the whole movement towards a strictly limited number of evangelistic tasks. The provision of objective criteria for measuring achievements helps to focus interest on them, and the skilful publicization of statistical records is useful in legitimating individual and collective targets. Yet this is only the more visible side of the matter; the movement's ideology also promotes activism by teaching, in effect, that it is one of the prerequisites of salvation.

It may seem surprising that an ideology based on deterministic millennialism could stimulate activism, and indeed this was definitely not the intention, nor perhaps the original dream of the movement's founder. But at the time when Rutherford was trying to weld the Bible Students together into an efficient, unitary body of separatist evangelists, the criterion of moral integrity lost priority to the measurable criterion of the amount of time and effort expended in active service-work. It was no coincidence, therefore, that Watch Tower ideologists began stressing the necessity to be energetic in evangelism at the same time as they were suppressing the vestiges of 'character development' among the descendants of Russell's Bible Student movement.

More obviously, Watch Tower ideology conduces towards activism through the teaching that Armageddon is imminent and that contemporary events constitute 'signs of the times' that 'the end of this present wicked system of things' is close. This sort of theme has proved a valuable catalyst in precipitating commitment to all millenarian movements, but its relevance for Bible Students and Jehovah's witnesses has been occasionally boosted by official predictions of prophetically significant dates. Thus, the level of millenarian expectations has usually been high among people subject to the influence of Watch Tower ideology, and, coupled with the movement's equation of salvation with activism, it intensifies the sense of urgency with which most Witnesses tackle their evangelistic tasks. By contrast, the schismatic groups of Bible Students that seceded during, or shortly after, the Watch Tower movement's quietist phase have persisted in a more fatalistic or resignatory outlook than have the heirs of Rutherford's reforms. This is a result of, *inter alia*, their refusal to equate salvation with activism. Comparison with other millenarians (e.g. the Christadelphians, Shakers, Mormons) points up the Watch Tower movement's distinctively activist orientation and its consequent ability to maintain high rates of membership-growth without compromising its commitment to millenarian doctrines.

The apparently paradoxical relation between deterministic millennialism and evangelistic activism can also be explained in terms of the particular *kind* of millennialism which the Watch Tower movement teaches. Yonina Talmon (1966) would probably include it under the heading 'post-millennialism' because it teaches that Christ's second coming has already taken place (albeit invisibly). The temporal separation of this event from either the Battle of Armageddon and/or the instigation of the millennium on earth, according to Talmon, encourages a 'gradualist' view of history and a relatively optimistic conception of the future. For the intervening period allows time for evangelism or, in the case of utopian millenarians, the gradual moral perfection of individuals. There is certainly more than a hint of this gradualism in Watch Tower teachings about the establishment of the Kingdom of God on earth—not so much (as one might expect from millenarians) as an *event* but more as a *process* for which Jehovah's witnesses are partly responsible—and it clearly legitimates the movement's unswerving orientation towards evangelism.

(d) *Rationalism*

'Rationalistic' is the most suitable term for describing a further aspect of Watch Tower ideology which produces distinctive effects on the behaviour and outlook of British Witnesses. We understand by 'rationalistic' (a) insisting on the necessary compatibility between beliefs and the canons of human reason, and (b) deliberately excluding the influence of non-rational factors on religious belief and practice. It is immaterial in the present context whether Watch Tower ideology does in fact satisfy these criteria of rationalism: what is of paramount importance is that Jehovah's witnesses consciously place a high evaluation on things that are rationalistic in these terms. The term 'rationalistic'[4] has the advantage of implying that *claims* to compatibility of their beliefs with reason are important for Jehovah's witnesses in respect of both their own *Weltanschauung* and of the propaganda that they disseminate.

We might even describe the movement's dominant 'cultural style' as rationalistic insofar as it deprecates mystery and affect while explicitly lauding certainty and reason. In this respect it clearly differs in cultural style from the majority of Christian, and particularly Adventist, groups. The Watch Tower conception of Jehovah, for example, is an unemotional amalgam of all principles of truth, reason and goodness. Similarly, the idea of death holds no mystery for them: it means simply a period of total unconsciousness terminating in the process of resurrection.

Nothing could therefore be less compatible with Watch Tower doctrines than the notions of a *deus absconditus* or of 'mysteries of the faith', because they imply that man cannot attain truth through the exercise of his reasoning faculties alone. Thus, *The Watchtower*, 1 February 1962:

> Those who desire to use their reasoning ability will find that God has provided evidence plentifully to aid the reasoner to establish (1) that God exists and (2) that his primary attributes are love, justice, wisdom and power . . . Right reasoning establishes faith.

The dispassionate character of its basic doctrines is echoed in the movement's ideology and organization, but our present interest is in the important consequences that it has for the *Weltanschauung* of individual Jeehovah's witnesses.

The centrality to Watch Tower ideology of the view that truth is unitary and absolute is essential for legitimating the Society's exclusive claims to authority over the Witnesses, and it is supported by the teaching that the alleged logicality of its doctrines and social arrangements is proof of its divine mandate. Its exposition of doctrines aspires towards so-called logicality in two ways. On the one hand, as outlined in Chapter 5, reason and logic are said to be the principal hall-marks of God's work and only teachings and social arrangements that display them should be considered 'true'. On the other hand, Watch Tower theology tends to be systematic in the sense that it can be expounded from a small number of basic assumptions which 'tie in with' pieces of Scriptural evidence to form what Jehovah's witnesses acknowledge as a self-contained, coherent system. Common to both arguments is the unusually high degree of *conscious* insistence by its followers on the so-called logicality of the Society's teachings.

The ideological argument states that, since absolute truth is unitary and exclusive of all relativisation, there can only 'logically' be one human organization to represent it.[5] Consequently, all other religious organizations are in error and are to be strictly avoided. The absolutist view of truth further implies that, since anything less than absolute truth can only corrupt and destroy it, there can be no justification for Jehovah's witnesses having any kind of association with other religionists—however sincere the motivation might be. The argument goes on to justify the highly organized, rational character of the Watch Tower movement in terms of its necessary affinity with the character of Jehovah. Finally, it can be worked into a justification for the intensely methodical and ruthless way of organizing evangelism on the grounds that rationality demands efficiency.

The principal reflection of the rationalistic character of Watch Tower ideology in the attitudes and behaviour of Jehovah's witnesses is the unemotional and didactic atmosphere of their meetings. Meetings consist predominantly of sober, matter-of-fact discussion of the Society's interpretation of biblical truth, and only a very small amount of time is spent on singing and prayer. Even these two devotions are practised in the most unemotional and perfunctory fashion. David Martin, for example, aptly describes the Witnesses as 'full of religious zeal but devoid of religious emotion'. (Martin, 1965, p. 188) Thus, the devotional and experiential dimensions of personal religiosity are under-developed among the Witnesses compared with the doctrinal, ethical and consequential dimensions. Even the Witnesses' prayers rarely amount to more than an offer of thanks for special benefits, and affirmation of dedication to Jehovah and a request for the necessary strength of will to remain dedicated. The language of their prayers, as of other types of liturgical symbolism, is uniformly down-to-earth and lacking in colourful or archaic embellishment. They entertain no hopes of a mystical experience of union with their deity nor do they expect to feel possessed by beneficent spiritual forces.

In brief, the major organizational implications and functional correlates of the Watch Tower movement's rationalistic ideology are: reduction of the likelihood of perfectionism, a more stable source of legitimation for the leaders' authority, a strong argument in favour of the necessity for individual Witnesses to remain in fellowship with the Watch Tower Society and a reinforcement of the view that evangelistic work is a condition of survival through Armageddon. The combined effect is to heighten the believers' dependence on the Watch Tower movement for the satisfaction of religious wants and to place narrow constraints on their *Weltanschauung*. Not surprisingly, as we showed in Chapter 4, the heavy emphasis on purely intellectual and evangelical components has a limiting effect on the warmth of social relations between Jehovah's witnesses in congregations and is partly responsible for a number of defections from the movement.

Incidentally, these remarks on the very limited emotionality of Watch Tower life, raise a general point about the alleged cultural appropriateness of such a form of religion for specific social classes. Unfortunately, Max

Weber's authoritative statement that, '. . . it is far easier for emotional rather than rational elements of a religious ethic to flourish' among 'the proletaroid or permanently impoverished lower-middle class groups who are in constant danger of sinking into the proletarian class' (Weber, 1965, p. 101) has been frequently misconstrued to mean that rationalistic religion is *exclusively* appropriate for non-proletaroid groups. Our findings have in fact shown that the extremely rationalistic aspects of Watch Tower religion do not deter working-class people from joining the movement.[6]

(e) *Authoritarianism*

Authoritarianism is as characteristic of Watch Tower ideology as is rationalism, but the combination of these two characteristics is not common among religious groups. The Society is principally authoritarian in denying *a priori* the legitimacy of all criticisms of itself and of refusing to institutionalize the means whereby internal criticism, or at least discussion, of its pronouncements could take place.

The individual Witness's *Weltanschauung* reflects ideological authoritarianism in *dogmatism*, i.e. the readiness to posit and to propagate doctrines without necessarily having completely adequate proof of their validity. In this sense, the whole corpus of Watch Tower doctrines is dogmatic because it is a rigidly structured set of assumptions and propositions that do not admit freely of change or reinterpretation. At the believers' level this has the consequence that most Jehovah's witnesses are not prepared even to entertain the possibility that their basic doctrinal assumptions could be revised in any way.

A further aspect of dogmatism is reflected in the extent to which the Witnesses conceive of their beliefs as a self-contained system that is 'closed' to criticism or influence from outside the Watch Tower Society's elite. In this way they insulate themselves against the potentially disturbing effects of everyday experience and of explicit anti-Watch Tower criticism on their faith. This, in turn, leads them to learn a number of specific disbeliefs (see Rokeach, 1960, chap. 2) which they associate with people out of sympathy with the Watch Tower outlook. Holding firm disbeliefs reinforces their tendency to assert positive beliefs with dogmatic rigidity.

As we tried to argue in Chapter 5 and earlier in this chapter, the authoritarianism of the ideology has its source partly in the nature of some basic Watch Tower doctrines. The perceived character of Jehovah, the historicist view of historical dynamics, the insistence on absolute truth, the prevalence of black and white ethical principles and the exclusivist intolerance of alternative outlooks could all be characterized as inherently authoritarian. But this argument is stronger if it is emphasized that ideological authoritarianism derives much of its force from the authority structure of the whole Watch Tower movement. The most fruitful way of analysing the situation then, is in terms of a symbiotic relation between ideology and social structure which produces appreciable effects on the *Weltanschauung* of individual Jehovah's witnesses. One of these effects is the high value placed upon what we shall call the paternalism pervading the social relations between them.

One of the most basic rules for the Witnesses holds that, *ceteris paribus*, females must defer to males and that a male should always fulfil the functions of head of the household. Legitimation for this paternalistic rule is claimed on the grounds that it mirrors the correct relationship between Jehovah and His creatures and echoes some Old Testament statements about the allegedly hereditary instability and defects of the feminine character. Since the 1890s Watch Tower leaders have consistently imposed stringent controls on the scope of women's functions within the movement's official structure of roles and offices, and present-day 'sisters' are only allowed to officiate in congregation meetings in the absence of suitably qualified men. Even when this condition is met, women must still wear a head-covering as a mark of respect for the men present. In the home wives are taught to be subservient to their husbands in all situations, and, surprisingly perhaps, this rule is held to apply in cases where the husband is not a practising Jehovah's witness. The logic of the rule demands that children also must submit to parental authority, and our observations of the Witnesses in their homes as well as in public have generally confirmed that their children are outstandingly obedient.

In general we observed that the hierarchy of authority relations within each congregation was respected by the Witnesses and did not appear to give rise to resentment or friction. Even more clearly apparent was the deference shown by congregation members towards visiting officers of the Watch Tower Society's regional or national organization; their commands, however critical of local conditions, were respectfully obeyed as far as we could judge. But both the history of the Watch Tower movement and an objective analysis of the logic of the situation lead us to believe that the potential for occasional rebellion, defection or secession is contained within existing arrangements. Dogmatic, black-and-white patterns of thought are so deeply engrained in the minds of Witnesses that even relatively slight differences of opinion among them can precipitate major divisions. The rejection of toleration, compromise and relativism are positively functional for the movement's pursuit of its goals just so long as unanimity characterizes its followers' opinions. But if they come to disagree on a point of doctrine or organization, the risk of rapidly escalating conflict is greatly increased. If a collective secession occurs, the exclusivist character of Watch Tower ideology ensures that neither party will tolerate the other in any respect, and the prospects of an eventual reconciliation are very remote.

(f) *Extremism*

Although, as we have endeavoured to demonstrate, Watch Tower ideology may be usefully analysed in terms of historicism, absolutism, activism, rationalism and authoritarianism, it is probably best known to the public for yet another characteristic—its extremism. But we shall now argue that the everyday behaviour of British Jehovah's witnesses betrays no signs of violent alienation from major social institutions or processes, and that their outlook could be more accurately described in other ways.

Firstly, it must be made clear that the Witnesses in this country do not typically concern themselves with the details of Armageddon's occurrence nor do they have articulate ideas about their anticipated millennial existence. As they believe that God's plan must be fulfilled, they have little sense of working towards an end whose realization may depend upon their active participation. Joining the Watch Tower movement is not so much a commitment to promote and expedite the millennium as an expression of faith in its ineluctable occurrence. Their position resembles that of the Jewish Hasidim during the second century BC or the Essenes at a slightly later date: they combined what David Martin called 'acute symbolic aggression' with 'political pacifism'. (Martin, 1965, pp. 28–9) Unlike the Zealots, their eschatological expectations did not induce them to join the fight for Jewish national independence. Rather, they were 'inclined to see the actual fighting as only a "little help" compared with the victory which was to come from God'. (Martin, 1965, p. 28) In this respect, then, the outlook of Jehovah's witnesses differs markedly from that of most political revolutionaries, for whom 'promoting' the revolution is usually taken to be an essential condition of its success.

Their situation is more closely analogous to that of many cargo-cult followers whose fantasies, according to I. C. Jarvie, are 'entirely rational attempts, within the native framework, to explain the 'incompatibility' (Jarvie, 1970, p. 56) between their wants and the available means of satisfaction. Their situation is also superficially similar to that of utopian millenarians (see Whitworth, 1971) who believe that God's bestowal of grace on them is conditional upon their loyalty to Him and to His schemes for establishing the Kingdom of God on earth. But the further consequences of this belief are very different in the two kinds of sect. For the utopians it means that, unless they carry out God's will, the world's gradual transformation into a perfect environment will not take place. For the Jehovah's witnesses, however, it means that Armageddon will take place regardless of their efforts, but that only through co-operation with the Watch Tower movement's work can *individuals* secure their personal survival through the testing period and help others to survive as well. Becoming a Witness can therefore be partly understood as a rational calculation of personal interests.

The fact that British Witnesses make only very selective reservations about compliance with the civil law-code implies that their alleged commitment to revolutionism finds only superficial expression in their actual behaviour. Their refusal to enlist in the armed forces, to accept restrictions on their alleged rights to evangelize in public without hindrance and to control the precise type of medical treatment for themselves or for dependants virtually exhausts the list of present-day sources of friction with secular authorities. What is more, the Witnesses readily resort to litigation in defence of their principles and are thereby willing to exhibit their faith in the value of due legal process. In Britain, therefore, Jehovah's witnesses have become so mild and conventional in their criticism of the prevailing political and legal arrangements that 'world indifference' more aptly describes their outlook than 'extremist' or 'revolutionist'.

The inclination of commentators on the Watch Tower movement to use such epithets as 'revolutionist' or 'aggressive' is partly the result of a failure to distinguish between the collective and the distributive applications of the terms. While the official Watch Tower outlook remains uncompromisingly revolutionary in the sense that the sect's propaganda has never ceased affirming the imminence of a shattering destruction of all known social structures, it is open to doubt whether the British adherents to the sect are individually conscious of a commitment to precipitate that destruction. That is to say, it may be misleading to call the sect 'revolutionist' when its followers are not revolutionarily-oriented.

The difference in meaning between the collective and distributive use of the term has widespread implications for the movement's structure and dynamics, but it also helps to account for the strength of middle-class support for a millenarian movement. It is possible that individual members join the movement because they are persuaded that its interpretation of the past, the present and the future is plausible and correct; the fact that it predicts a revolutionary situation in the near future is not what convinces middle-class people of its correctness. Armageddon is simply entailed by other beliefs, but does not serve as a prominent attraction in the early stages of a neophyte's interest-arousal. The majority of British Witnesses are nothing more than 'revolutionaries in spite of themselves', and we have endeavoured to show in this chapter that their outlook is basically conservative and fully congruent with their social and material status. The combination of an officially revolutionary ideology with a membership of actually conservative members has consequences of the highest importance for many of the movement's sociological characteristics.

Our findings on the social class composition of the British Branch of the Watch Tower movement and on the paradoxically unrevolutionary commitment of the followers of this 'revolutionist' sect are in line with Frank Parkin's general characterization of the difference between middle-class and working-class radicalism. (Parkin, 1968) Parkin distinguishes between middle-class radicals who envisage far-reaching social reforms based on moral considerations and working-class radicals who envisage reforms of an economic or material kind. We have shown that the Witnesses in Britain are typically motivated to join the sect by considerations of a moral rather than a materialistic nature, and it is clear that they have no systematized beliefs about the structure of property or authority relations after Armageddon. Their behaviour, adopting Max Weber's terminology (Weber, 1964, p. 115), is more conspicuously *wertrational* than *zweckrational*, and their radicalism centres mainly around ethical, rather than materialistic, concerns. This brand of radicalism is undoubtedly appropriate to a movement which was founded largely by middle-class people and whose following has more recently been drawn from a wider range of social classes. The compensatory benefits offered by the millennial upheaval are outweighed for most British Witnesses by the satisfaction deriving from its alleged historical inevitability and its moral unambiguity.

These considerations on the relation between religious ideology and social stratification call in question the kind of automatic relation that S. M. Lipset suggests between religious (or political) extremism and the lower classes. (Lipset, 1963) Support for our argument can also be drawn from D. P. Walker's study of the eighteenth-century Philadelphians, (Walker, 1964) Gusfield's study of the American Temperance movement, (Gusfield, 1963) Shepperson's findings on nineteenth-century millennialism in Britain, (Shepperson, 1962) and, less clearly, Worsley's analysis of cargo cults. (Worsley, 1957)

There remains, of course, the objection that the Watch Tower movement warrants the designation 'extremist' by virtue of its theological doctrines, but this argument rests upon certain normative assumptions that have no justifiable bearing on a sociological study of religion. In one sense, for example, Jehovah's witnesses and Christadelphians are both extremists as far as their doctrines for the end of the world are concerned, but they differ enormously in the respective ways of putting their extremism into social practice. The former have a highly centralized and auto-cratic organization, whereas the latter have chosen a diametrically opposed form of organization. It cannot be helpful, therefore, to begin an analysis of their sociological characteristics from an assumption about their so-called extremism. Paradoxically, the same point also emerges from Talmon's (1966) discussion of the social correlates of millennial beliefs and from Martin's (1965) delineation of characteristic Christian responses towards warfare. The paradox lies in the fact that both of these authors clearly believed that it *was* sociologically useful to proceed from a logic of extremist doctrines to a typology of social responses.

THE SOCIOLOGY OF KNOWLEDGE

The development of a theoretical argument in this book has now reached a critical juncture at which it is necessary to draw together several dis-parate threads. In an attempt to locate the process of conversion to the Watch Tower movement in as comprehensive a sociological context as possible, we have reviewed the influences of a large number of distinct factors. Some have been found to exercise independent effects on the conversion-process, while others seem to have been largely irrelevant. But the pattern that has slowly emerged from the findings raises a more general problem about explanation in sociology. In particular, it calls in question a number of propositions basic to the Sociology of Knowledge, that is, the attempt to specify the relation between ideas and social struc-tures or processes. In order to steer a clear passage through the myriad complications and difficulties of this subject, we shall confine ourselves to a narrow critique of a recent study that set out to tackle it directly—G. Schwartz's *Sect Ideologies and Social Status* (1970).

The first point to establish is our disagreement with Schwartz's general view that,

> As an intervening variable, ideology specifies the meaningful con-nection between religious belief and social action. It mediates between an actor's position in the social structure and his status expectation, on the one hand, and his religious outlook, moral code and secular behaviour on the other. By conceiving of ideology in this manner, we can ask how objective social realities are translated into subjective religious experiences. In what ways do various amounts of wealth, prestige and power transform an individual's perception of his immediate social situation into a religious vision of the good and proper life? (Schwartz, 1970, p. 51)

Our major objection to the passage is that it encourages the sociologist to overlook what we have found to be the crucial factors intervening between the 'actor's position in the social structure' and 'his religious outlook'. To leave out of consideration such factors as the design of evangelism, the nature of the interaction between evangelist and audience, or the structure of the evangelistic agency's organization is to run the risk that research findings will be compressed into intuitively plausible explanations which in fact do no more than perpetuate common stereotypes and prejudices.

With special regard for the study of Jehovah's witnesses an examination of their 'wealth, prestige and power' in order to discover how these attributes are 'transformed into subjective religious experiences' would excessively narrow the scope of research and would, as it happens, be an unhelpful line of inquiry. It would overlook the often-neglected fact that the Watch Tower Society's policy and practice are to introduce its ideas into the minds of people whose 'position in the social structure' would not necessarily conduce a particular 'religious vision of the good and proper life'. The findings of Chapter 7 testified to the Society's success in mobilizing recruits from a wide range of social strata, thereby casting doubt on what Schwartz presumes to be a straightforward relation between 'objective social realities' and 'subjective religious experience'.

Another consideration that would seem to be excluded in Schwartz's programme is the variety of ways in which the Watch Tower Society has presented its message at different moments in time. During the years of the Depression, for example, its ideology was suffused with threateningly aggressive symbolism, but in recent decades, partly in response to changing internal and external circumstances, the tone of its ideology has become less raucous and more irenic. These changes have affected the type of person attracted to the Watch Tower movement and have incidentally produced a stratification of its following which reflects the ascendancy of different social strata at different times.

A still more serious objection can be levelled against Schwartz's belief that,

> Sect ideologies support and to a certain extent, create social conduct which has adaptive consequences for their adherents. More specifically, these ideologies serve as a means of formulating and dealing with status problems which are beyond immediate instrumental solutions, given the technical facilities available to the actor . . . (Schwartz, 1970, pp. 52–3)

Unless it can be specified what it is that religious ideologies are supposed to help their adherents to adapt to, the proposition is either vacuous or, more probably, tendentious in that it covertly implies that there are universally valid standards of human performance which are beneficial to those who attain them, i.e. the adapted. A further implication is that 'adaptation' is considered the normal state of human affairs and that sectarian ideologies serve the interests of normality. We reject the normative assumptions of Schwartz's argument and question the usefulness of asking whether the consequences of sect adherence are 'adaptive'. We also reject the naively rationalistic implication that the 'adapted' person would solve his 'immediate status problems' in an instrumental manner whereas the 'maladapted' needs to resort to religious means. Schwartz apparently believes that the 'normal' solutions to such problems are instrumental but that only those with 'limited economic and social means' may be obliged to adopt a different type of solution. He is clearly judging the behaviour of sectarians against his own common-sense assumptions and explaining their (to him) strange behaviour in terms of an inability to attain the standard of rationality with which he operates. In its mildest formulation our disagreement with Schwartz disputes that his generalizations from evidence about Seventh-day Adventists and Pentecostals are applicable to British Jehovah's witnesses. But there remains the stronger objection that his proposals for conceptualizing the relation between religious ideologies and social structure would have a harmful effect on any objective attempt to account for the structure and dynamics of *any* religious group. Indeed, if the present findings have a general import at all, it is the lesson that relations of theoretical symmetry between ideas and social structure cannot be presumed to hold independently of the influence of a wide range of intervening factors. The unforeseen, if not actually paradoxical, nature of the relation is more sociologically interesting than the expected and the plausible.

NOTES TO CHAPTER 10

1. Our use of 'historicism' leans heavily on the work of Sir Isaiah Berlin (1955) and Sir Karl Popper (1969).

2. Alan Westin (1964, p. 204) says of the John Birch Society, for example, 'Its image of world events and American politics is wholly conspiratorial.'

3. This is most clearly illustrated in the Watch Tower Society's bluff dismissal of the theory of evolution. See *Did Man Get Here by Evolution or by Creation?*, 1967, esp. pp. 186-7.

4. Our reasons for shunning the term 'rational' are expounded by Jarvie (1970).

5. 'There must be only one kind of worship, one religion, that is right. This is the one in harmony with the absolute truth. Since there is just the one that is true,

set against so many hundreds of others that prove to be false, it follows that those who adopt and practice the true must necessarily be in the minority.' *What Has Religion Done for Mankind?* (1951), p. 16.

6. For further evidence of working-class participation in rationalistic religious groups, see Mews (1972).

CONCLUSION

This book has been written in the conviction that scientific knowledge normally progresses through a process whereby propositions are asserted, checked, criticized and possibly reformulated in the light of fresh information. It follows that findings such as we have advanced above can never aspire to more than provisional truth. Indeed, one of the in-built presuppositions of our method of research was that subsequent studies should be able either to process our data in different ways or to suggest a completely novel way of approaching the problem. For this reason our exposition of arguments about concepts, theories and results may seem to have been unduly schematic, but final judgement on our general strategy must depend not only upon the present findings but also upon its heuristic usefulness in other contexts.

PROBLEM AREAS

Of course, scientific progress can only come about if research is focused on *problems*. Continuity in research, comparability in findings, and, ultimately, progress in knowledge are best served by clear identification of useful questions to be asked. In the interest of clarity, therefore, we shall review briefly the four major problem areas that have occupied our attention.

With regard to the Watch Tower movement at the highest level of generality, instructive questions concerned the specification of sociological factors that influenced its organizational and ideological development. Its relations with a changing intellectual (and especially theological) matrix, political conditions, economic circumstances and moral 'climate' threw some light on the main problems of why this movement developed when it did and in the way that it did. But internal factors were no less significant: the assertive control over the movement's development by competing factions within an oligarchy and the imposition of bureaucratic means of control were shown to have severely limited its range of responses to the 'external' factors. Finally, the need for identity-maintenance and for legitimation of the leaders' authority elicited responses which reflected the sociological distinctiveness of the Watch Tower movement and called in question some *idées reçues* about the dynamics of religious organizations.

A second major problem area concerned the specification of factors associated with the processes of proselytism, recruitment and socialization. A number of hypotheses were tested with a view to discovering their potential to account for the reasons why people become Jehovah's witnesses. Straightforward confirmation of the most widely diffused explanations was not forthcoming and it was necessary to turn to cognitive and social factors that emphasized the creative and positive, rather than the negative and reactive, aspects of conversion. But, above all, the problem of explaining converts' behaviour was found to be inseparable from an understanding of the recruiting group's strategies and tactics for evangelism. Approaching the Watch Tower Society as a mass-movement helped to resolve the sociological problem more plausibly than did any of the deprivation theories that were examined.

The third set of problems was associated with the Sociology of Knowledge. Our findings suggested that the relation between religious ideas and social structures was considerably more complicated than some sociologists had allowed. Starting from the view that the relation was problematic rather than self-explanatory, we found reason to understand the role of Watch Tower ideology as an important and intrusive mediator between individuals and their *Weltanschauungen*. Analysis of the ideology proved more enlightening about the sect's historical development and the social situation of its recruits than did an *ex post facto* search for the logic of congruence between so-called objective social situations and subjective outlooks. This was a further confirmation of the necessity to take into consideration the concerted policy and practices of religious organizations in 'marketing' an ideology that might cut across the expected relation between ideas and social groups.

The final problem area to which this study was oriented concerned the difficulties of conceptualization, definition and classification of religious sects. Our proposed solution was to cut through the morass of recurrent obstacles to comparative research by laying bare the explanatory assumptions and mechanisms that have been merely implicity in previous uses of the term 'sect'. The resultant delineation of theoretical traditions and derived hypotheses facilitated explicit, though imperfect, testing of the explanations for sectarian behaviour that have hitherto been obscurely encapsulated in definitions of the term.

An equally important reason for tackling this particular problem is that changes in the general situation of religious organizations, particularly since the Second World War, changes in the organizational rationales of Western secular organizations and changes in the dominant cultural symbolism of industrial societies have all contributed to the blurring of what had seemed at the beginning of the twentieth century like a fairly clear-cut distinction between two principal types of religious group— church and sect. For the findings of Chapter 4 demonstrated the fruitless-ness of treating the Watch Tower *organization* as essentially different from that of some church-like groups. A more fruitful way of approaching the sociological study of contemporary religious groups *from the specific viewpoint of their organization* is to abandon the conceptual opposition between so-called sects and so-called churches (or denominations, estab-lished sects and cults) and to analyse them all in the same terms. This has the advantage of facilitating not only comparison between religious groups but also the application of general sociological theories of organizations to them.

SECULARIZATION

At several junctures in this book there was scope for a digression about the implications of our findings on Jehovah's witnesses for questions of wider sociological significance. Although some of these issues deserve far more intensive consideration than space permits, it will be worthwhile to review them briefly because they help to situate the Watch Tower move-ment in a broader societal context. In the first instance, we shall discuss the bearing of sociological propositions about secularization on the development of this particular group.

The fact that the number of British Jehovah's witnesses continues to rise steadily is not necessarily incompatible with the view that 'religious thinking, practice and institutions' are losing 'social significance'. (B. R. Wilson, 1966, p. xiv) It may simply imply that 'real religion' is thereby breaking through the constricting bounds of ossified, institutional forms of Christianity. In other words, matters of definition and ideological *partis pris* are clearly crucial to these opposing interpretations of statistics, and it might be more helpful to consider other aspects of the question. Certainly, the numerical expansion of Watch Tower adherents is con-sistent with Bryan Wilson's prediction that only religious sects will temporarily resist the force of secularizing influences and will prosper at a time when more orthodox and larger religious groups will wither away or lose their corporate identity in ecumenical mergers. Less certain is the confirmation of what other sociologists have understood as further signs of secularization. For example, L. Shiner's (1967) view that the process of secularization may entail a shift from 'other-worldly' to 'this-worldly' orientations was not clearly reflected in our findings. The evidence on the Witnesses indicates that their orientation has always been ambiguous in this respect: their evangelistic orientation and organizational rationale are this-worldly; their doctrines are largely other-worldly; and their general outlook is world-indifferent. Whether their world-indifference is a sign of secularization or of de-secularization is again a matter of definition and ideological standpoint. But there has never been a time when the Watch Tower movement was 'engaged' in its host societies in the sense of trying to influence the direction of their political development.

If one defines 'secularization' more widely in terms of the growing differentiation or disjunction between religious and secular institutions in modern Christian societies, then the position of the Witnesses still remains ambiguous. On the one hand the development of the Watch Tower movement represents an instance of social differentiation by virtue of its doctrinaire self-sufficiency and separateness from 'outside' agencies. But on the other hand Watch Tower ideology derives much of its persuasive power precisely from its scathing criticism of the differentiation of 'true religion' from secular affairs. Furthermore, it encourages and constrains Jehovah's witnesses to integrate all aspects of their private lives around the central notion of their commitment to Jehovah's service. This could be seen as an attempt to restore the sacral unity of individual and group in opposition to the forces operating towards atomism outside the sect. But it must be emphasized that the potential for turning the Watch Tower movement into a State within a State is counteracted by its 'mass-movement' characteristics: sharp distinction and wide social distance between elite and mass; obstacles to formation of intermediate groups between mass and elite; and systematic disparagement of democratic notions. For the same reasons it is unlikely that the Watch Tower movement could ever serve as the sacralizing agent for a whole society. Thus, the Watch Tower movement both instantiates and villifies the same process.

The de-mystification or de-sacralization of the natural environment that is sometimes alleged to characterize the process of secularization elicits another ambiguous response from Watch Tower ideology. On the assumption that human and divine reason are perfectly compatible, Jehovah's witnesses teach that the world contains no 'real' mysteries but is wholly understandable in terms of the Bible's account of God's plans for the World. As in the case of 'true religion' the use of a persuasive definition is crucial for the rhetorical success of their argument. Again, the Watch Tower movement enthusiastically 'promotes' or 'sponsors' de-mystification but it also benefits in a paradoxical or parasitical fashion by recruiting many people who had been perplexed by the so-called rationality and impersonality of contemporary social life.

A less problematic approach to the study of secularization is via the allegedly concomitant process of 'pluralization'. Berger and Luckmann (1967) understand by this term a process whereby the monopoly previously exercised by one inclusive religious institution in a society gives way in the face of social-structural changes to a plurality of competing religious and ideological interest-groups. They argue that the pressure of purely economic considerations eventually obliges religious bureaucrats to form protective cartels between religious groups with a view to reducing the number of competitors and to establishing common ground rules for peaceful interrelations. They conclude that pluralism results in extensive standardization of religious 'products' and only minimal marginal differentiation between them. A second strand of the argument is that, since it is the clients who now determine the economic prosperity of a religious group in a pluralistic situation, they become the major determinants of production policy in so far as religion must be marketed to suit their personal needs.

If one suspends judgement on Berger and Luckmann's assumption that secularization ('the process by which sectors of society and culture are removed from the domination of religious institutions and symbols') (Berger, 1967, p. 107) begins with the on-set of pluralism, their theoretical interpretation of the recent history of Christian institutions in modern societies throws some interesting light on the significance of the Watch Tower movement's development. The most obvious observation is that for generations Jehovah's witnesses have been consistently and vigorously mounting a campaign of resistance against the incursions of secularization and pluralism in their opposition to all forms of ecumenism. Secondly, Watch Tower leaders have never ceased to make ideological capital out of their ruthless attacks on what they term the worldliness and political complicity of the ecumenical bureaucracies. Thirdly, the Watch Tower movement's propagandists have persistently challenged and ridiculed the marginal differentiation that characterizes the range of Christian outlooks in the Western world. Finally, the 'interiorization' of contemporary religion and the current vogue for 'peace of mind' literature (in the United States particularly) provide Jehovah's witnesses with yet another stick with which to beat what they consider to be the Satanic corruption and emasculation of Christianity.

In these various ways the Watch Tower movement has reacted *against* what Berger and Luckmann have identified as the dominant trend in modern religious phenomena. To that extent, Jehovah's witnesses may seem to have escaped from the effects of secularization. But in other respects they can be said to have instantiated the same trend in their own organization. In the first place, as we emphasized in Chapter 1, the Watch Tower movement was from its origins conceived of partly as a rational business enterprise for the production and dissemination of religious literature. The instrumental and pragmatic character of its primary goals naturally entailed a correspondingly purposive social organization, and the same underlying rationale has characterized Watch Tower organization ever since. In this sense, one could argue that the movement was secularized from its inception by virtue of its correspondence with the dominant organizational mode of the contemporary secular world. Furthermore, from the point of view of societies as wholes, the exclusiveness and separateness of Jehovah's witnesses may function as catalysts of the differentiating or pluralizing process—thereby contributing to the progress of secularization.

For reasons associated with problems of both operationalization and definition it is impossible to specify more accurately at present the significance of secularization for the Watch Tower movement or *vice versa*. It is possible and instructive, however, to consider the continuing numerical expansion of Jehovah's witnesses against the background of other contemporary changes in British religious phenomena.

NEW RELIGIOUS MOVEMENTS

Foremost among contemporary changes is the current vogue of so-called new religious movements which embody, either in isolation or in combination, such characteristics as communitarianism, Orientalism, manipulationism or moralism. Despite the bewildering variety of new religious manifestations, the provision of cognitive certainty and the arrangement of social life according to fixed principles are two of the principal 'services' offered by nearly all the new movements. A sacred canon usually functions as an authoritative source of guidance and legitimation, permitting relatively intensive study or exegesis. Recruits seem to transcend social class and status boundaries, but they are largely confined to the under-thirty age-group. High levels of public commitment and activism characterize a sizeable proportion of the membership, and many of the groups evince at least a formal interest in solving some pressing social problems. (See, for example, Robbins, 1969; Robbins and Anthony, 1972) Above all, the new movements display a form of organization which is not exactly hierarchical but none the less quite rigidly structured. The notions of congregational autonomy or of representative democratic control seem to be alien to the new movements—even in cases of communitarian living.

It is immediately apparent that in respect of organizational structure and the provision of cognitive certainty the Watch Tower movement is similar to, and perhaps even heralded the advent of, some new religious initiatives. The consequences of participation are also alike in entailing the observance of explicit principles and rules of behaviour. In terms of the social background of recruits, moreover, the only link between them is the transcendence of social status group boundaries. Indeed, whereas the formal organizational aspects of the two types display considerable similarities (with the exception that the Witnesses lack a charismatic leader) their respective 'constituencies' are very different. The fact that the Watch Tower movement contains a more or less even distribution of age-groups, for example, is connected with a range of salient divergencies from the style and symbolism of most of the new movements. Jehovah's witnesses do not therefore use symbols deriving from the American youth culture or counter-culture, nor is their version of Christianity in any way syncretistic. Finally, the new movements often provide substitute family environments for recruits, whereas Watch Tower ideology is nowadays supportive of life in natural families.

Our conclusion is that the Watch Tower movement's organization and methods of evangelism are echoed in the latest upsurge of religious activity in Western societies, but that the substantive content and cultural styles of the new movements are at variance with the earlier model. The former point can be seen as partial confirmation of the pragmatic appropriateness of Watch Tower organization for modern societies. The latter point does not imply that Watch Tower teachings are now out of date: on the contrary, it is doubtful whether the theology of the new movements will prove to be an adequate basis for a long-lasting, continually energetic religious movement. Our guess is that Biblical literalism, evangelicalism and unemotionality are a better recipe for long-term, organized activism than heightened emotion and syncretism.

'THE END OF THIS SYSTEM OF THINGS'

Sociologists and social-psychologists have asserted a small number of propositions about the conditions which allegedly favour the survival of religious groups whose prophecies for the end of the world receive no clear empirical confirmation at the critical time. Prophetic disconfirmation (as we shall call this situation) may first lead to momentary disappointment and loss of enthusiasm on the members' part. The initial shock is frequently followed by a period of renewed evangelistic activism and an increase in the mutual dependence of members on each other. But successive disconfirmations usually destroy the fabric of social relations in the group and entail its eventual disbandment. The Watch Tower movement has already survived several prophetic 'crises' with varying degrees of group disturbance, and these episodes provide reasonably good grounds for inferring what will happen if the Witnesses' current belief about the eschatological significance of 1975 is not obviously borne out by observable events.

The way in which the prophecy for 1975 has been announced, defended and qualified in Watch Tower literature implies that some of the dangers of disappointment are being prophylactically forestalled. For example, the futility of making precise predictions about the form that events will take in 1975 has been a common theme in recent publications of the sect. An alternative tactic has been to suggest that full understanding of the events may be available to Jehovah's witnesses only a long time after 1975. Clear warnings have been issued about the dangers of expecting observable, dramatic upheavals or the instant promotion of all Witnesses to highly privileged positions in the post-Armageddon world. In these and other ways, then, Jehovah's witnesses are being skilfully prepared for prophetic disconfirmation at an elementary level of comprehension.

Anyway, the character of Watch Tower eschatology is such that it does not encourage frequent speculation among the Witnesses about the detailed outcome of Armageddon. As we argued in Chapter 7, their beliefs about the end of the World have greater importance for the group's retrospective understanding of human history than for its anticipation of the future. An extreme view would be that the search for certainty in history automatically entails the need for a clear-cut conclusion to the perceived pattern of past events, but that the actual shape of the future is of relatively little immediate interest. A further characteristic of their eschatological views that helps to detract from the potentially crucial significance of prophecy is the two-fold belief that the physical conditions of life will not alter beyond recognition during Armageddon and that the Watch Tower Society will continue to function as a social entity afterwards. It follows for the Witnesses that the Society is presently justified in maintaining and even expanding its material effects on earth right up to the anticipated end of the present system of things and that the envisaged smoothness of transition through Armageddon for faithful Witnesses will possibly make it difficult for them to know whether a cataclysmic event will have taken place or not.

Even if it is correct that prophecy nowadays serves a largely formal function in Watch Tower ideology, it is imperative to bear in mind the distinction that we proposed in Chapter 7 between the distributive and the collective modes of referring to the Witnesses. For it may well be that *individuals* will experience acute disappointment if their expectations are not visibly fulfilled in that year (or thereabouts), but it is unlikely that *as a group* they will manifest signs of disappointment. Rather, the supportive structure of social relationships among Witnesses will protect their shared beliefs (see Festinger, 1957) and ensure that whatever happens will be assimilated into the collective belief-system without serious damage.

Social-structural features of the movement also make it unlikely that Jehovah's witnesses would suffer greatly from the disconfirmation of prophetic beliefs. Doctrine has always emanated from the Society's elite in Brooklyn and has never emerged from discussion among, or suggestion from, rank-and-file Witnesses. To be a Witness is therefore to have accepted the legitimacy of the doctrinal rulings that issue from head-quarters and are diffused through official publications. The habit of questioning or qualifying Watch Tower doctrine is not only under-developed among the Witnesses: it is strenuously combated at all organiza-tional levels. Providing, then, that authoritative interpretations of events continue to be 'handed down', there is little possibility or likelihood that cognitive dissonance will result in mass dissent or defection among the Witnesses.

The enormous scale of the Watch Tower movement's present-day operations and the huge investment that it has in both material and human resources have created a sense among the Witnesses of its institu-tional 'momentum'. If C. T. Russell was able to put the 'argument from momentum' to good ideological effect in alleviating prophetic disappoint-ment among the Bible Students in the 1880s, how much more effective must it be today. For just as the publication of impressive growth statistics has been helping to retain the commitment of Jehovah's witnesses for several generations, so the same figures can serve to obviate by anticipa-tion the dangers of disruption in the future. Watch Tower propaganda has therefore created in the minds of Witnesses the notion that the evident success of the movement is proof that it must be divinely guided, correct in its interpretation of prophecy and consequently certain to weather whatever storms may occur in 1975 or thereafter.

Nothing is better calculated to give added weight to the movement's momentum than the unremitting orientation towards public evangelism on the part of every member. If such an evangelical programme had been instigated solely in response to the immediate urgency of Armageddon it might prove to exacerbate feelings of disappointment in the event of prophetic disconfirmation. But this has been the primary orientation of the Watch Tower movement for so long that, on the contrary, it constitutes a factor for stability. Constant evangelism distracts the Witnesses' attention from a potentially harmful obsession with the details of Armageddon as an event and provides scope for group-affirming social activism during the anticipated event itself. It thereby commutes the *event* into a lengthier *process* with a consequent reduction of all concomitant anxieties and crises.

Yet, the weight of doctrinal, ideological and social-structural arguments for the view that the Watch Tower movement will not suffer violent disruption if prophetic disconfirmation occurs in 1975 must be to some extent counterbalanced by other considerations. In the first place, we must make it plain that the disappointment or despondency of some individual Witnesses will undoubtedly lead them to cease active participation; others may 'resign' simply out of distaste for specific prophecies, preferring instead to leave it to Jehovah to usher in Armageddon whenever it suits Him. There can be little doubt that defection will occur among those Witnesses who, either in anticipation of millennial blessings or in fear of the physical disturbances of Armageddon, have already abandoned their houses and livelihoods and migrated to remote parts of the country in order to await 1975 in tranquility. These people will surely be vulnerable to acute feelings of despondency if their expectations are confounded, but the number of such defectors is unlikely to be sufficiently high to cause other Witnesses to entertain doubts about the Society's divine function. There is certainly no likelihood of massive defection immediately after 1975, but it is possible that subsequent years might witness a slow trickle of people away from the movement. The evidence from earlier prophetic 'incidents' suggests that the full implications of a specific prophecy take years to become manifest in such a large organization. In this respect, then, the important factors are the speed with which the elite can propagate a comprehensive, retrospective interpretation of events and the degree of resoluteness with which it sponsors programmes of future activity.

Finally, on the assumption that the movement will survive the testing year of 1975 the question arises of what form it will take in the long-term future. The most important consideration is that the apparent 'invulnerability' of the Society's elite from internal, and most forms of external, attack or social pressure looks like remaining the organization's dominant characteristic. So long as this remains the case, the movement's primary goal will probably continue to be the mobilization of maximal resources in evangelism. This, in turn, entails the recruitment of people from an extremely wide range of social classes, status groups, age-sets and nationalities. It follows that the common process whereby a distinctive religious message or vision becomes associated with one major social division or interest-group is unlikely to occur and that, consequently, the challenging or 'prophetic' nature of its message for the world will probably go undiluted. This expectation is based on the general notion that the distinctiveness and radicalism of moral, political or religious protest are usually dissolved through excessively close association with one social group for too long. So long as the collectivity of Jehovah's witnesses retains its mass-movement features, however, the chances of its accommodation to a narrowly specific set of interests are remote.

In order to complete the chain of reasoning, we should add that the same 'mass' features also favour the privileged isolation of the Watch Tower elites and, thereby, the untrammelled assertion of their primary goal. Only a radical change of outlook among the elite, *ceteris paribus*, could alter the movement's general character and orientation, but this possibility is rendered remote by the stringency of checks on elevation to this tiny group. Thus, unless social conditions in all parts of the world change in such a way as to dispose of the market for comprehensive religious ideologies, the Watch Tower movement will continue with its distinctive work in its distinctive manner.

BIBLIOGRAPHY

The bibliography contains only items that are referred to in the text. For a much more extensive coverage of works on the sociology of the Watch Tower movement, see Beckford (1972b) and Rogerson (1972).

For the sake of convenience all works published under the auspices of Zion's Watch Tower Tract Society or the Watch Tower Bible and Tract Society are included in Section I. It contains works signed by Russell and Rutherford as well as some of the anonymous publications that the Watch Tower Society has produced. Unless otherwise stated, all of these items were originally published in Brooklyn.

Section II contains all the items referred to in the text but not published by the Watch Tower Society.

SECTION I

C. T. Russell

(1873) *The Object and Manner of Our Lord's Return.* Pittsburgh.

(1881) *Food for Thinking Christians.* Pittsburgh.

(1887) *Three Worlds or Plan of Redemption.* (In collaboration with N. H. Barbour). Pittsburgh.

(1886–1904) *Studies in the Scriptures* (until 1904 the title was *Millennial Dawn*). Pittsburgh. There have been several editions of this series, but all references in this book are to the edition published by the Laymen's Home Missionary Movement, 1960. Copyright is in the name of P. S. L. Johnson, Pennsylvania, 1937.

Vol. 1: *The Divine Plan of the Ages.* (1886)

224

Vol. 2: *The Time is at Hand.* (1889)
Vol. 3: *Thy Kingdom Come.* (1891)
Vol. 4: *The Battle of Armageddon.* (1897)
Vol. 5: *The Atonement between God and Man* (1899)
Vol. 6: *The New Creation.* (1904)

J. F. Rutherford

(1921) *The Harp of God.*
(1927) *Freedom for the Peoples.*
(1940) *Religion.*

Anonymous

(1890) *Poems and Hymns of Millennial Dawn.* Pittsburgh.
(1914) *The Photo-Drama of Creation.* (Scenario of the film-strip).
(1943) *A Course in Theocratic Ministry.*
(1945) *Theocratic Aid to Kingdom Publishers.*
(1946) *Equipped for Every Good Work.*
(1950) *The New World Translation of the Christian Greek Scriptures.*
(1951) *What Has Religion Done for Mankind?*
(1955) *Qualified to be Ministers.*
(1959) *Jehovah's Witnesses in the Divine Purpose.*
(1961) *The New World Translation of the Holy Scriptures.* (Revised edition)
(1961) *Blood, Medicine and the Law of God.*
(1966) *Life Everlasting in Freedom of the Sons of God.*
(1967) *Did Man Get Here by Evolution or by Creation?*
(1968) *The Truth that Leads to Eternal Life.*

Periodicals

Zion's Watch Tower and Herald of Christ's Presence. July 1879–December 1907.
The Watch Tower and Herald of Christ's Presence. January 1908–October 1931.
The Watchtower and Herald of Christ's Presence. October 15th 1931–December 1938.
The Watchtower and Herald of Christ's Kingdom. January 1939–February 1939.
The Watchtower Announcing Christ's Kingdom. March 1939–
The Golden Age. October 1919–September 1937.

Consolation. October 1937–July 1946.
Awake! August 1946–
The Yearbook of the International Bible Students Association. 1928–32.
The Yearbook. 1933.
The Yearbook of Jehovah's Witnesses. 1934–

SECTION II

Aberle, D. (1966) *The Peyote Religion among the Navaho*. Chicago, Illinois, Aldine Publishing Co.

Abrams, M. (1968) *Education, Social Class and Readership of Newspapers and Magazines—1968*. Institute of Practitioners in Advertizing.

Albrow, M. (1970) *Bureaucracy*. London, Macmillan.

All England Law Reports. Vol. 3, 1956.

Anon. (1917) *Light After Darkness*. Brooklyn, Pastoral Bible Institute.

Anon. (1923) *The Laodicean Messenger, being the Memoirs of the Life, Works and Character of that Faithful and Wise Servant of the Most High God*. Chicago, Illinois, Bible Students Book Store, 3rd edition.

Argyle, M. (1958) *Religious Behaviour*. London, Routledge & Kegan Paul.

Banks, J. A. (1972) *The Sociology of Social Movements*. London, Macmillan.

Becker, H. S. (1963) *Outsiders. Studies in the Sociology of Deviance*. New York, The Free Press of Glencoe.

Beckford, J. A. (1972a) 'The embryonic stage of a religious sect's development: the Jehovah's witnesses', pp. 11–32 in: M. Hill ed., *A Sociological Yearbook of Religion in Britain*, no. 5, S.C.M. Press.

(1972b) 'A sociological study of Jehovah's witnesses in Britain', unpublished Ph.D. thesis, University of Reading.

(1973) 'A Korean evangelistic movement in the West', pp. 319–35 in: *The Contemporary Metamorphosis of Religion?*, Acts of the 12th International Conference for the Sociology of Religion, The Hague.

(1975) 'Religious Organization', *Current Sociology*, vol. XXI, No. 2.

Bell, C. (1969) *Middle Class Families*. London, Routledge & Kegan Paul.

Bendix, R. (1967) 'The comparative analysis of historical change', pp. 67–86 in: T. Burns and S. Saul eds., *Social Theory and Economic Change*, London, Tavistock.

Bendix, R. and Berger, P. L. (1959) 'Images of reality and problems of concept formation in sociology', in L. Gross ed., *Symposium on Sociological Theory*, New York, Harper & Row.

Berger, P. L. (1967) *The Social Reality of Religion*. London, Faber & Faber.

Berger, P. L. and Luckmann, T. (1967a) *The Social Construction of Reality*. London, Allen Lane, The Penguin Press.

Berger, P. L. and Luckmann, T. (1967b) 'Aspects sociologiques du pluralisme religieux', *Archives de Sociologie des Religions*, 23: 117–27.

Berlin, I. (1955) *Historical Inevitability*. Oxford University Press. Reprinted in P. Geyl, *Debates With Historians*. London, Batsford, 1955.

Bernstein, B. (1971) *Class, Codes and Control. vol. 1. Theoretical Studies Towards a Sociology of Language*. London, Routledge & Kegan Paul.

The Bible Student (1914–24) Edited by W. Robertson, Edinburgh.

Box, S. and Ford, J. (1971) 'The facts don't fit; on the relationship between social class and criminal behaviour', *Sociological Review*, 19, 1: 31–52.

British Government White Paper. *Germany no. 2. Papers Concerning the Treatment of German Nationals in Germany 1938–39*. Cmd. 6120.

Buckle, R. (1971) 'Mormonism in Britain: a survey', pp. 160–79 in: M. Hill ed. *A Sociological Yearbook of Religion in Britain*, no. 4, London, S.C.M. Press.

Budd, S. (1967) 'The loss of faith. Reasons for unbelief among members of the Secular Movement in England 1850–1950', *Past and Present*, 36: 106–25.

Burns, T. and Stalker, G. (1961) *The Management of Innovation*. London, Tavistock.

Campbell, C. B. (1967) 'Humanism and the culture of the professions: a study in the rise of the British Humanist movement, 1954–1963', unpublished Ph.D. thesis, University of London.

Carrier, H. (1965) *The Sociology of Religious Belonging*. London, Darton, Longman & Todd.

Chamberlayne, J. H. (1964) 'From sect to church in British Methodism', *British Journal of Sociology*, XV, 2: 139–49.

Clark, E. T. (1929) *The Psychology of Religious Awakening*. New York, Macmillan.

(1949) *The Small Sects in America*. New York, Abingdon Press.

Cohn, W. (1955) 'Jehovah's Witnesses as a proletarian movement', *American Scholar*, 24: 281–98.

Cozin, M. (1973) 'A millenarian movement in Korea and Britain', pp. 100–21 in: M. Hill ed. *A Sociological Yearbook of Religion in Britain*, no. 6, London, S.C.M. Press.

Curran, J. (1970) 'The impact of television on the audience for national newspapers 1945–1968', pp. 104–31 in: J. Tunstall ed. *Media Sociology*, London, Constable.

Czatt, M. S. (1933) *The International Bible Students: Jehovah's Witnesses*. Yales Studies in Religion no. 4. Mennonite Press, Scottdale, Pa.

Demerath III, N. J. (1965) *Social Class in American Protestantism.* Chicago, Illinois, Rand, McNally & Co.

Demerath III, N. J. and Hammond, P. (1969) *Religion in Social Context.* New York, Random House Inc.

Dencher, T. (1966) *Why I Left Jehovah's Witnesses.* Oliphants.

Douglas, M. (1973) *Natural Symbols.* Harmondsworth, Penguin Books.

Edgar, Minna (1918a) *The Memoirs of Dr. John Edgar.* Glasgow, Morton Edgar.

(1918b) *The Memoirs of Aunt Sarah.* Glasgow, Morton Edgar.

Edgar, Morton (1910) *Great Pyramid Passages and Chambers.*

Eister, A. W. (1967) 'Towards a radical critique of church-sect typologising', *Journal for the Scientific Study of Religion,* 6, 1; 85–90.

(1972) 'Outline of a structural theory of cults', *Journal for the Scientific Study of Religion,* 11, 4: 319–33.

Embley, P. L. (1967) 'The Plymouth Brethren', pp. 213–43 in: B. R. Wilson ed., 1967.

Etzioni, A. (1961) *A comparative Analysis of Complex Organizations.* New York, The Free Press of Glencoe.

Farr, A. D. (1972) *God, Blood and Society.* Aberdeen, Impulse Books.

Fawcett, T. (1970) *The Symbolic Language of Religion.* London, S.C.M. Press.

Fenn, R. K. (1972) 'Towards a new sociology of religion', *Journal for the Scientific Study of Religion,* 11, 1: 16–32.

Festinger, L. (1957) *A Theory of Cognitive Dissonance.* Illinois, Row, Peterson & Co.

Festinger, L., Riecken, H. and Schachter, S. (1964) *When Prophecy Fails.* New York, Harper Torchbook.

Fichter, J. (1961) *Religion As an Occupation.* Notre Dame, Indiana, University of Notre Dame Press.

Fletcher, W. (1970) 'Britain's national media pattern', pp. 79–91 in J. Tunstall ed., *Media Sociology,* London, Constable, 1970.

Froom, L. E. (1946–54) *The Prophetic Faith of Our Fathers.* Vols. 1–4, Washington, Review & Herald Publishing Co.

Gellner, E. (1973) 'Post-traditional forms in Islam; the turf and trade, and votes and peanuts', *Daedalus,* 102, 1: 191–206.

Glass, D. V. ed. (1954) *Social Mobility in Britain.* London, Routledge & Kegan Paul.

Glock, C. Y. (1964) 'The role of deprivation in the origin and evolution of religious groups', pp. 24–36 in R. Lee and M. E. Marty eds., *Religion and Social Conflict.* New York, Oxford University Press.

Glock, C. Y., Ringer, B., and Babbie, E. (1967) *To Comfort and to Challenge.* Berkeley, California, University of California Press.

Goen, C. C. (1970) 'Fundamentalism in America', pp. 85–93 in P. E. Hammond and B. Johnson eds., *American Mosaic*. New York, Random House.

Gouldner, A. (1955) *Patterns of Industrial Bureaucracy*. London, Routledge & Kegan Paul.

Gusfield, J. (1963) *Symbolic Crusade: Status Politics and the Temperance Movement*. Urbana, Illinois, University of Illinois Press.

Harris, N. (1968) *Beliefs in Society*. London, Watts & Co.

Harrison, P. M. (1959) *Authority and Power in the Free Church Tradition; a Social Case Study of the American Baptist Convention*. Princeton, N.J., Princeton University Press.

Hébert, G. (1960) *Les Témoins de Jéhovah*. Montreal, Editions Bellarmin.

Hudson, W. S. (1961) *American Protestantism*. Chicago, Ill., University of Chicago Press.

Isichei, E. A. (1964) 'From sect to denomination in English Quakerism', *British Journal of Sociology*, XV, 3: 207–22.

Janis, I. L. and King, B. T. (1954) 'The influence of role-playing on opinion change', *Journal of Abnormal and Social Psychology*, 49: 211–218.

Jarvie, I. (1964) *The Revolution in Anthropology*. London, Routledge & Kegan Paul.

(1970) 'Explaining Cargo Cults', pp. 50–61 in: B. R. Wilson ed., *Rationality*. Oxford, Blackwell.

Kaufmann, R. (1964) *Millénarisme et Acculturation*. Brussells, Institut de Sociologie de L'Université Libre de Bruxelles.

Kessin, K. (1971) 'Social and psychological consequences of intergenerational occupational mobility', *American Journal of Sociology*, 77, 1; 1–18.

Klapp, O. E. (1969) *The Collective Search for Identity*. New York, Holt, Rhinehart & Winston.

Kornhauser, W. (1960) *The Politics of Mass Society*. London, Routledge & Kegan Paul.

Lenski, G. (1966) *Power and Privilege*. New York, McGraw-Hill.

Lippmann, W. (1970) 'The breakdown of religious authority', pp. 269–78 in P. Hammond and B. Johnson eds., *American Mosaic*. New York, Random House.

Lipset, S. M. (1964) *Political Man*. Mercury Books. 1st ed. 1963.

Lipset, S. M. and Bendix, R. (1959) *Social Mobility in Industrial Society*. Berkeley, California, University of California Press.

Lofland, J. (1966) *Doomsday Cult; a Study of Conversion, Proselytization and Maintenance of Faith*. Englewood Cliffs, N.J., Prentice-Hall.

Long, N. (1968) *Social Change and the Individual*. Manchester, University of Manchester Press.

Luckmann, T. (1967) *The Invisible Religion*. New York, Macmillan.

MacMillan, A. H. (1957) *Faith on the March*. Englewood Cliffs, N.J. Prentice-Hall.

Mann, W. E. (1955) *Sect, Cult and Church in Canada*. Toronto, University of Toronto Press.

Manwaring, D. (1962) *Render Unto Caesar. The Flag Salute Controversy*. Chicago, Ill., University of Chicago Press.

Martin, D. A. (1962) 'The denomination', *British Journal of Sociology*, XIII, 1: 1–14.

Masterman, C. F. G. (1909) *The Condition of England*. London, Methuen.

Messinger, S. L. (1955) 'Organizational transformation: a case study of a declining social movement', *American Sociological Review*, 20: 3–10.

Mews, S. P. (1966) 'The effects of the First World War on religious life and thought', unpublished M.A. thesis, University of Leeds.

(1972) 'Reason and emotion in working-class religion, 1794–1824', in D. Baker ed. *Schism, Heresy and Religious Protest*. Studies in Church History, vol. 9. Cambridge University Press.

Mulder, J. and Komisky, M. (1942) 'Jehovah's Witnesses mould constitutional law', *Bill of Rights Review*, 2, 4.

Munters, Q. J. (1971) 'Recruitment as a vocation: the case of Jehovah's Witnesses', *Sociologia Neerlandica*, 7, 2: 88–100.

McKenzie, J. L. (1969) *The Roman Catholic Church*. London, Weidenfeld & Nicolson.

McKinney, J. C. (1966) *Constructive Typology and Social Theory*. New York, Appleton, Century, Crofts.

McLoughlin, W. G. (1967) 'Is there a third force in Christendom?', *Daedalus*, 96, 1: 43–68.

Newton, K. (1966) *The Sociology of British Communism*. London, Allen Lane, The Penguin Press.

Niebuhr, H. R. (1957) *The Social Sources of Denominationalism*. New York, Meridian Books. 1st ed. 1929, New York, Holt, Rhinehart & Winston.

Parkin, F. (1968) *Middle Class Radicalism*. Manchester, Manchester University Press.

Parliamentary Debates: Hansard, House of Commons Official Report.

Parsons, T. and Shils, E. (1951) *Toward a General Theory of Action*. Cambridge, Mass., Harvard University Press.

Patrides, C. A. (1972) *The Grand Design of God and the Literary Form of the Christian View of History*. London, Routledge & Kegan Paul.

Persons, S. (1961) 'Religion and modernity, 1865–1914', in: J. W. Smith and A. L. Jamison eds., *Religion in American Life*. Princeton, N.J., Princeton University Press.

Pike, E. R. *Jehovah's Witnesses*. New York, Philosophical Library.

Piker, S. (1972) 'The problem of consistency in Thai religion', *Journal for the Scientific Study of Religion*, 11, 3: 211–29.

Poblete, R. (1960) 'A sociological approach to the sects', *Social Compass*, 1, 5–6: 383–406.

Popper, K. (1969) *The Poverty of Historicism*. London, Routledge & Kegan Paul.

Portes, A. (1971) 'On the logic of post-factum explanations; the hypothesis of lower-class frustrations as the cause of leftist radicalism', *Social Forces*, 50, 1: 26–44.

Rauschenbusch, W. (1907) *Christianity and the Social Crisis*. New York, Macmillan.

Robbins, T. (1969) 'Eastern mysticism and the resocialization of drug users. The Meher Baba cult', *Journal for the Scientific Study of Religion*, 8, 2; 308–17.

Robbins, T. and Anthony, D. (1972) 'Getting straight with Meher Baba: a study of mysticism, drug rehabilitation and postadolescent role-conflict', *Journal for the Scientific Study of Religion*, 11, 2: 122–40.

Roberts, B. (1968) 'Protestant groups and coping with urban life in Guatemala City', *American Journal of Sociology*, 72: 753–67.

Rogerson, A. T. (1969) *Millions Now Living Will Never Die*. London, Constable.

(1972) 'A sociological analysis of the origin and development of the Jehovah's witnesses and their schismatic groups', unpublished D. Phil. thesis, Oxford, University of Oxford.

Rokeach, M. (1960) *The Open and Closed Mind*. New York, Basic Books.

Runciman, W. G. (1966) *Relative Deprivation and Social Justice*. London, Routledge & Kegan Paul.

Scalf, J. H., Miller, M. J. and Thomas, C. W. (1973) 'Goal specificity, organizational structure and participant commitment in churches', *Sociological Analysis*, 34, 3: 169–84.

Schnell, W. J. (1957) *Thirty Years a Watch Tower Slave*. Marshall, Morgan & Scott.

Schwartz, G. (1970) *Sect Ideologies and Social Status*. Chicago, Ill., University of Chicago Press.

Sears, C. (1924) *Days of Delusion*. New York, Houghton Mifflin.

Séguy, J. (1966) 'Méssianisme et échec social: les Témoins de Jéhovah', *Archives de Sociologie des Religions*, 21: 89–99.

Selznick, P. (1948) *T.V.A. and the Grass Roots*. Berkeley, California, University of California Press.

(1957) *Leadership in Administration*. New York, Harper & Row.

(1960) *The Organizational Weapon*. New York, McGraw-Hill. 2nd ed.

Shepperson, G. (1962) 'Comparative study of millenarian movements' and 'Nyasaland and the millennium' in: S. Thrupp ed. *Millennial Dreams in Action: Essays in Comparative Study*. Supplement no. 2, *Comparative Studies in Society and History*, The Hague, Mouton.

Shepperson, G. and Price, T. (1958) *Independent African: John Chilembwe and the Origins, Setting and Significance of the Nyasaland Native Rising of 1915*. Edinburgh, Edinburgh University Press.

Shiner, L. (1967) 'The concept of secularization in empirical research', *Journal for the Scientific Study of Religion*, 6, 2: 207–20.

Sibley, M. Q. and Jacob, P. E. (1952) *Conscription of Conscience*. Ithaca, N.Y., Cornell University Press.

Simon, H. A. (1957) *Administrative Behaviour*. New York, Macmillan. 2nd ed.

Smyth, C. P. (1864) *Our Inheritance in the Great Pyramid*. Isbister & Co.

Sprague, T. W. (1942) 'Some problems in the integration of social groups with special reference to Jehovah's Witnesses', unpublished Ph.D. thesis, Harvard University.

(1943) 'Some notable features in the authority structure of a sect', *Social Forces*, 21, 3: 344–50.

Starbuck, E. D. (1899) *The Psychology of Religion*. New York, The Contemporary Science Series.

Starbuck, W. H. (1971) *Organizational Growth and Development*. Harmondsworth, Penguin Books.

Stark, W. (1966–72) *The Sociology of Religion*. London, Routledge & Kegan Paul. 5 vols.

Stevenson, W. C. (1967) *Year of Doom, 1975*. London, Hutchinson.

Stroup, H. H. (1945) *Jehovah's Witnesses*. New York, Columbia University Press.

Sunday Telegraph.

Talmon, Y. (1966) 'Millenarian movements', *Archives Européennes de Sociologie*, 7, 2: 159–200.

Thompson, K. A. (1970) *Bureaucracy and Church Reform*. Oxford University Press.

Thouless, R. H. (1971) *An Introduction to the Psychology of Religion*. Cambridge University Press. 3rd ed.

The Times.

Tomsett, V. (1971) *Released from the Watchtower*. Lakeland Press.

Toupin, R. (1958) 'Le dossier du "pasteur" Russell', *Sciences Ecclésiastiques*, 10, 3: 497–519.

Vorwaller, D. (1970) 'Social mobility and membership in voluntary associations', *American Journal of Sociology*, 75, 4: 481–95.

Waite, E. F. (1944) 'The debt of constitutional law to Jehovah's Witnesses', *Minnesota Law Review*, 28, 4.

Walker, D. P. (1964) *The Decline of Hell*. London, Routledge & Kegan Paul.

Warburton, T. R. (1966) 'Comparative study of religious groups with special reference to holiness and related movements in Britain in the last fifty years', unpublished Ph.D. thesis, University of London.

Weber, M. (1964) *The Theory of Social and Economic Organization*. Translated by A. M. Henderson and T. Parsons, New York, The Free Press of Glencoe.

(1965) *The Sociology of Religion*. Translated by E. Fischoff. London, Methuen.

Westin, A. (1964) 'The John Birch Society' in: D. Bell ed. *The Radical Right*. New York, Doubleday & Co.

White, J. W. (1970) *The Sokagakkai and Mass Society*. Stanford, California, Stanford University Press.

White, T. (1967) *A People for His Name*. New York, Vantage Press.

Whitworth, J. McK. (1971) 'Religious utopianism: a comparative study of three sects', unpublished D.Phil. thesis, University of Oxford.

Wickham, E. R. (1969) *Church and People in an Industrial City*. London, Lutterworth Press, paperback ed.

Williams, R. (1961) *The Long Revolution*. London, Chatto & Windus.

Wilson, B. R. (1955) 'Social aspects of religious sects: a study of some contemporary groups with special reference to a Midland city', unpublished Ph.D. thesis, University of London.

(1959) 'An analysis of sect development', *American Sociological Review*, 24: 3–15.

(1961) *Sects and Society*. London, Heinemann.

(1963) 'Typologie des sectes dans une perspective dynamique et comparative', *Archives de Sociologie des Religions*, 16: 49–63.

(1966) *Religion in Secular Society*. London, Watts & Co.

(1967) ed. *Patterns of Sectarianism*. London, Heinemann.

(1969) 'A typology of sects' in: *Types, Dimensions et Mesures de la Religiosité*. Actes de la Xᵉ Conférence Internationale de Sociologie Religieuse, Rome.

(1973) 'Jehovah's Witnesses in Africa', *New Society*, 25, 562: 73–5.

Wilson, J. (1966) 'The history and organization of British Israelism; some aspects of the political correlates of changing social status' unpublished D.Phil. thesis, University of Oxford.

Winter, G. (1968) *Religious Identity; the Organization of the Major Faiths*. New York, Macmillan.

Worsley, P. (1957) *The Trumpet Shall Sound*. London, MacGibbon & Kee.

Yeo, S. (1973) 'A contextual view of religious organization', pp. 207–34 in: M. Hill ed. *A Sociological Yearbook of Religion in Britain*, no. 6, S.C.M. Press.

Yinger, J. M. (1970) *The Scientific Study of Religion*. New York, Macmillan.

Young, F. W. (1960) 'Adaptation and pattern integration of a California sect', *Review of Religious Research*, 1, 4.

Zald, M. N. (1970) *Organizational Change: the Political Economy of the Y.M.C.A.* Chicago, Ill., University of Chicago Press.

Zetterberg, H. (1952) 'The religious conversion as a change of social roles', *Sociology and Social Research*, 36: 159–66.

(1957) 'Compliant actions', *Acta Sociologica*, 2.

Zuercher, F. (1939) *Croisade contre le Christianisme*. Paris, Editions Rieder.

Zygmunt, J. F. (1967) 'Jehovah's Witnesses. A study of symbolic and structural elements in the development and institutionalization of a sectarian movement', unpublished Ph.D. thesis, University of Chicago.

(1972) 'Movements and motives', *Human Relations*, 25, 5: 449–67.

AUTHOR INDEX

SUBJECT INDEX